Praise for *Balm in Gilead*

"The great virtue of this book is the preference for storytelling rather than abstract argument. . . . *Balm in Gilead* is a daughter's loving witness to a mother's important healing life."
—Robert Coles, *The New Republic*

"It is in the explosive area of skin color and its particularly destructive impact on blacks that Lightfoot stands tallest. She unflinchingly and honestly describes the hierarchies of skin color that permeated life for her mother."
—*The Philadelphia Inquirer*

"Enchanting . . . reflective rather than rancorous . . . the narrative pays more attention to challenges overcome than to injustices suffered."
—*The New Yorker*

"The story of a daughter's spiritual and emotional journey to discover her own identity by attempting to understand her mother's life . . . Lightfoot admits that the opportunity to collaborate with her mother on this book was a rich and rare experience. So it is also for the reader."
—*The Nation*

"A superb biography, filled with gentle humor, understanding, and decorous anger at racial prejudice."
—Doris Grumbach, *Chicago Tribune*

"Combining the passion of a family member with the skepticism of a social scientist, [Lightfoot] raises the standard of authenticity in African-American biography."
—Nell Irvin Painter, *The Washington Post Book World*

"A deeply moving portrait. . . . This is a book about courage and healing and strength and love."
—Carol Gilligan

PENGUIN BOOKS

BALM IN GILEAD

Sara Lawrence-Lightfoot is the author of the much praised and critically lauded *I've Known Rivers: Lives of Loss and Liberation* and several other books. A sociologist, she is a Professor of Education at Harvard University and was a 1984 recipient of the prestigious MacArthur Prize Award which she used to write this book. She resides in Boston, Massachusetts with her family.

Balm in Gilead

JOURNEY OF A HEALER

Sara Lawrence-Lightfoot

PENGUIN BOOKS

PENGUIN BOOKS
Published by the Penguin Group
Penguin Books USA Inc., 375 Hudson Street, New York, New York 10014, U.S.A.
Penguin Books Ltd, 27 Wrights Lane, London W8 5TZ, England
Penguin Books Australia Ltd, Ringwood, Victoria, Australia
Penguin Books Canada Ltd, 10 Alcorn Avenue, Toronto, Ontario, Canada M4V 3B2
Penguin Books (N.Z.) Ltd, 182–190 Wairau Road, Auckland 10, New Zealand

Penguin Books Ltd, Registered Offices: Harmondsworth, Middlesex, England

First published in the United States of America by Addison-Wesley
Publishing Company, Inc., 1988
Published in Penguin Books 1995

1 3 5 7 9 10 8 6 4 2

THE LIBRARY OF CONGRESS HAS CATALOGUED THE HARDCOVER AS FOLLOWS:
Lightfoot, Sara Lawrence.
Balm in Gilead: journey of a healer/Sara Lawrence Lightfoot.
p.   cm.—(Radcliffe biography series)
"A Merloyd Lawrence book."
Includes index.
ISBN 0-201-09312-X (hc.)
ISBN 0 14 02.4967 2 (pbk.)
1. Lawrence, Margaret Morgan, 1914—.   2. Women psychiatrists—
United States—Biography.   I. Title.   II. Series.
RC339.52.L39L54   1988
616.89′0092′4—dc19   88–14519
[B]

Printed in the United States of America
Set in 12-point Granjon
Designed by Janis Capone

THIS BOOK IS WRITTEN

In memory of my father,
Charles Radford Lawrence II,
Who traveled the long road with my mother,
Who nurtured the healer
And celebrated her journey.

And for my children,
Tolani and Martin David,
Whose laughter and love
Brought me closer to home.

There is a balm in Gilead,
To make the wounded whole.
There is a balm in Gilead,
To heal the sin-sick soul.

NEGRO SPIRITUAL

How can I bear my sorrow?
I am sick at heart . . .
I am wounded at the sight of my people's wound,
I go like a mourner, overcome with horror.

Is there no balm in Gilead,
  no physician there?
Why has no skin grown over their wound?

JEREMIAH (8:18–8:22)

Contents

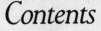

CONTENTS

Acknowledgments

It is rare, I think, for parents to let their children—of any age—grow up and become peers. My parents, Margaret and Charles Lawrence, encouraged their three children's autonomy and equality, making it possible for each of us to feel both closer to and more separate from them as we grew older. That combination of intimacy and identity made this book possible. I thank my parents for their enthusiastic participation in this project—their eagerness to tell their stories, their courage in revisiting old haunts and uncovering family secrets. But mostly I feel indebted to them for the strength of our relationships, which allowed me to mix the roles of daughter, inquirer, and narrator, and to blend the passion of a family member with the skepticism of a social scientist.

This kind of project is a family affair and could not have gone forward without the support and blessings of everyone concerned. Before I dared approach my mother for permission to tell her story, I sought out my brother, Chuck, and my sister, Paula. Both of them embraced the idea, dug through their attics and drawers for precious materials, read drafts of chapters, helped put together historical puzzles, and lived with my interpretations and perspectives, which were not always theirs.

My own family "of procreation" (as my father, the sociologist, always said) offered their patience and humor. Orlando, my husband, tolerated my weekly geographic departures to my childhood home, and the psychological departures that pulled me into the past and filled me with historical echoes. His quiet, generous support, his unyielding belief that this book was worth doing, sustained me throughout. And my children, Tolani and Martin David, put up with my seclusion in my study ("Mom's Tree House"), asked the best and toughest questions about why they should care about "long ago stories," and gained a lively appreciation for history and roots. It was for them that I wrote this book.

Beyond my immediate family, a few people played critical roles and deserve credit and praise. The love, devotion, and good judgment of Pam Frey, our children's nanny and very much a part of our family, gave me the ease and space to write. Wendy Angus, my assistant, is a skilled, sensitive, and loyal colleague who traveled the long road with me—transcribing tapes, collecting documents, and typing and retyping the manuscript. Pamela Gerloff, my research assistant, gathered and reviewed background materials, wrote thoughtful summaries, and was an insightful and probing reader of early drafts, paying attention to the ideas and the language. Merloyd Lawrence, my editor, worked for clarity and understanding, with a gentle/strong touch and a discerning eye.

Friends and colleagues cheered and criticized. I thank Stephen Arons, Derrick and Jewel Bell, Sissela Bok, Kay Cottle, Caroline Ellis, Helen and Jay Featherstone, Carol Gilligan, Barbara Gordon, Patricia Graham, Judyth Katz, Lee Schorr, and Stone Wiske. My first audience, they were careful of my vulnerabilities and believed in my strength to persevere.

Finally, I am indebted to the John D. and Catherine T. MacArthur Foundation, which awarded me a MacArthur Prize Fellowship in 1984, giving me the time and resources to do this work and the courage to depart from familiar paths and pursue a new adventure.

S. L. L.

Family Tree

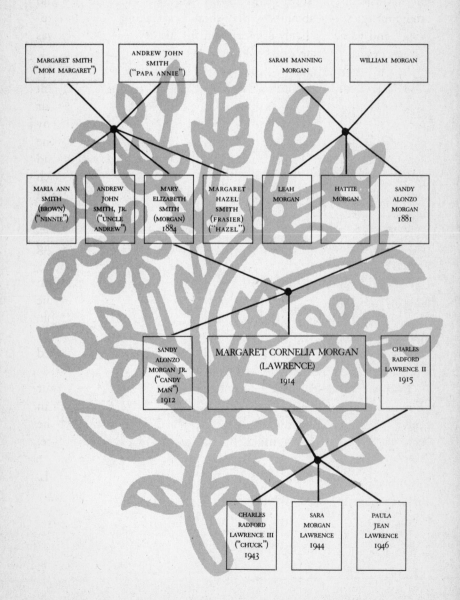

| MARGARET SMITH ("MOM MARGARET") | ANDREW JOHN SMITH ("PAPA ANNIE") | | SARAH MANNING MORGAN | WILLIAM MORGAN |

| MARIA ANN SMITH (BROWN) ("NINNIE") | ANDREW JOHN SMITH, JR. ("UNCLE ANDREW") | MARY ELIZABETH SMITH (MORGAN) 1884 | MARGARET HAZEL SMITH (FRASIER) ("HAZEL") | LEAH MORGAN | HATTIE MORGAN | SANDY ALONZO MORGAN 1881 |

| SANDY ALONZO MORGAN JR. ("CANDY MAN") 1912 | MARGARET CORNELIA MORGAN (LAWRENCE) 1914 | CHARLES RADFORD LAWRENCE II 1915 |

| CHARLES RADFORD LAWRENCE III ("CHUCK") 1943 | SARA MORGAN LAWRENCE 1944 | PAULA JEAN LAWRENCE 1946 |

Beginnings

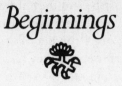

D R. Margaret Cornelia Morgan Lawrence stands on a podium, ready to address her fellow psychoanalysts. Her long black hair, laced with silver, is braided into a soft crown around her head. Her brown skin is serene and unlined. She looks silently at her audience before she speaks. Her loose, rust-colored dress hangs in graceful curves and amber earrings dangle halfway to her shoulders, casting light patterns, the only sign of motion in her calm presence.

As I watch my mother from the audience, I can feel the peacefulness that she emanates, but I also know that inside she is nervous with anticipation. She feels the confidence to speak before her colleagues because she has a message they need to hear, and because she inherited eloquence and authority from her father, an Episcopal priest from Mississippi. But she would rather be doing psychotherapy with children—making up puppet shows and plays, finger painting, throwing water balloons—than talking about the theories behind her work. As a psychiatrist, she is engaged by immediacy; her genius lies in the messiness of practice, with all its ambiguities. Now I see her hands tremble slightly against the pages of the paper she is preparing to read. Just before speaking, Margaret makes sure that her half-moon glasses are on securely and gives one more direct and purposeful look at her audience. She believes in "the Word" and hopes to communicate, not merely entertain or fill time in a professional ritual. These are her colleagues, and she is used to the way they look—mostly white, middle-aged, and male, in tweed jackets and ties; many balding and bearded; several chewing on unlit pipes. They are psychiatrists and psychoanalysts, and they are used to listening. A noncommittal glaze settles over their eyes, a monotone expression on their faces. It is hard to get a rise out of this group; they have been trained not to reveal surprise, and they anticipate a certain language and set of assumptions from others in their inner circle.

Margaret stands tall, her back kept strong by years of morning yoga. She amazes her six-year-old granddaughter when she shows her the headstand toward the end of her morning ritual. "How old do you have to be to do that, Nana? ... Are you the only Nana who wears a purple leotard?"

Steady behind the podium, Margaret finally digs in, her voice strong with feeling and energy. She is not the distant, removed analyst— she sees herself, her family history, her culture, her experiences, as dimensions of her craft, and she asks the same of others as she opens her talk. "Know the long sweep of your own history," she urges, "know the values embedded in your cultural perspective; know the inner workings of your own psyche ... *before* you dare to ask others for stories." She goes on to say:

> Actors who meet in a play are human beings who share a time in history, and have access to common symbols, myths, dreams, and hopes. ... The action takes place in the office, hospital ward, or therapeutic nursery; in the street, court of law, or home.

For Margaret, the "play" to which she refers is not bound by social class or privilege. In all her patients—of many colors, origins, and classes—she sees the universal themes of humankind. The rich, she points out, do not necessarily have a "richer" interior life or a greater capacity for identifying and expressing feelings. The poor do not necessarily have "impoverished" emotional lives, although such is often the assumption in her field.

> Psychotherapy among poor populations asks of the therapeutic "self" the freedom to join the act, the "play," the event ... Our engagement in vital action with the poor is a caring, loving use of ourselves which derives its force from our own life stories. ... Most people in poor settings have had sufficient interactions with "good-enough

caregivers" to bring reverberations, awareness of being lovable or worthy of love, when exposed to expectations from the therapist.

The therapist's work with patients, Margaret points out, is not designed simply to maintain the status quo, to make impoverished people feel comfortable with their deprived state. When therapy is successful there will be social and cultural ripples, if not waves. Individual health inspires a changed view of old, unproductive conditions. There is a strong, if complicated, relationship between psychotherapy and social change. Margaret Lawrence's voice gains intensity as she offers her colleagues this moral challenge, with full awareness of the barriers that stand in the way of its realization. The challenge mirrors a deep commitment of her own:

> Necessary social change reflects acts of caring among human beings. Participation in social change can result from the collaborative efforts of family and therapist. . . . Yet poor families collaborating with health, including mental health, workers must recognize the limitations of their collaborative efforts given society's failures. Families of the poor and those who share their concerns require access to the halls of decision making. This too is part of our commitment for the common good.

Because these proclamations seem empty without evidence from real human lives, and because she feels more at home describing a concrete scene, Margaret gives life to the values that guide her clinical work by telling a story. She chooses the plight and treatment of the Browns, a family who sought help at the Developmental Psychiatry Clinic that she directed for years at Harlem Hospital. I see my mother's face brighten as she moves into the narrative. She can picture the Browns on their first visit to the clinic. She can feel their fears and their hopes, and see the innocent, troubled face of their four-year-old son, Tchikaya.

> The Brown family had never been seen before in our clinic. Mrs. Brown's friend, the transportation aide at our therapeutic nursery, had urged her to bring the children to the clinic. Mrs. Brown had been raped. Mr. Brown had been out of town, and the two boys

witnessed the attack. Mrs. Skinner, the clinic's psychiatric social worker, and I decided that treatment for this family should be immediate and that a full evaluation should follow.

Little was known about Mr. and Mrs. Brown. They had had a common-law marriage for almost nine years. Mr. Brown's work as a musician took him out of town occasionally, and Mrs. Brown remained at home except for rare part-time jobs and a high-school course. At those times she would hire a babysitter. Tchikaya (Victory), the four-year-old, attended a day-care center at which we consulted. Akeloba (Gracious Love), the two-year-old, showed an obvious developmental lag and had been observed in another hospital since the age of five months.

Mr. and Mrs. Brown, the two boys, a child psychiatry resident, and I sat around a children's nursery table. Mrs. Brown held Ake, and Tchikaya sat in a small chair next to his mother and close to her knee. On the other side of Tchikaya was his father, at first stiff and silent, gazing out of the window. I sat across from the four-year-old. The resident physician sat to the side and somewhat behind me.

I asked Mrs. Brown what had happened five nights before. She first avoided discussing the rape by dwelling instead on Ake's problems. With our encouragement, she then told of the events leading up to the incident and of the rape itself. Two weeks prior to the attack both parents had been home one night when a girlfriend visited them whom they did not know very well. She brought along her boyfriend and another couple. The man of this couple reappeared two weeks later while Mr. Brown was away. It was evening, and the two boys were with Mrs. Brown. At the door the man said, "You remember me," and pushed his way in. He grabbed Mrs. Brown, pushing her into the bedroom and onto the bed while he tore off her clothes. Mrs. Brown recalled that the children were jumping up and down, screaming.

A large two-story dollhouse made to represent an inn had been placed on the round table. I told Tchikaya that I would start a play, just like on TV, and would ask him to finish it. We were sitting very close to one another. Tchikaya could look directly at both of his parents. I asked him to help me to be sure that I had all of the people that I needed: I chose mother, father, big brother Peter, and the baby brother. "Is there another man?" I asked Tchikaya. "Yes," he answered, handing me a man doll, "here's the Big Boss."

I began. "The Big Boss is walking up the stairs." "He gonna ring the bell," said Tchikaya quietly but a little breathless. I continued. "The mommy says 'Hi,' and the Big Boss comes right in the door."

Tchikaya hung over my shoulder as I moved the dolls. I pulled him around to my left side where I put my free arm around his waist. He was also close to his mother. "Oh, oh, he pushed her in there; he's pulling at her clothes; he's pushing her on the bed. Where's Peter? Where's the big brother?" I asked. "Here he is," answered Tchikaya, "right by the door." "He's scared," I continued. "What's the Big Boss going to do to Peter's mommy? Peter is angry with the Big Boss. He's angry with his mommy. Maybe Peter thinks he's a bad boy, but Peter is not a bad boy. He loves his Mommy very much, but he's angry with his mommy. You take Peter. What's he going to do? What's he going to say?" Tchikaya paused only a moment. "Peter's getting in the car. He's gonna go around the house and get his daddy. Here comes the daddy. He's gonna beat that Big Boss up. Pow! Pow!" Tchikaya threw the Big Boss doll across the table and looked at me. "Let's make the play again," I said. Putting things back in order, I repeated the entire play word for word. At the appointed time Tchikaya accepted the Peter doll, and spoke even more vigorously than before, "Peter's gonna get his daddy now." This time I restrained his hand mildly, saying, "Oh, Peter's daddy has gone away. He's gone away on a trip." "No, he's not!" shouted Tchikaya. "He's coming home with Peter. He's beating the Big Boss up." This time the furniture and people were thrown around violently.

I repeated the story a third time, simply announcing that we would make the play, just one more time. The third time around I again handed Tchikaya the Peter doll. Tchikaya put the Peter doll in the car and, looking at me, said firmly, "He's gonna get his daddy." "Not yet Tchikaya. His daddy is away on a trip." Tchikaya looked fearful, and I held him close. Looking at Mrs. Brown, I asked, "Didn't Tchikaya scream?" "Did he scream!" she exclaimed, smiling. "He screamed, and I screamed, too. We screamed so loud that the neighbors came, banging on the door. That man flew out of there. They caught him, though. He's in jail now."

"Let's finish the story," I said, looking at Tchikaya. "Let me have Peter a minute. That Big Boss is still there. Peter is scared. He's looking for his daddy. He can't find his daddy. Daddy is on a trip. He's angry with his daddy. He loves his daddy, but he's angry with his daddy. Peter is a fine, strong boy. He just screams as loud as he can. His mommy screams too. Even the baby brother screams. That Big Boss jumps and runs away. You take Peter." "Ain't the daddy coming?" asks Tchikaya. "He sure is. Here comes the daddy."

"Where have you been, Daddy?" said Tchikaya. "The Big Boss been here. Daddy got that Big Boss. He beat him up, Pow! Pow!

Pow! Peter's going out to play now. He's gonna play with his friends." Tchikaya picked up another boy doll and pushed each in turn down the toy sliding board. Mr. Brown broke the silence very quietly: "I could have broken his legs," he said. "I'm glad he's in jail."

Margaret goes on to describe her follow-up session with Tchikaya, and how the crying and nightmares of which his mother complained following the attack began to disappear. She carefully outlines her evaluation of Tchikaya's responses to the incident, and the consultations with the resident child psychiatrist and the staff of Tchikaya's day care center.

Margaret's description of the Browns—read from the written page, presented literally for her audience—feels somewhat static to me. I have watched my mother at work and there is so such more to see. In the live portrayals, the catharsis, with all its passion and drama, explodes before me. I see Margaret cutting through the murky complex of feelings, listening for the patient's tortured story, for old family patterns that have echoes in the present. Out of the long, convoluted tale, she draws the simple truths and recovers the potential for change and growth.

In her speech to her colleagues, I miss the gestures, the nuances, the smells and noises that rise up from the streets below and drift through the crack in the hospital window. I see my mother sitting comfortably on a tiny child's chair, pulling play people and cars and balloons out of her large African bag. The big woven bag sometimes contains a loaf of her homemade "Maggie Bread" to be broken into bite-sized pieces for a hungry child. I miss her serious, nurturant gaze that gains trust from the child. I miss her special blend of intimacy and fearlessness as she tries to make use of every second of time. I can imagine the parents' bodies relaxing as they listen to the soothing authority of the doctor's voice and begin to appreciate the intelligence and bravery they can now perceive in their son. Above all, I miss the *reverence*, for the child and his family, that can always be felt in her small conference room.

Even as a young child, I knew both the passion and the reverence my mother brought to her work. At the dinner table, while protecting the privacy and anonymity of her patients, she would reenact the dramas of the clinic, providing enough details for us to get caught up in the story. I would hear tightness and anger in her voice when children and their families got hopelessly wrapped up in bureaucratic red tape, or when a colleague, out of fear or ignorance, acted unprofessionally. Sometimes I would feel waves of jealousy and abandonment when my mother would go off to help a child in trouble, leaving her three "real" children behind. A Saturday family adventure would be shattered, a cooking project stopped in the middle, the pansies half-planted. I always screamed loudly as she walked out the door, her cape streaming, her gait purposeful. When she returned to us, leaving the clinical emergencies safely out of our view, we would confront her with "how we felt" about her leaving, and she would carefully and candidly explain her devotion to her work *and* her mother-love for us. Didn't we know that the latter was deeper, that it would last "forever"?

From time to time, I remember my mother saying, without sentimentality, "I love my work," a statement I puzzled over as a child. It made me imagine a day at the office full of pleasure and sunshine. Since the home scene, with all its love and laughter, had its inevitable crises and struggles, I occasionally worried whether my mother liked going to work more than staying home. Many years later, I understood everything she meant by that brief affirmation. Her work—with its frustrations and imperfections—offered endless challenges and a few victories, offered her the chance to use her wisdom and skills, and offered her the "privilege" of healing others. Now that I am middle-aged, and "loving my work" as well, I know even more clearly how much my mother gained fulfillment from balancing work and family. And I also understand some of the high costs of this balance, and of her struggle with many unyielding institutions to live out these deep, dual commitments.

This realization was just one of the ways in which my feelings and attitudes toward my mother were transformed as I grew older. For most of my life, I was regarded as my father's daughter. My likeness to my father, in appearance, temperament, and style, was always contrasted with my sister, who was seen as my mother's mirror image. "You're just like your dad," people would say after giving me just one hard look. "Paula is the spit and image of your mom." For those people who insisted upon attaching labels to children, Chuck, my brother, was perceived as the embodiment of both parents. "He is the combination of Margaret and Charles. . . . You can see his mother's eyes, his father's nose, his mother's quiet, his father's posture. . . ." I remember feeling that my brother's combined label gave him more room, a more generous repertoire of ways to be, while staying "in character."

Mostly I enjoyed the parallels people drew between me and my father. I knew they saw him as handsome, vigorous, and intelligent, and I longed to inherit those fine qualities. But there was a part of me that yearned to be like my mother. People described her as serene, beautiful, and wise—like a clear, still pond. I thought that in being outgoing and energetic like my father, I was missing the mystery, the softness, the feminine *grace*, of my mother. Over the years, the perceived similarities were underscored, exaggerated, and I would alternately welcome and resist them. When, in my mid-twenties, I chose my vocation and my husband, my father joked: "Now I know Sara is thoroughly identified with me. She became a sociologist and she married a psychiatrist."

But by then the likeness was largely family myth. Over the years, without anyone noticing, changes began to take place, until one day I was met by a total stranger on the streets of New York who recognized me because of my mother. From way at the other end of a long block, she watched me striding toward her, *my* cape billowing out behind. As we came closer, she stopped me with a smile and a look that said, "I know you from somewhere." She searched her mind while I waited, feeling no familiarity but believing in hers. After a few moments, her brow relaxed. "You must be Margaret's daughter. You look *just* like her!"

A few years later, I stood for an artist's portrait and watched as she uncovered a presence within me that was my mother. In my last book, I wrote about this experience and the troubling and surprising portrait that emerged:

> It was difficult, wearing work trying to hold my pose, with arms hanging long and loose and hands clasped softly. At first the stance

would feel natural, then I would lose my ease. My arms would stiffen, my fingers would press each other until the red showed through my brown skin, and my jaw would grow tight. The painter would notice the slow stiffening of my body and she would offer a break, sometimes a cup of tea. But we would soon return to the task and she would encourage me to relax and think good thoughts. Finally, the artist discovered the words that would produce the expression she wanted. "Think of how you would like your children to remember you," she said earnestly. Still not thirty and not yet a mother, I found the request overly sentimental, and almost incomprehensible. I did, however, try to produce a look that conveyed goodness, nurturance, care, and understanding.

The portrait passed through several phases and my image was transformed in front of my eyes. The transformations were all unsettling, even when the emerging image offered a prettier, more likable portrayal. With a sensitive eye, a meticulous brush, and enduring patience the artist painted me "from the inside out," the skeleton sketched in before the bulky frame, the body contours drawn before the layers of clothing. I did not see the final product until months after its completion when my husband and I quickly bought the piece fearing it would be sold, and I would be hanging in someone else's living room.

When I saw it I was shocked, disappointed, and awed all in the same moment. I had the odd sensation that the portrait did not look like me, and yet it captured my essence.... Although many of the details of this representation seemed wrong, the whole was deeply familiar. She was not quite me as I saw myself, but she told me about parts of myself that I never would have noticed or admitted. More important, I had the eerie sensation that she anticipated my future and echoed my past. I could look at her and see my ancestors, and yes, see myself as my children would see me. In these troubling features there was an ageless quality. Time moved backward and forward through this still and silent woman.

When my husband brought the large canvas home he leaned it up against the wall and gave it a sharp and skeptical look. His first comment, "It's not you." His second, "It's a family portrait . . . all of you women are in her." Both his observations seemed right to me. I did not see Sara alone . . . but I did see my mother Margaret, my sister Paula, my grandmothers Lettie and Mary Elizabeth— women who have had a profound influence on my life, women who have shaped my vision of myself, women who have known me "from the inside out." And when my mother Margaret saw the portrait for the first time, she stood in the doorway of the dining room where it hung, her arms loosely hanging, her hands lightly clasped, her head slightly tilted, and her gaze maternal. A look of recognition swept over her face and tears shot to the corners of her eyes. "That's a picture of me," she said with wonder. And at that moment her posture and aspect made her look remarkably like the woman in the picture. The artist had caught my attempt to look maternal, a replica of the motherly eyes that had protected me all of my growing up years.

By the time I was in my mid-thirties, with two children of my own, the identification with my mother was complete. Now I became a baker of "Maggie Bread," the hearty whole wheat variety, with my own embellishment of raisins. Now I wore colorful shawls like my mother always did, draped for warmth and drama. Now I plaited my daughter's brown braids and could feel the sensations of my mother's soothing hands on my head as I laid mine on my daughter's. Now I tried to put the pieces of my own too-busy life together, racing home to place bright napkins and candles on the dinner table, to create the appearance that I had been there all day. Now I heard my children's harsh complaints or watched their silent resignation when I flew off to distant places to deliver speeches, attend meetings—to do my version of the teaching/healing legacy. Now I could feel so keenly the mothering I was replaying, while being aware that the father in me had not disappeared.

This slow discovery of identification with my mother became intriguing to me. I recognized the ways I incorporated her style and her values, sometimes unknowingly, sometimes on purpose. I began to think of writing her story. If I could learn about her origins, her childhood, her dreams, her fears, I might have greater insight into my own life. If I could move beyond family myths—so static and idealized—to trace the actual events of my mother's life, I might uncover the historical patterns that give shape to my own.

My interest in telling my mother's story, however, was charged by more than my emerging identification with her. I wanted to explore beyond the myth of Margaret Lawrence. All families have elaborate tales that stand as models of courage, wisdom, strength, or loyalty for their members. The tales are told and retold, in long embroidered versions or in family shorthand. Everyone is comforted by their familiarity, the promised punch line, but no one would claim that these tales are the whole story. Bigger than life, they have turned into legends, morality plays. For as long as I can remember, my mother had been an idealized figure in our community, put on a pedestal, spoken of with awe and envy. Parents of my friends, neighbors, teachers, shopkeepers in town, would speak about my mother's serenity and quiet intelligence, about the way her very presence seemed to ease their pain. Sometimes their veneration made me wonder.

I remember the day my mother and I went to the Corsette Shop on Main Street to buy my first brassiere. I was twelve and "ample," as my father would say diplomatically. I had been walking around self-consciously for months, enduring my bobbing breasts as a horrible humiliation, and had begged my mother to let me get a bra. She had quietly, but stubbornly, resisted. My mother had never worn a bra, had refused to use the one thrust upon her at age fourteen, and seemed to regard them as nothing but sham and artifice. After weeks of my lobbying, she reluctantly gave in. I think she wanted me to avoid the abuse of my peers, several of whom had sported bras since the fourth grade. The two of us made a special trip to town to search for the most natural, least pointed kind. The Corsette Shop ladies greeted my mother with fanfare, oozing delight out of every pore. "Dr. Lawrence, we are so *thrilled* to see you!" The chatter continued while the ladies passed selections through the green curtains of the dressing room and I fumbled with snaps and straps and "cups." Occasionally one of them would come in unannounced to inspect the fit. During one of those unwelcome intrusions (my mother had gone out briefly to put a nickel in the parking meter), I remember waiting for the inevitable refrain—"Your mother is the loveliest woman I've ever met . . . she's as good as gold." I could be anywhere, even here in this underwear shop, under these embarrassing conditions, and I'd be treated to this familiar litany.

The worshipful praise always seemed genuine, but even as a child I recognized that it came at some cost. People did not always like the image that they had created of Margaret Lawrence. It made them feel inadequate or graceless in contrast. For some, the image of her goodness led to resentment. "How does your mother do it all?" asked the mother of one of my fellow Girl Scouts. "And she always looks so good." Each word of praise bore an edge of cynicism, and I could hear both, having learned early to catch these double-edged inflections.

The world's image of my mother never squared with mine. Yes, I knew she was different, even special, an achiever. I knew of no other mother who seemed to put so many pieces together; whose work seemed to require so much passion, who managed all her competing commitments. But rather than the serenity the world perceived, I saw my mother on the move, beads of sweat above her upper lip, her fingernails filled with paint and clay, brow furrowed, muscles sore and eyelids drooping by days' end. When I bothered to look, I saw a grown-up life that was hard and demanding, that left no time for frivolity. What others saw as peacefulness, I saw as my mother's chief survival strategy—complete concentration. I am sure that the dissonance between the idealized perceptions of Margaret and a daughter's nonheroic view must also have fueled my interest in exploring her life. I mistrusted the legend that seemed, in its grandeur, to diminish me.

Years later, having written other books that tried to get beyond surface and stereotypes, I felt the impulse to look at my mother's life more deeply, to tell of her grace against odds, of the pain that accompanied achievement, the loss of laughter that came with single-minded pursuits. Not only would the story focus on her triumphs, it would also show how her life was filled with very ordinary twists and turns, with moments of traumatic defeat . . . and slow, purposeful recovery. I wanted to explore the family silences, the breaks in family stories that emerge because people have simply forgotten, because memories have faded with time, because images have had to be repressed in order to move on with life, because people have chosen to hide a piece of the truth for their own peace of mind. In tracing my mother's development, I wanted to undo the caricatures that never wholly fit my view of her. I was particularly fascinated by the way she had transformed hardship into strength, and loneliness into sensitivity and introspection.

The project seemed less daunting than it might have because I expected my mother to be able to tell her story well. As an only child with a ruminative temperament, Margaret had watched the family drama and recorded everything within. She turned the images over in her mind, trying to make sense of the mysteries and silences. In her mid-thirties, when Margaret experienced "the couch" for the first time, she was amazed at how her well-developed introspective capacities translated so easily into the psychoanalytic process, how once she decided to "put it out there" it all came so naturally. Free association was much like the uninhibited, wandering fantasies she had enjoyed as a child, like the unspoken questions and observations she silently harbored as an adolescent and young adult. It was not hard for her to dig into her past, to revisit old haunts and enjoy the fuzzy, refracted quality of early images that she calls "screen memories."

Seventy years later, Margaret can draw a detailed plan of the church and rectory at Widewater, Virginia, a remote, tiny cross-in-the-road that no one can find on a map. She can feel her father's large hand holding hers as they take the slop to the pigs. She has been well practiced in exploring these early experiences, and her belief in their power is deep. As she said in her talk to her fellow analysts, her own childhood stories, their pain and their resonance, are central to her therapeutic work with children and their families. She uses that self-knowledge to gain access to her patients' lives and histories.

For my mother, our collaboration is a psychological and spiritual journey. The journey back through time feels like a tunnel, dark, mysterious, and finally luminous. In one of her books, Margaret described the cultural and religious origin of values that give shape to her work with patients, as well as to our work together:

> In the crisis of death, adolescence, or when a husband ran away, the black people I knew in the urban and rural Mississippi of fifty years ago turned to religion for comfort in the literal sense of the word; that is through religion they "joined" their strength, body, mind, and soul: "You took my feet out of the mirey clay and placed them on a firm foundation." Each individual, man or woman, boy or girl, became the "tool" of his own reconstruction. "Soul" was a matter of depth of being, as compared with more superficial feelings or emotions, although these more superficial expressions of feeling

accompanied the deeper sense of "soul." Expression of soul was free, and further enhanced in community.

Young Inner City Families, 1975

For a year and a half my mother and I met weekly to talk about her life. Until his death three-quarters of the way through this project, my father told me his story as well, bravely battling his illness to piece together a coherent narrative. The days were long. In the early morning, I would fly from Boston to New York, then drive the hour and fifteen minutes to my parents' home thirty miles northwest of the city. At day's end, I would retrace the miles, landing in Boston after my children were sound asleep. One night, a soft kiss on my six-year-old daughter's brow woke her. She wiped her eyes clear and asked in a pleading voice, "Mom, why can't you just call Nana and Papa on the phone to learn about their lives?" Before I could begin to reply, she answered her own question: "Oh, I know, you have to see their faces so you can know what they mean." With that insight, she dropped off into a deep sleep.

The interviews with my mother were all held in her office, a suite of rooms connected to her house, but separated by a garage and workroom and by a psychological distance that makes it feel as if the office were across town from the kitchen. Over thirty years later, I can still hear my mother's firm tone of voice, saying to us as she headed over to her office, "Do not disturb me unless it is an emergency." Despite scraped knees, sibling battles, and injured spirits, we did not test this boundary.

When Margaret first started her private practice, her office was a small room in our newly built house. During office hours, the family bathroom converted into a raucous playroom for activities with water and paint. There was no space for a separate waiting room, so the living room became off-limits to family. Very early, we children learned not to look at arriving patients (we and they entered different doors), and to respect their need for privacy and anonymity. Even if we stole secret glances and chose not to forget them, we never spoke about her patients, not even to each other. We managed to allow them their privacy and dutifully avoided *our* living room when it became *their* waiting room. We didn't manage, however, to escape resentment of these strangers, these "other children," invading our family space. Occasionally, I would lash out in anger, often at something else that was not the cause. As my mother would help me peel back the layers of my rage, we would discover the accumulated frustration that had grown up around the patients' invasion. Everyone was relieved when several years later my parents were able to save enough money to build a separate office for Margaret—an addition of three rooms that was carefully designed with work and family boundaries in mind. Our home was our own again. We no longer had to share our precious space or behave with such cautious discretion.

Margaret's office is dominated by "the playroom," a big open space with a larger-than-life-sized clown whose face is pocked with dart holes, a long red counter for art and clay work, a sink for water play, a punching bag, a handmade wooden cradle that fits big bodies as well as small, cabinets several feet above adult height that can become a tree house or a secret hideaway. There is also a drain in the floor—useful after the fierce games with water balloons. Everything in this room is sturdy, tough, able to withstand a child's exuberant or angry behavior. The one exception is the plate glass windows that take up one long side of the playroom. Here the doctor draws the line. "You can do anything you want here—paint the walls, flood the floors, make as much noise as you like—you are not even expected to clean up after you make a mess. . . . But you may not hurt yourself or me, and you may not break the windows." In thirty years of working with patients in this room—years of violent tantrums, elaborately staged plays, messy experiments, carpentry projects, and water fights—never have the windows even suffered a crack.

The playroom is a child's (any child's, not just a troubled child's) dream. It is also Margaret Lawrence's dream. She designed it carefully, planning an environment that would allow for movement, expression, drama, privacy, and confrontation. The consultation room, where we meet for our interviews, is a smaller, more adult space full of treasures that reflect Margaret's history and passions. Family photographs are carefully arranged to allow everyone's face to be seen. There are African Mkonda statues, a redwood image made by a sculptor friend of "Mother and Child," a calendar picturing beautiful

brown Indian women with babies on their backs, a miniature porcelain black infant, and a handwoven hanging from West Africa that
covers an entire wall. Because this is where Margaret sees her adult
patients, there are the more typical doctor's office furnishings: a
medical degree from the College of Physicians and Surgeons, Columbia University, 1940; a Master of Science in Public Health degree
from the Columbia School of Public Health, 1943; diplomas from
the American Board of Pediatrics, 1948, and the New York Psychiatric Institute, 1950; and a Certificate in Psychoanalysis from the
Columbia Psychoanalytic Clinic for Training and Research, 1951. An
answering machine with lots of buttons and buzzers sits on top of a
small teak desk. The analytic couch does not resemble its Freudian
prototype. A handsome black leather two-seater, it is partially covered
by a friendly quilt.

An entire wall is covered with books and journals. The two books
Margaret has written, *The Mental Health Team in the Schools* (1971)
and *Young Inner City Families* (1975), are sandwiched among hundreds
of volumes on child development, psychiatry and psychoanalysis, and
public health. Although her professional life is largely devoted to
clinical practice, Margaret has made time to document the pioneering
programs in child psychotherapy that she has developed in schools,
day-care centers, and hospital clinics. In her file drawers are half-
written monographs based on observations she has collected while
visiting families and child-care centers in the southern United States
and in countries in West Africa. These are part of a cross-cultural
search, tracing the connections among historical and cultural forces,
community context, family dynamics, and the development of ego
strength. "No matter what I'm writing about, that is the theme that
keeps surfacing, *ego-strength.*"

As we talk, I sit in the chair used by most of my mother's patients.
It is a comfortable, simply designed Danish chair with green woven
fabric, placed to face the doctor directly. Margaret Lawrence likes to
see her patients. This arrangement permits no obstruction and no
escape between doctor and patient. As she sits at her desk, Margaret
can also look out into the woods. She calls the view "dreamy" and
seems to derive nourishment from this direct connection to nature.

As she listens to her patients, she watches the change of seasons: new buds, full summer lushness, reddening maples. When winter comes, she can follow the winding path of a brook several yards from her office.

Margaret's body settles into her chair; she straightens her back for comfort, clasps her hands in her lap, and fixes her eyes on me. She is ready. I feel her full attention and eagerness to proceed. She looks forward to our sessions, for the chance to sit together uninterrupted, for the excuse to focus on her own life. I turn on the tape recorder, prepare to take notes, and remind her of where we traveled during our last session. Once she gets located in time, Margaret needs little prompting. She pauses as she reflects on the many paths converging in her head. She picks one and sets forth. The story gains in feeling and intensity as she proceeds, churning up fantasies, dreams, and new detours. If I insist on a literal tale or stop her for the facts, she loses her momentum.

Margaret moves through time and space in her own characteristic way. Her mind is poetic and playful, not literal or analytic; she rarely follows strict chronology, rarely remembers dates but never forgets history. She speaks directly from feelings, from emotional content. Her mind puts things together that others see as disparate or unconnected. She can make patterns from stray remnants of all shapes and colors. Hers is an intelligence exquisitely suited to a psychoanalyst who must help the patient integrate fragments of history, gathering loose threads from the distant past.

Margaret's memories are not edited. Only twice in all of our sessions together has she censored herself. At one point, she spoke about a woman we both know, who had appeared in a fascinating and murky dream, and had second thoughts. "You'd better check with her first before you recount the dream ... even though it is my dream, it speaks about her." Several months later, after describing an aunt's dalliance with a male suitor, she worries out loud. "There's more ... but it's all gossip and I'm reluctant to repeat it." Usually Margaret does not restrain the images and feelings that seem to tumble out of her mouth "of their own free will." She does not hold back tears or rage or laughter. More than once, Margaret exclaims softly, "This feels like a second analysis." After every session we are exhausted—sometimes exhilarated by discovery and memories of victory, sometimes saddened by images of defeat and humiliation.

We travel together across time and space, tracing Margaret's ancestry, her parents' marriage, her childhood and adolescence, school and college, her own marriage and early years as a parent. We journey hundreds of miles from the Deep South to New York; from all-black Magnolia High School in Vicksburg, Mississippi, to an integrated elite classical girls' high school in New York; from the middle-class Negro society of Vicksburg, where "white folks were totally irrelevant," to the all-white, professional circles of the Columbia Psychoanalytic Clinic; from a deeply religious family whose members "were in touch with the spirits" but "never talked about feelings" to training in a field where religion is denigrated and considered childlike and where feelings are the currency of discourse; from a family dominated by powerful women who were merciless to men to a marriage defined by respectful and loving equality. Margaret's journey travels a great distance but returns to the same place; "I've never really left Harlem," she reminds me.

As I travel with my mother, I am most interested in her interior journey. I listen for how she feels about the family drama, not for bare facts. I listen for how she perceives community, prejudice, illness and healing, not for an objective rendering of the sociohistorical contexts. Her narrative is enriched by hundreds of letters she has saved, by diaries, school records, fellowship applications, medical reports, and photographs. I am able to contrast her voice with her written work: published articles, essays, and books and unpublished poetry.

My mother and I carefully separate our book interviews from our family talk, vigilantly marking the boundaries so that the work will keep its integrity and momentum and so that we can recapture our familiar mother-daughter patterns. This is not as hard as we feared. We walk from the office to the kitchen and feel ourselves moving back into the present and back to family habits. My mother provides the cues as she spots a thirsty plant ("Maybe I'm giving it too much direct sun") or asks about her four-year-old grandson ("How is Martin? Is he loving nursery school?"). Soon we are putting the finishing touches on dinner, back in the old groove together. My mother anticipates my visits by fixing special feasts. The veal stew, the shrimp stir-fry, are both bountiful and beautiful, and we are always hungry after our work. We make it through these days, I realize, much the way we manage our lives—living fully in the moment, concentrating completely, and providing markers that define the occasion. Dinner is ready, the table is set with a golden tablecloth and burnt-orange napkins. We sing grace, two women's voices praising the journey.

Richmond

THE FIRST MARGARET

MARGARET Elizabeth Duke Smith stood at the center of her family, radiating power in all directions. Deep olive–skinned, ample bodied, stern, "Mom Margaret" dominated her children with a mighty will. She had won the dependence as well as the devotion of each one. The oldest of her three daughters, Maria Ann (known as Ninnie), did not dare to marry until after Mom Margaret's death. Harvey Brown courted her for more than thirty years. He would arrive with his fat cigar and his *New York Times* every Sunday morning and sit on the living room couch until he was served Sunday dinner, patiently waiting for Ninnie. Not much conversation, just a long wait. It had been made clear to him that Ninnie would not be available until her mother died; and he persevered quietly and patiently. By the time Mom Margaret was dead, they were both in their early sixties. Ninnie never recovered from the sadness of losing her mother, and Harvey was never taken completely into her heart. Even after their marriage, he still seemed to be waiting on the couch, a wait that by now anticipated very little. After all, no man could fill the place once occupied by Mom Margaret.

Mary Elizabeth, the bravest of the Smith girls, secretly married Sandy Alonzo Morgan at the house of one of their friends. Although brave enough to marry, she didn't dare leave home immediately. Mary knew that her mother would not tolerate being abandoned by her children. Marriage was the most devastating abandonment. Mary returned home after her simple wedding and told only her older sister Ninnie, swearing her to secrecy. A few days later Ninnie, who enjoyed her role as the "good daughter in the family," leaked the news to their mother. She looked forward to the fireworks. Mom Margaret waited for the moment when she and Mary were together preparing dinner in the kitchen. Almost before Mary heard her mother's raging words, she watched Mom Margaret pick up a teacup and hurl it at her head. The daughter's reflexes were quick—she had grown used to her mother's sudden outbursts of anger—and she ducked just in time to avoid the cup and hear it shatter against the wall behind her. As the chips of china spilled to the floor, she felt her heart break. She knew then she would always yearn for the old bonds. No matter how far she traveled, she would always be drawn back to her mother, always want to feel secure in her love.

Even more than abandonment, Mom Margaret dreaded the men her daughters might choose. All three Smith girls—Maria Ann, Mary Elizabeth, and Margaret Hazel—were beautiful women, valued for their white skin and "good hair." Ninnie had "the best-quality hair," silky, straight, and smooth, but all three girls had long hair reaching down to their waists that they coiled into neat buns for going out. Margaret Hazel's hair, helped along with a little coloring, was bright red; Ninnie's was a medium brown; and Mary's could look brown or reddish depending on the light and shadows. All of them "could pass for white," and their mother recognized her good fortune in producing such gorgeous daughters. She raised them to believe in their beauty and to appreciate the status their light skin afforded them. In Richmond, Virginia, the Smith girls walked with pride; they dressed well, excelled in school, and joined the right society clubs, gathering places where the "black bourgeoisie" of Richmond came for tea, conversation, and occasional demure parties. Both Maria Ann (who later changed her name to Marie Lillian when she moved to New York because she thought her given name was too southern and too old-fashioned) and Mary Elizabeth became schoolteachers, and Margaret Hazel (always called Hazel) went to seek respectable work in New York City. Since respectable work was then rarely available for Negroes, she "passed" as white and always dreaded the day when she would look into the eyes of another "colored person" and her secret would be found out. For the Smith girls, dignity and whiteness were deeply intertwined. For their mother, whose skin was darker, their whiteness needed to be carefully protected. As far back as the girls could remember, Mom Margaret warned them to be suspicious of the advances of men. Men were not to be trusted. They would tempt you with sweet words, woo you with generous affection, hook you, and leave. The daughters should make sure not to be seduced or tricked by male attentions if they wanted to maintain their status and dignity. But most important, railed Mom Margaret over and over again, they should not marry black men. Black was bad. Black was devious. You couldn't trust black.

When Mom Margaret hurled the teacup at Mary, she was raging not only at her abandonment but especially at Mary's choice. Her second oldest daughter had chosen to marry a man Mom Margaret considered black (actually a dark brown–skinned man) who might ravage the hard-earned status of the family. And in their turn, all three sisters, despite their mother's grim admonitions, chose and married dark-skinned men. Maria Ann, the last to fall from grace, did not want to have her mother endure the shame one more time; so she waited for her to die. Harvey Brown was the blackest of all— as black as his fat, black, smelly cigar.

The anger that Mom Margaret unleashed on her daughters and their men spilled over in torrents from her own desperation. Her husband, Andrew John Smith, strikingly handsome and dapper, was the son of a black slave and her English master. From his father's side he had inherited white skin, silky hair, and sharp features. "Papa Annie" was lovely to behold, and he knew it. For years he was headwaiter at one of the posh clubs in Richmond. All dressed up in his coat and tails, he looked gorgeous. Mom Margaret loved him to distraction; but her love would turn to violent rage when he would suddenly disappear and leave her alone with the children. Without a word, he would leave, travel from Richmond to New York where he would have the time of his life, enjoying the philandering that came easily to him, taking advantage of his beauty and his seductive powers.

Home in Richmond, Virginia, Mom Margaret tried to hold herself and her family together until she could no longer restrain her fury. When the combined forces of love and hate grew too powerful to resist, Mom Margaret would head north in search of her wandering husband. Sometimes she would take her children with her and they would scour the city together. The children could feel their mother's pain and her seething anger as they pounded the streets in search of their father. They would always find Papa Annie but the search could go on for days. When they found him, his charm would turn to guilt and apology, and his wife's rage would melt into tears. The reunions were passionate affairs filled with lust and rage. Papa Annie and Mom Margaret would return to Richmond with new promises and hopes. They would make another baby together, and he would leave again when her belly began to swell.

When she was eighty-six years old, Mary Elizabeth replayed "the search" over and over again. Now living with her own daughter, Margaret, and her daughter's husband, Charles, she would rise out of bed in the middle of the night and her mind would take her back more than eighty years. She would pound on Margaret and Charles's bedroom door searching for her mother and father. Then she would tell her daughter the story as if she were living it just then. Margaret remembers those haunting nights. "Her memory was of finding Papa Annie in a boardinghouse; of her mother and Papa Annie sleeping beside her on a bed, while she, a three-year-old, slept on top of a nearby trunk. Part of this memory was a fantasy that she could still reach her mother and father who were in the bed beside her involved with each other. . . . Months before her final illness she would come out in the hall and knock on our door, wanting to get to *the other* Margaret and her father, knowing they were engaged with one another."

Certain that Papa Annie would leave her again, Mom Margaret always worked ferociously to support her family. At one point she built a thriving laundry business for actors and actresses in touring companies. She hired several women to help her with the washing, starching, and ironing and became known as someone who could prepare fancy costumes in quick time. This was a fast business. Mom Margaret would catch a train in the morning and travel some distance from Richmond. Then she would change to the train bringing actors and actresses to Richmond and go from car to car picking up their laundry so she'd be ahead of anybody else that might offer to do laundry in Richmond. Mom Margaret would bring the laundry home, and she and the other women would work at a feverish pitch to have it done by performance time. She would then rush to the theater, usually carrying along some of her children. Mom Margaret would have them sit quietly backstage while she distributed the costumes. When Hazel, the youngest Smith child, was about five, her mother found her a dark corner and told her to wait there. Hazel could hear the hum of the actors' voices on the stage and soon drifted off to sleep. Suddenly the sound effects called for a roll of thunder and flashes of lightning. Hazel, startled out of her sleep, was terrified in this strange dark place and began to cry out for her mother. The audience heard the child's wails even above the thunderous roar, until Mom Margaret came tearing back to collect her frightened child.

The laundry work appealed to Mom Margaret's impatient and competitive temperament. She liked moving quickly and beating out the competition. She liked being on the edge of the theater world, participating backstage. And she liked not being under the direct domination of a boss. Although she was serving lots of people, they were always moving on to the next place and she never had to assume a long-term subservient role in relation to them.

The laundry business was certainly better than the job she had had several years earlier as the matron of a "poorhouse." This came at "a low point" in Mom Margaret's life. Papa Annie had deserted her and she already had two children, Maria Ann and Andrew, her only son, named after his father. Desperate for work, Mom Margaret took the children to live with her in the poorhouse, a horrible asylum for the poor, the sick, and the elderly, who each fed on the other's infirmities. This was no place for children, and their mother alternated between wanting to protect them from the horrors to wanting to be rid of them. She was deeply distressed and isolated and had no energy for their lively spirits. Andrew was an active fellow who liked to explore the place. His noise disturbed the old folks, who often grew impatient with him. When Mom Margaret could no longer bear his noise, she would lock him in the basement. When Margaret tells this family story, her face winces at the terror of it. "Andrew was about seven or eight, and Mom Margaret would put him in the basement of the poorhouse, which was the morgue, locking him in there with dead bodies.... He grew up to be psychotic; this was enough to account for it." Mom Margaret's anger at the boy's father came down heavily on her son. The Andrews became merged in her mind. Rage at the abandoning father was mirrored in her abuse of the helpless boy. "I think that Mom Margaret, having had such troubles with Papa Annie, found the boy child hard to take.... Here she had to work to keep them alive and couldn't tolerate any misbehavior or aggressiveness on Andrew's part ... at this job her children had to be with her."

When Mom Margaret was pregnant with her third child, Mary Elizabeth, her desperation grew almost unbearable. Another appearance from Papa Annie; the passionate reunion; another pregnancy; another baby to care for. Papa Annie was gone again. With the newborn bundled in her arms, she roamed the house, reckless with despair. Her mother, who was visiting for the birth, suddenly could not find her daughter and new granddaughter. She called out for them and then searched anxiously in every room of the house. Where could they have disappeared? "Finally she decided to try the attic. When Mom Margaret saw her mother she burst into tears, and her mother said, 'What are you doing?' She had completely undressed the baby and had her lying naked on a bed in the attic. She said, 'I can't take care of another baby.' "

Mom Margaret did manage to raise and care for Mary Elizabeth, and then after her Margaret Hazel—four children in all. She would always manage to raise herself up out of the ashes and live on. She was strong and resilient, a survivor. But the energy and courage required to persevere brought her a fierce and unforgiving nature. In Margaret's memories, she is large and imposing. "I have many stories about my grandmother. I remember walking down the street with her when I was about five years old and my grandmother stopping at a pushcart with peaches. She would lean over, pick up a peach, hand it to me, and say, 'Let's go.' As we walked off, the man would say, 'Hey lady,' and Mom Margaret would say, 'I just want a peach for the little girl' as she continued to walk away. That was my grandmother!"

Years later, when Margaret was a teenager living in Harlem with her Aunt Ninnie and Mom Margaret, she respected and avoided her grandmother's indomitable will. They lived together in the Dunbar Apartments on 149th Street and Eighth Avenue, an elegant housing complex for middle- and upper-middle-income black residents. Margaret remembers the uncompromising directives that Mom Margaret would issue daily. "My grandmother would send me to the A&P Tea Company and she would say 'Get me a half a pound of Oolong and a half a pound of Gunpowder (Oolong was black and Gunpowder was green), and don't get them mixed. I'll mix them.' From time to time I would forget or I would be too embarrassed to ask, and they would mix and weigh them. When I arrived home with the teas mixed, Grandmother would tell me to take them back and I did."

But sometimes Mom Margaret tried to push her power too far and Margaret would resist. When Margaret arrived in New York from Mississippi to live with her aunt and grandmother, she was fourteen years old and not in the habit of wearing a bra. Her body had been fully developed since she was eleven or twelve years old, but her mother had never encouraged her to buy a bra and Margaret found them strange and inhibiting to wear. But here in the big city, Aunt Ninnie and Grandmother insisted that she wear one. They wanted to "contain" this adolescent girl, get her under tight wraps. Margaret's refusal was silent. She simply hid the thing. "I would tuck it under the mattress and springs of my bed." This quiet resistance worked with the struggle over underwear, but she had to confront another intrusive directive from her grandmother more directly. This time the Margarets clashed and the younger one was victorious. "Once my grandmother went too far and she said to me, 'Margaret, I know about girls and I want to see your napkin every month.' I said, 'What? I'll *never* do that. I won't show it to you!' And she never said another thing to me. I was another Margaret. *That was going too far.*"

The sense of discovering the limits of power, "of going too far," is something Margaret herself had experienced. Uncle Andrew lived in the New York household with Grandmother and Aunt Ninnie. By the time Margaret moved from Vicksburg to New York, Andrew, then in his fifties, had become seriously psychotic. The horrifying experience of being locked in the morgue at seven years old, the anger from his mother that he received as the only boy child of his philandering father, the long loneliness of his father's absences, all combined to break his spirit. He became increasingly disturbed, more noticeably so around his thirtieth birthday, and his mother suffered with guilt and remorse. In the Dunbar apartments, Andrew stayed on a cot in the dining room. He spent endless hours silently peering out the window of the dining room into the courtyard below, his eyes empty, his face passive, his body immobile. The long silences would be interrupted by his hallucinations, loud talk, and gestures of punching the air. Margaret grew used to the vacant silence, but she couldn't stand the loud, eerie noise.

"Andrew would talk to himself out loud, and I had a strong feeling that he could do something to control this. I was very self-righteous with absolutely no understanding of what had happened to him and no understanding of mental illness. . . ." One day Andrew's wild screaming did not just annoy and disturb Margaret but touched a raw nerve. She was enraged. "Stop making all that noise!" she yelled at the top of her lungs. "Stop it, you sissy!" Andrew lost control. "He lunged at me, and I realized that *I had gone too far*." Like Margaret in relation to her grandmother, Andrew would not allow himself to be abused. When the intrusiveness turned to assault, even Andrew fought to protect himself in the household. Margaret's choice of words had stung. Even in his hallucinatory state, he could hear the implied emasculation. "Sissy meant to me that you're not a man."

Margaret's attack on Andrew came out of a deep sense of humiliation. "I was embarrassed by him. I never wanted to bring anyone home with him making his noise." Margaret also identified with her grandmother's pain. She was angry with Andrew for the distress he caused Mom Margaret. "I know how my grandmother suffered. . . . We all realized that Grandmother had this strong involvement and concern for her boy. You have to understand that it was not that she hated having a boy child; she *loved* having a boy child just like she loved her husband. But she had disrespect for a male who reminded her of her husband. . . . Andrew's relationship with his mother was obviously very rough, but he was her heart." Andrew consumed much of Mom Margaret's passion and energy, leaving less for everyone else. Fifteen-year-old Margaret was enraged by the way Andrew robbed the rest of them.

Mom Margaret had been born and raised in Richmond, Virginia.

The oldest family legend is a tender tale of Mom Margaret, a young girl of seven, sitting on the street curb at the end of the Civil War when Grant entered Richmond. "The legend goes that her father, Papa Duke, had gone fishing the day Grant's army came into the streets of Richmond. My grandmother remembers sitting on the curb as the army passed by and weeping with fear. A soldier stopped and offered her candy from his pocket. He said, 'Don't cry, little girl. Go home and tell your people they are free.' " The story brings tears to the eyes of Mom Margaret's granddaughter, now seventy years old. Tears for that young girl at the beginning of her life with all its possibilities and for the struggles and despair she would face as the years went by. Tears for another Margaret, fearful of the sound of the soldiers' boots hitting the pavement, but brave and resilient, able to move through fear and beyond it.

Mom Margaret loved Papa Duke and took him into her home when he was old, sick, and dying. She loved his strength, his manliness, and his devotion to his family. Now grown, married, and the mother of four children, Mom Margaret nursed her father during his final days. "One of the famous stories about them was about the gathering in the house when her father died. There was Aunt Ria, who was the oldest, Uncle Willy, Mom Margaret, and Aunt Vic, who was about the same age as Aunt Ninnie (Mom Margaret's oldest child). Aunt Ria came from the country on a wagon with her many children all weeping and wailing. The noisy procession reached Mom Margaret's house and went in. Aunt Ria, seeing her younger sister, cried out sorrowfully, 'Margaret, Margaret, our father is dead!' They were hugging and crying, and Aunt Ria said through her tears, 'Margaret, where are father's gold-rimmed spectacles?' And Margaret responded, 'I've got them and I'm going to keep them!' "

Mary Elizabeth Smith was introduced to the Reverend Sandy Alonzo Morgan by a mutual friend in Richmond. A graduate of Richmond Colored High and Normal, Mary was a dedicated and caring teacher. Sandy Morgan had recently completed his studies at the Bishop Payne Divinity School, an "Episcopal Seminary for Negroes" in Petersburg, Virginia. Upon graduation he joined a rare breed of black Episcopal priests serving Negro communities in the Deep South. A photograph of his graduating class shows six serious and determined men all dressed in their black clerical garb. But the camaraderie and competition among the classmates were lively. "My father told a story of everyone sitting around in somebody's room trying to decide who was blackest. After comparing the variations in their blackness, they decided on a winner. The fellow who won was black on the palms of his hands and the soles of his feet." Margaret's father would throw his head back in laughter each time he would describe this scene. He never tired of his favorite stories, and this one seemed to capture something about the spirit and sense of humor in this small male group. It also reminded Reverend Morgan of his joyful commitment to the ministry; how wonderful it felt to find work that was fulfilling and important.

Until he enrolled in the seminary, Sandy Morgan's school experiences had not been particularly satisfying. Graduating from the public high school in Richmond, he had enrolled in Hampton Institute, a "sort of high and normal school" in nearby Hampton, Virginia. Like Tuskegee Institute in Alabama—the school started by Booker T. Washington—Hampton had a militaristic flavor. The young men were expected to be highly disciplined, cleanly and neatly dressed, punctual and mannerly. Not only was it a highly controlled environment, it was also dominated by Washington's ideology: a set of values that urged "Negroes" to be industrious and patient, that saw agricultural work as their chief economy, and that stressed the separation and contrasting competencies of blacks and whites. The spit and polish and the restricted atmosphere turned Sandy Morgan off, and he spent a good deal of energy plotting an escape. At Hampton, there was a woman doctor, called Doctress Walden, who cared for the sick students. Sandy Morgan would often visit Doctress Walden's office with one complaint or another. These frequent appearances made the Doctress suspicious, so she finally decided to check his temperature. Sandy met the challenge by learning to "blow up" the thermometer to make it register a fever.

When his various attempts to leave gracefully met dead ends, he became bolder. "My father was caught smoking on the school grounds, and that was considered a terrible offense. There were several boys out in the dark smoking, and my father claims he wasn't smoking but was huddled in the shadows with the group. The commandant came along and said, 'Who is there?' and the boys scattered in all directions. My father started running and he never came back. That was when he left Hampton for good."

The next stop was St. Paul's College in Lawrenceville, Virginia, another normal school that was not as committed to military styles and regimented order. It was a brand new school, and the students learned carpentry skills through working on the institution's buildings. As they learned to hammer nails and lay brick, slowly the modest buildings rose around them. Industry and perseverance mattered at St. Paul's, but the discipline did not feel as stultifying as it had at Hampton. Sandy Morgan did not enjoy the carpentry work, but he was proud of the building on which he was put to work and on which his name remains carefully engraved along with his fellow builders. "My father never loved physical work," Margaret remembers with a smile, "but one of the jobs he was given at St. Paul's was to work on the chapel." Already committed to the ministry, he could tolerate the sweat and toil because he was engaged in building the Lord's house. "My father tells the story of learning how to saw and the teacher saying to him, 'You've been working on that same board all day long, and it takes everybody else about three minutes to do it. You're not a carpenter.'"

His instructor's judgment did not greatly disturb Sandy Morgan, for he knew that his skills lay elsewhere, in social and intellectual realms. He enjoyed reading and talking and meeting and greeting. He liked reaching out to people, guiding them through tough times. He relished ritual and ceremony and being center stage. And he was drawn to spiritual life, to the sacred dimensions of human encounter, and to the healing of mind, body, and soul.

Sandy Morgan had been drawn to the ministry since childhood. His father, William, died when he was a few years old, and his mother, Sarah, was left to support her family of four children. "Here again was a woman holding her family together," says Margaret as she sees the parallel life struggles of her maternal and paternal grandmothers. "Grandma Sarah," who had come to this country from Guyana, was of Carab Indian ancestry, with high cheekbones, aquiline nose, and thick, silky black hair. Since Grandma Sarah died when she was three, Margaret's memories of her are sparse—not nearly as strong as her images of Mom Margaret. A very large sepia-colored photograph of Sarah Morgan still hangs in Margaret's living room and invites fantasies of this handsome woman. She appears both strong and graceful, forceful and feminine. Sarah's eyes, which seem to inquire as well as protect, were inherited by her granddaughter Margaret.

When her husband died, Sarah Morgan went to work as the "janitress" of a white Lutheran Church in Richmond. She would clean the church and parish house, maintain the church grounds, and on Sundays she would pump the organ. Sandy, her third child, would usually go along. He loved being around Sarah as she polished the pews and shined the silver candle holders, and he loved the sense of solace and peace he felt inside the big church. When he got to be old enough, he inherited the job of organ pumper. Sometimes, during the Sunday service, the ritualized voice of the minister would sooth him to sleep and he would have to be awakened for the hymns. The Lutheran minister took a liking to the young boy and noticed his attraction to church life. Thinking this interest should not be wasted—it was so unusual to see a youngster enamored of church—the minister suggested to Sandy's mother that he introduce her son to a priest in the black church. The priest Sandy met was affiliated with the "colored" Episcopal Church in Richmond, and the boy began to attend his church regularly. In Sandy Morgan the priest saw great interest and potential, and he soon began to mold the boy for the priesthood. "Sandy took to it like a duck to water," says his daughter. "Here's a white minister who sees a nice little black boy with no father and introduces him to the black minister. The black minister took him under his care and wanted him to do well. I think if somebody does that, there is an expectation ... children respond to that sort of thing."

Besides responding to the care, attention, and expectation, Sandy Morgan saw in the ministry—particularly the relatively high status Episcopal ministry—the opportunity for a respectable career. His mother deeply valued education, dignity, and decorum in her children, and insisted through her will and energetic example that they become upstanding citizens. Sandy felt the responsibility of her message, and so did his older sisters Hattie, who became a teacher, and

Leah, who married a successful lawyer and gained status through him. "By being an Episcopal minister he got a good deal of respect from his family," says Margaret. "Aunt Hattie and Aunt Leah both expressed great pride in their brother's chosen vocation."

This family admiration felt good to the young minister, but a deeper pleasure in the ministry grew out of a match between his temperament and his vocation. He had a personality that seemed to thrive on the gregarious, reciprocal nature of the ministry, giving *and* receiving! Often he would say, "He's a great person and he thinks the world of me." "My father was very outgoing with his parishioners; people liked him." He reached out to people beyond the Episcopal church. "My father was *ecumenical* long before anybody used the word. He would go on occasion to the Baptist church, or the Methodist church, and the ministers would say, 'Oh, I see that Reverend Morgan is in the congregation. Come on up here, Reverend Morgan.'" He reached out to people on the other side of the tracks. "My father would go anywhere to see his parishioners, or to see anybody who expressed an interest in the church. . . . He would go over to the Red Light District on Mulberry Street in Vicksburg. He was always careful to take me along with him . . . so that no one would misinterpret his reasons for being there. I loved my father . . . I think I had a feeling of being on his side." Father and daughter would go out together to minister to the community; Reverend Morgan always dressed in his formal clerical garb, and his daughter in a neat, starched dress.

Sometimes the ministry would take them to homes that felt mysterious and ominous to the young girl. "I have a memory of going on a streetcar to a house near Magnolia Avenue High School, to see a lady named Miss Harrison. We went in, and I noticed she was wearing a wig which to me had a sense of utter falsehood. (As a child I was so unforgiving.) Maybe I thought my father shouldn't have been visiting. . . . There was some question in my mind of how she lived. My mind raced . . . Was she one of the ladies of the evening from Mulberry Street? . . . She brought out beaten biscuits, and I was very afraid to eat them. Beaten biscuits are very hard and flaky, very brittle, and I was afraid to eat them . . . afraid of what might happen to me." Even in this scary place, the girl would watch her father reach out, listen, and counsel. The strange lady with the wig received the same caring attention as the upper-middle-class Negroes who lived on the hill close to the church. So Margaret sat quietly and patiently beside her father, watching him work; waiting to get out of there; courteously avoiding the biscuits.

Occasionally Reverend Morgan's travels took him to places where he hadn't planned to go. He would set out to visit one place and feel compelled to change his plans. "Something would tell him" that he was needed elsewhere, and he would let "the Spirit" (the Holy Spirit) direct him to the unplanned destination. "My father had feelings which led him. One day he was walking down the street toward downtown and something said to him, 'Go and see Mr. Jones,' and Father said out loud to himself, 'No, I can go to see him another time. I'm going to the bank.' Again he started across the street to the bank, stopped again, and thought he'd better go and see Mr. Jones immediately. He cuts off, walks maybe a mile to this man's house. Vicksburg is on a lot of bluffs and he has to climb up and up. When he finally arrives he knocks on the door, but nobody answers. The door is ajar, so he pushes it open and there sits the man dead." Reverend Morgan counted on spiritual forces to guide and direct him in his work. "He might have even said that he was in touch with the man's soul." Although he would sometimes resist for a moment "the feelings that led him" and arrive too late, he had great respect for them. "Apperceiving [being conscious of perceiving] 'that of God' in himself and others was just one of the aspects of his life," explains his daughter as a way of describing how her father naturally incorporated the Spirit into his everyday life.

Sandy Morgan believed in the laying on of hands, the healing powers of prayer, but he did not practice "the healing ministry" publicly. He did not regard himself as an evangelist who could make the lame man suddenly rise and walk or make the blind child see. His view of healing was something more subtle: a belief in the healing power of prayer; a belief in the deep connections between spiritual and physical recovery. Occasionally he would have a series of healing sessions with one of his parishioners in the church study. "He knew better than to lay hands on women, but he would lay hands on male friends," says Margaret who was moved by what she saw—the slow evolution toward health, the power of caring and praying.

When Mary Elizabeth and Sandy Morgan married, they each carried into the union a single-minded purpose. Mary wanted to continue to teach children to read and write and "figure." She was dedicated to teaching. And Reverend Morgan saw his life deeply committed to the ministry. But the outlook on the world that each brought was very different. When Mary finally disentangled herself from Mom Margaret's tight hold, she brought along the reticence and shyness that were part of her character and the sadness of separation from her powerful mother, a sadness that never seemed to leave her. He brought along his outgoing, adventurous spirit and his optimism about the inspiration and fulfillment to be found in the ministry. Their first stop was Fayetteville, North Carolina, where Reverend Morgan became the minister for a small black "charge." "There were plenty of black charges in North Carolina and Virginia, in every sizable town," explains Margaret. These places were not full-blown churches. They were tiny outposts of the Episcopal church, with modest buildings, minimal resources, and meager congregations. They often seemed like lonely, isolating places to Mary, who was raised in the Richmond urban society. These desolate places with dusty roads depressed her and made her long for the company of her mother and sisters. She missed the company of women and would grow quietly angry at her husband for stealing her away from them.

In Fayetteville, the young couple had their first child, a beautiful boy whom they named after his father, but who inherited his mother's coloring. They called him "Candy Man" because of his white skin and blond curls. To both parents the baby seemed like a glorious miracle, so gorgeous he was. But for eyes that could have seen, there were warnings of disaster when he was born—a congenital illness that was never fully understood or explained. Less than a year later, Candy Man was dead. There was nothing any doctor could do. Their beautiful, first born son died in Mom Margaret's arms, his arms and legs flailing wildly and then collapsing into a silent heap. The sadness filled the Morgans' household and lingered there forever, rarely mentioned. The sadness moved with the Morgans from church to church, house to house, following them around like a shadow. Each time they moved, Candy Man's picture would be hung in the central spot in the living room over the couch. From this lofty position Sandy Alonzo Morgan, Jr., would gaze down on his family.

Soon after Candy Man's death their second child was on the way. By then the Morgans had moved from Fayetteville, North Carolina, to Portsmouth, Virginia, Mary reluctantly and Sandy optimistically. Mary was thirty when her second child arrived, and her husband was thirty-three. Several weeks before the baby was due, Mary traveled north to be with her mother during childbirth. She wanted the baby to be born in a fine northern city hospital. She didn't want to risk the casualties that might occur in the South, where medical care for blacks was very poor. Margaret Cornelia, a beautiful brown baby girl, was born on August 19, 1914, at Sloan's Hospital for Women in New York City.

Widewater to
Vicksburg
❀

PREACHING AND TEACHING

MARGARET's memories do not reach back to Portsmouth, Virginia, the place where she and her mother returned several weeks after her birth. But her memories do stretch back much farther than most people's, and they form visual pictures that she can retrieve with astounding ease. Her hands draw pictures in the air as she describes the scene. She does not worry about the memory's accuracy. The truth she is searching for is by now a rich mixture of recollection, legend, and fantasy. Her very first memory is of Newbern, North Carolina. The Morgan family had moved from the black charge in Portsmouth months after Margaret's birth and paused in Newbern long enough for Margaret, not much over a year old, to record the picture. "What I remember was that the church was next to the house with a covered cement walkway in between and that you had to come out of the church on the side. My *fantasy* is that I was a baby and somebody dropped me on the cement ... someone was caring for me and dropped me on the hard pavement ... I think I remember the fall ... I didn't walk until I was two and a half ... whether I really got injured and that caused the delay in my walking, or whether I just got scared, I don't know." The fall is all that she remembers of Newbern. "By the time I was three, I was in Widewater, Virginia."

Widewater was another small rural town, dreary and isolated, and Mary dreaded the move. Reverend Morgan, in typical fashion, saw it as a new opportunity and was ready to leave Newbern. "My father would stay a year or a year and a half at a place and then get a call to go somewhere else. If the people didn't suit him, he shook the dust off his feet and moved on. It was fairly easy to get a call. You just had to let the bishops know that you were ready to move and somebody would call you." Sandy Morgan's optimism was mixed with impatience and some measure of ambition. Maybe the next place would offer the new challenges and opportunities he was looking for. He was running from boredom and repetition. As soon as she would hear the awful news that her husband had received the bishop's call, Mary would fall into a deep sadness. She hated to go, hated to sever the tenuous roots she had begun to set down in the strange soil. Before she could even find her bearings, they were on the move again. Mary would slump into depression, and her husband would busy himself with getting the house packed. She had no energy for the move; he seemed to find new vigor in dismantling the house and packing boxes.

When the Morgans arrived in Widewater, Mary took to her bed. Each uprooting had disastrous effects on her energy and spirit. Mary would go to bed and stay there for weeks, unresponsive, unavailable, "with her face to the wall," "as though she were dead." The father and the daughter would have to fend for themselves. Margaret's memories of Widewater are vivid. "I can see a crossroads between Quantico and Washington," says Margaret, sketching the geography on a desk. "The church is on the main road and along a side road nearby. On a knoll is the two-story house where we lived. There was a big apple tree in the front. Somewhere between the church and the house was a two-story barn. There was a swinging bridge over the brook, and the pigs were on the other side of the bridge." The scene, which Margaret calls a "screen memory," is connected to more painful memories of family struggles in this remote, country town. "My father had no experience whatsoever with rural living and neither had my mother. . . . I don't know how long she stayed in bed. I remember there was a living room near the front door, a dining room, and steps going upstairs to the bedrooms. I remember going up the steps when I was three years old, knowing my mother was in that room, and I wouldn't go in. She was like dead and I was too scared to go in." Margaret's face reflects the anger and pain of seventy years ago, of the young child whose mother was closed up in the room, "like dead."

When his wife went to bed, Reverend Morgan took care of Margaret, and his care expressed his devotion to both his daughter and his ailing wife, and his anger at the circumstances. He would rise in the morning, put on his heavy robe, and begin the sloppy ritual of cooking oatmeal. Margaret remembers his seething rage as he fiercely stirred the thick gray mixture, spilling the stuff on the stove and dripping it all over his robe. When he finally finished cooking the lumpy, slimy porridge, it was utter punishment to eat. Each morning he would put it in front of his young daughter with the instructions that she should eat it without complaint, and Margaret would suffer every spoonful.

Just as Margaret can remember the awful texture of her father's oatmeal, she can also bring back the feeling of her hand in his as they would walk out back to feed the pigs. The squeeze of his large dark hand was not reassuring. It was hard and scared; she could feel his desperate worry. "I can remember him holding my hand and bringing slop to the pigs on the other side of the small bridge . . . walking along and saying, 'My God, can you imagine . . . here I am, my wife in bed, a three-year-old child, taking slop to the pigs . . . that is the *last* thing I want to be doing.'"

The neighbors and parishioners were generous country folk who felt sorry for the minister. "They offered their help to Reverend Morgan whose wife was sick. They didn't think emotionally sick; she was just sick." Margaret remembers the neighbors filling their house, the warmth and comfort of their talk and laughter. "The neighbors were good people. They came over and helped shuck the corn and kill the hogs—that memory is just as fresh today as it ever was. My mother was still in bed and the house was full of people downstairs. A round tin tub was full of chitterlings in the dining room, and hanging from the ceiling was a big balloon. It was a hog bladder. Somebody had hung it up there and while nobody was looking I got up on a chair and reached for the balloon. The chair slipped and I fell in the chitterlings." From head to toe, Margaret was smeared with the repugnant smelling slime. The neighbor women rescued her from the big pot and began the restoration project. "My mother wasn't there, so the women stripped me and put me in a tin bathtub. The house was full of people downstairs; hog-killing time was a big time ... and I could hear their voices rising as the ladies scrubbed me down."

There was only one thing that would make Mary rise out of her sick bed; one thing that would finally lift the terrible depression. She would rise to teach. After weeks lying motionless in bed, one day Mrs. Morgan would peel the covers back, put her feet down on the floor, and decide it was time to teach. In Widewater she rose up to teach all the black children within shouting distance—children of all ages. And she taught with devotion and love. "She was a *fierce* teacher," says her daughter proudly. "You see, she was a teacher from the beginning—from before she met my father—and she *wanted* to teach. She was forceful. . . . You *had* to learn with my mother . . . when I was three years old she taught me how to read. . . . She was a very involved teacher ... there was never a slow learner for my mother. . . . She stayed late if somebody was having trouble learning something. Sometimes she'd put a book under her pillow and see if she could dream about the best way to teach some arithmetic lesson that somebody was having trouble with." Even as a very small child, Margaret recognized her mother's uncommon devotion to teaching. Nowhere else did her mother show the same aggressiveness and commitment. Nowhere else did she seem as alive as she was in the classroom—outgoing, demanding, and strong. This reticent woman would transform herself into a spirited, charismatic teacher. In teaching she found her own calling, her chosen work, and her spirit soared. Then, after an energetic week of teaching, Mary would sometimes collapse in bed on Friday and not rise until Monday morning. "But when Monday morning came, she was up and at 'em. I recognized that as a child I made some judgment about how sick my mother really was based on whether she was up and dressed on Monday morning."

When Mary Morgan taught, she worked with few props. In Widewater, one end of the church became her classroom. She and her students sat on the hard wooden pews; they huddled around the wood stove for warmth in the winter; they used borrowed and ancient books; they saved paper and used their pencils until they were tiny stumps. But the students had their teacher, and her skill and caring sustained them. "I can remember sitting on a bench around the stove in winter, with the steam rising up from the children's warm underwear." Mary Morgan was not only interested in developing skills. She also wanted her students to have poise and possess a strong sense of self-esteem. She took these country children, shy and awkward around adults, not practiced in language and decorum, and insisted that they learn how to perform onstage. Practice, drill, and discipline were part of her curriculum as she readied her students to present themselves publicly and show what they had learned in school. When the night of the program arrived, Mrs. Morgan's students would perform with a practiced dignity and a newly acquired grace. These were proud moments. Parents marveled at the transformations in their children. Margaret remembers the terrible moment when she, the youngest child at three years, stood up on the stage and froze. "I can remember getting up there onstage, looking out at the audience, panicking, and closing down."

Mary Morgan showed her aggressiveness in one other way: in her driving. In Widewater the Morgans owned a horse and buggy, which Mary liked to drive very fast. The horse was gray and named George. One day Mary and Margaret set out in the buggy to visit their neighbors, the Daggs. The Daggs used to go down to Quantico and get fish heads for the Reverend and his family. "I don't think my father was very fond of fish heads," observes Margaret, remembering her father's polite but unenthusiastic response to the Daggs' offering of this local delicacy. On this day Margaret and her mother were probably stopping by their friends' house to pick up the fish heads. "We were clipping and clopping along the road when my mother's broad-brimmed hat blew off. My mother said, 'Whoa, George,' and put the reins in my lap. She hopped down from the buggy and said, 'Sit here while I go get my hat!' . . . I can see her running back. Here I was, sitting with the reins in my lap . . . I don't remember thinking about it, but I hear myself saying, 'Git up, George!' What do you think George did? He went tearing down the road at top speed. I looked back and could see my mother running behind the buggy. She couldn't catch up." Margaret throws her head back and laughs. Then the smile of the mischievous girl appears on her face. "Mrs.

Daggs was standing at the top of the hill, yelling, 'Don't worry, he'll stop when he gets here.' George Horse knew that his feed came from the Daggs, so when he arrived at the brink of the hill just in front of their house, he stopped dead away.... My poor mother; *I* was delighted!" My mother laughs again, and I wait to hear about Mary's fury and the reprisals that followed. But Margaret says happily that her "screen memories" allow her to savor the delight but block out the repercussions. "I have no idea what my mother did. I remember only my own pleasure, not what she felt about it. It could well have been my way of getting back at her for staying in bed so long. I must have been angry with her."

The photograph, taken in Richmond where the Morgans had traveled for Grandma Sarah's funeral, shows three-year-old Margaret in high-top shoes, kneesocks, and a starched white dress, with her smooth black hair tied in white ribbons. The photographer has directed her to assume an adultlike pose—standing tall with her right hand placed on a chair and her left hand held poised at her waist. Her face is still, but her eyes are lively, penetrating. Margaret looks long and hard at herself seventy years ago. "This little girl is *aware* of all sorts of things ... she senses conflict ... she doesn't say anything, but she is very much aware." She takes another studied gaze at the photographer as if trying to bring back the little girl's interior thoughts. "I'm looking at my top lip," Margaret explains slowly, "trying to discover whether I see anything there ... I fell down the stairs on that trip to Richmond ... probably down the front stairs at Aunt Leah's house. I still can have a fear of falling, even now. I can feel it now ... suddenly going down, frightening ... I think my mother was there and available, but I suspect that something was happening. Suddenly I'm falling ... and I get the sense that it is related to something else." Margaret struggles to bring it into focus. The "something else" is elusive, but associated with feelings of family conflict, of battling between her mother and father.

"My mother and father always had words," says Margaret as a way of describing the tensions and difficulties between her parents. "They would fight about anything." Some years later, when Margaret was nine or ten years old, the fights had taken on a ritualized pattern. "They would start arguing, and I would hear my father walking down the hall, talking out loud, 'Confound it, you white bitch!' . . . that was the worst—'*confound it*' was like 'damn!'—but it always went with 'white bitch.' " When Sandy Morgan uttered these horrible words, his daughter knew he had been driven to the limits of his rage. They could be arguing about anything, but his fury was related to all the ways his wife was deeply connected to her mother and sisters. Those "entangled ladies" formed a psychic fortress that excluded men. Even though Mary's mother and sisters were hundreds of miles away in New York, and even though Mary "got a cup thrown at her head and managed to get out from under her mother," the Smith women had a powerful pull. "It was very much a family for women," and Mary always "saw herself alone" when she was at home with her husband and child. So on those occasions when Sandy Morgan raged at the "white bitch," he would always follow his name-calling with a phrase that placed Mary in the company of her women. "You're just like the rest of the Smiths." He used to refer to the ladies as "The Smithies," his voice filled with cynicism and anger. "He felt that their world was *the enemy*, really."

Although Sandy Morgan was more vociferous in his anger than Mary, Margaret usually felt that her mother had quietly and subtly driven her father into his rage. She would needle and poke and prod until the cumulative provocations caused an explosion. Then Margaret would hear the heavy footsteps down the hall and the words spoken through clenched teeth, "Confound it, you white bitch." When the battle lines were set, Margaret would feel drawn to her father. "From way back I adored him." And his choice of words, "white bitch," put Margaret and Sandy on the same side of the color line. They were both brown and Mary was "white." Their struggles arose from temperamental differences and familial pulls, but they never could be disentangled from the feelings attached to color. Mary's sense of superiority derived from her fair skin, and Sandy's feeling of rejection was always related to his dark skin.

Just as Sandy Morgan never felt as if his wife gave fully to him, so Mary Morgan was always suspicious of her husband's wandering affections. Her anxiety would cause Mary to punish her husband in almost invisible ways. For a child the punishments were difficult to detect. They could be felt, however: a vague sense of her mother withholding, of her mother acting "alone" even when she was with her husband, of her mother's great energy flowing into teaching with so little left for her family. Mary's imperceptible but deeply felt assaults seemed to flow from her fears of abandonment. "My mother was very often suspicious that my father was seeing another woman. I never knew my father (and I was around him a good bit) to have anything to do with another woman; but my mother would suspect this." Margaret would see her mother kneeling and praying beside her bed, asking God to protect her from her husband's infidelities. When the praying was not enough to sooth her anxieties, she would go searching for him "up and down the streets of Vicksburg." "She would take me along to look for my father. We never found him anyplace that was suspicious."

The urgency of her searching, the relentless anxiety about abandonment, were echoes of her own childhood, of the trips she took with Mom Margaret from Richmond to New York in search of Papa Annie. When the three of them reunited, slept in one room in a boardinghouse, Mary on the top of a traveling trunk, she was no doubt aware of their lovemaking. As Margaret the child analyst reflected on this later, she saw her mother as "a little Electra wanting the love of her papa, herself . . . but also wanting to keep the love of her mother." Echoes of these painful times when Papa Annie deserted the family never left Mary: echoes of her mother's hurt and rage, echoes of their footsteps tracing the streets of New York, echoes of the enraptured reunion. These echoes, not formed into conscious thoughts, drove Mary to the streets of Vicksburg to search for Reverend Morgan.

When Mary insisted that her daughter join her in searching for her father, Margaret's heart would be torn. Margaret resented her mother's suspicious ways and went along with great reluctance. Her mother would hold her hand tightly, demanding that they be allied in their suspicions, in just the way she herself had been dragged along by Mom Margaret. In remembering these searches, at first Margaret is uncharacteristic in her momentary understatement: "This was not a helpful thing for her daughter." Then her voice rises to match her feelings. "I didn't appreciate it; I loved my father to distraction; I very much identified with him. Everyone told me I looked like him.... When I was a preadolescent I was forced into identifying with my mother because she was telling me about these other women who existed in her mind.... Apparently these suspicions had been going on for most of her married life." With hands clasped on their searches, Margaret could not wholly resist her mother's anxieties. She would be disbelieving and harshly skeptical at first. Her fine father, the man she loved so much, would never do such a thing! But the search would slowly undo her determination not to join in her mother's suspicions and she would begin to feel identified with her mother's passionate concern. She twisted under the divided allegiance. Even as she fought off the suspicions, she began to feel the seeds of distrust for her father and for the male species in general. "There was enough identification with my mother that I wondered."

Mary's suspicions also caused Margaret to worry in another direction. Could it be possible that her mother was attracted to other men? Did her fears about her husband mean she felt temptations within herself? Had she ever been drawn to other suitors? Did she want to be seduced? And most important, would her mother one day be carried away in another man's arms? This last fantasy haunted Margaret: fear that her mother would fly away with a stranger and abandon her daughter. Margaret's worries were stirred by Mary's preoccupation with infidelity, but were also linked to the "issue of color." "I thought something about my mother's fair skin would make her attractive to men ... and maybe make her vulnerable to their invitations." So on Mary's searches, Margaret was forced to wonder about her father's possible philandering ("which I had no cause to suspect") at the same time as she concocted fantasies of her mother's wandering affections ("which also seemed to have no basis in reality").

The Morgans had left Widewater when Margaret was five and moved to a parish in Mound Bayou, Mississippi. Mound Bayou, an all-black town of about two thousand people, had been started by a black pioneer named Isaiah T. Montgomery as a place of welcome and retreat for southern blacks. It was a young, spirited town, and the only thing that Margaret recalls from their two-year sojourn in Mound Bayou is meeting the proud and determined founder. By the time Margaret was seven, her father was feeling restless again, ready to move on. This time when he got the bishop's call, he was even more optimistic than usual. This time he would be going to a real city—Vicksburg, Mississippi. With twenty thousand people, it was more than a dreary little town and it represented great possibilities for building a lively and rewarding church community.

As usual, the Reverend's enthusiasm was matched by his wife's sadness. She had felt welcome and protected in Mound Bayou. She had even managed to find a good and trusting friend. Mrs. Mosely, Margaret's piano teacher and the wife of the school's principal, had become Mary's close confidante, and their alliance had sustained her through two years in Mound Bayou. "A good friend you could depend on," Mary used to always say with a kind of force that seemed to convey how the presence of a close woman friend helped to anchor her and ward away the great gulfs of sadness. Mound Bayou must have felt safe to Mary, because she had not "gone to bed" while there. Her life as teacher and minister's wife went smoothly, and she had not been immoblized by the depression that had consumed so much of her life in Widewater. Margaret suspects that recollections of Mound Bayou were sparse precisely because of her mother's healthy existence there. Her early memories of the places they lived are always linked to Mary's illnesses. "I remember the places where my mother went to bed. . . . In Widewater, I could draw you a picture of the stairway up to *my mother's room* where she was laid out in bed—I guess it was my mother and father's room. I only remember it as my mother's room . . . I have no idea where *my* room was." Margaret remembers Widewater as the place where Mary was "like dead." Mound Bayou is a blank, empty of her mother's intrusive illness.

Not only did Mary Morgan have her usual apprehensions about the move from Mound Bayou to Vicksburg, she was also terrified by her neighbors' warnings. The people in all-black Mound Bayou told the Reverend's wife of the horrors of racism in the Deep South. They warned her that Vicksburg was no place for a dark-brown-skinned man to go with his white-looking wife. "The neighbors told my mother horror stories of Vicksburg, some of them accurate . . . scary tales about how people were lynched there. They would say to my mother, 'Mrs. Morgan, if you go there looking as white as you are and Reverend Morgan as dark as he is, he's going to get

in trouble.' " Their tales took away every bit of Mary's waning courage. "The move," normally a painful uprooting, felt this time like a
horrifying journey to the depths of hell. The moment they got to
Vicksburg, Mary took to her bed. Her seven-year-old child could
feel the new edge of fear in her mother. "My mother was terrified . . . and that's a frightening thing for a child. When my mother
went to bed, that meant things were bad and she wouldn't face them."

When Mary did manage to rise and teach, she was still haunted
by the terrors painted by her Mound Bayou neighbors. She left her
house each day with fear and caution, always expecting the worst.
Margaret can remember her mother's trembling body, her darting
eyes, her tight lips, as they walked to the stores in downtown Vicksburg. "I can remember walking back from town with my mother
on Jackson Street near First North. Suddenly she grabbed me and
shoved me off the sidewalk and onto the grass because a white man
was approaching from the other direction. She was frightened of
staying on the sidewalk." Young Margaret knew why her mother
was trembling. She, too, had heard the neighbors' warnings and
carried them with her to Vicksburg. If it was unsafe for her fair-
skinned mother to be with her dark-skinned father, what might
happen if she and her mother ventured out together on the Vicksburg
streets? "I recognized that I was like my father—that I was the same
color or close . . . I recognized that for me to be with my mother was
almost as bad as for my mother to be with him. I was frightened
because she was frightened."

Sandy Morgan had not listened to the horror stories told by his
Mound Bayou parishioners. He simply discounted them as exaggerated fears and refused to be intimidated. The Reverend depended
on his own abilities and character to carry him successfully into every
experience, and he didn't expect Vicksburg to be any different. His
entry onto a new scene always combined aggressiveness and humility.
"My father was an outgoing person . . . he made contacts with people
fairly easily . . . people *loved* Reverend Morgan. He was aggressive,
but he passed himself off as being humble. During church occasions,
I can remember my father (who was a relatively short man) walking
across the floor from one side of the room to the other. He would
walk bent over as if he had to reduce his height so he wouldn't

impede anybody's sight. This was his way of being humble." His daughter gets up to demonstrate the Reverend's gait—head slightly bowed, shoulders sloped in a walk of studied meekness. She smiles softly at the ways in which her father's barely masked assertiveness seemed to draw people to him. "He would always sign his letters to the bishop 'Your humble servant.' At the same time he was pretty outspoken . . . I think he didn't think about it much. It was just the way he was."

Reverend Morgan's reaching out had a fearless quality. He did not expect to be rebuffed or rejected. He assumed that people would be drawn to him; and within reason, he assumed that the white folks he reached out to would do him no harm. He was, of course, selective about which white folks he drew into his orbit. "I never thought of him as afraid of white people. Certainly I didn't think of him as having the fears my mother did." One day an acquaintance from church came to visit, uttered some words of concern to Reverend Morgan, and offered him the protection that a man in his position needed. " 'Reverend Morgan, you ought to have a gun.' It was just that any self-respecting man ought to have a gun . . . as a minister's family people were always giving us things." Sandy Morgan graciously accepted the gun but never expected to use it. "He would laugh and say he was scared to shoot it." One New Year's Eve he told his wife and daughter that he was going to celebrate the occasion by firing off a shot. Cautiously, he carried the gun out to the backyard, pointed it toward the sky, held his breath and pulled the trigger. "It took all his courage," says Margaret, remembering the tremors that shot through her father's body as he came back into the house.

But Mary was glad that one of their parishioners had been wise enough to give them the gun. She felt some relief knowing it was there, and she felt ready to use it on unwelcome intruders, although the occasion never presented itself. "The person who took over the gun was my mother; she usually put it under the bed; and sometimes during the day she'd move it under the pillow so it wouldn't be seen. My mother felt the need for a gun and my father accepted the gun." For Margaret, the gun was foreboding and ominous. She shared her father's anxiety about its presence in the house. "It was pretty big with a wooden handle. It was larger than a pistol. I didn't like the

Margaret Elizabeth Duke Smith
"Mom Margaret"

Andrew John Smith
"Papa Annie"

Sarah Manning Morgan
"Grandma Sarah"

Mary Elizabeth Smith,
ca. 1904

Graduating class, Bishop Paine Divinity School, Episcopal Seminary for Negroes,
Petersburg, Virginia, ca. 1906;
The Reverend Sandy Alonzo Morgan, second row, top left

Sandy Alonzo Morgan, Jr.
"Candy Man,"
1912

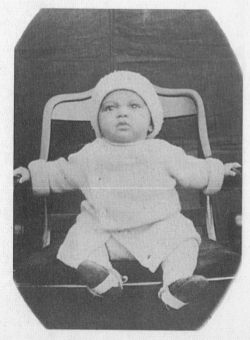

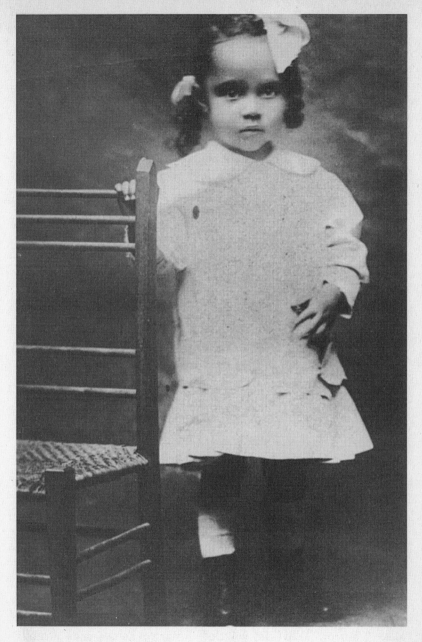

Margaret Cornelia Morgan, 1917

looks of the thing. If I was making my parents' bed I felt a little panic every time I touched it."

When the Morgans first arrived in Vicksburg, they lived on Main Street in "the Bottoms." Vicksburg is a city built on bluffs, and the various elevations marked distinctions of class and race. In the Bottoms, at the foot of the bluffs, lived blacks from working-class and lower-middle-class origins. On the bluffs lived the more affluent Vicksburg residents, both black and white. Like many cities and towns in the Deep South, the residential segregation did not appear to be clearly drawn. That is, neighborhoods were often inhabited by both blacks and whites, the races living side by side. But this apparent color mixture was misleading. It did not reflect integration or easy relationships across color lines. It reflected the fact that the southern psyche had so fully incorporated the caste system between races that there was no need for geographic boundaries. The map of segregation resided in the minds of blacks and whites, and there was no need to draw it on the land.

The Bottoms, being in the utter depths of the town, had only blacks, and the Morgans moved into a modest place that Sandy called a "shotgun house." This gray wood-framed house had one room lined up behind the other so that if a bullet went through the front door it could follow a straight path through the house and out the back door. The house was raised from the ground on tall stilts. A boardwalk connected the front door of the house to the street, and underneath the house was a wonderful place to hide and play with friends. Margaret remembers the mischief and magic of that private space where adults rarely ventured. "My naughtiness usually took place under the house. I would be playing there with my friends and they'd dare me to do something ... and I would do it, knowing very well that there would be consequences. ... Once I cut my hair off. I wore my hair in three braids, one in the front and two in the back, and my friends dared me to cut off the front one. I took up the challenge and cut it off. I remember coming upstairs and my mother's look of horror. 'What did you do?' " Margaret's tale ends abruptly as I wait to hear the terrible trouble that followed. But like the episode in Widewater with George Horse, Margaret's screen memories bring back the child's mischief but not the adult fury. "That's all I remember," says Margaret thankfully.

Memories of the Bottoms are filled with friendship and freedom. In this part of town there were lots of playmates and lots of adventures. Children were rarely hounded by watchful adults. "I can remember Mrs. Coffey's store, where the children from school would go and get a can of salmon for five cents and a loaf of bread for five cents. Two people would go together and then each cut open a half loaf of bread and put the salmon in. If you didn't want to do that, you could get some big pickles for a nickel and several peppermint sticks and put a peppermint stick down in the pickle. It was a great treat! It was not off-limits for children to go down and get what they had money for."

The "shotgun house" was next door to the Vicksburg Industrial School, also called St. Mary's Episcopal School, which was church sponsored and run. A large two-story brick building, it was one of three elementary schools for black children in Vicksburg, the other two being the local public school and the Catholic parochial school. When Reverend Morgan took over as priest at St. Mary's, he also assumed the role of school principal. Mrs. Morgan became one of the school's regular teachers. St. Mary's Church was located several blocks from the school on Grove Street. Life for the Morgans centered on home, school, and church; the boundaries between these worlds were fluid, creating a seamless existence.

Perhaps because of this undifferentiated quality, Margaret strains to picture the inside of the shotgun house. She can't remember the number and location of the rooms. But she can see and feel the night scene, sleeping in the same room with her parents. She wonders why: "Wasn't there another bedroom available in the house?" But all she can see is her parents' double bed and her single one next to theirs, in the same room. "I can remember waking up and being aware of my parents' bed moving. I don't think I looked; I think I pretended to be asleep. I assume that they were making love in the bed and it was moving, but I don't think I looked. . . . These memories are like a dream you cut off at the crucial point."

As soon as he arrived in Vicksburg, Reverend Morgan began making connections with people. He was willing to begin modestly, but he had bigger plans for his work in this city. Vicksburg held out possibilities that he had not envisioned in the other places they had moved through. Maybe this was a place that he would settle, grow roots, and dig in. Soon after his landing in Vicksburg, one of the key acquaintances Sandy Morgan made was Mrs. Fanny Johnson, a white widow, a millionaire with deep loyalties and commitments. Reverend Morgan began his pursuit carefully and strategically with conversations about his work in the church community. His approach was gracious and always appropriate—a charming mixture of assertiveness and humility. Mrs. Johnson was soon drawn to this energetic young black priest. She herself was an Episcopalian, a member of the white Christ Church, and she saw Reverend Morgan as a good conduit for her sense of social obligation to the black community. "Mrs. Johnson wanted to do something for the colored people. She had a colored chauffeur, Mr. McCarthy, and Mrs. Johnson thought of colored people in terms of her fondness for her chauffeur."

Her first act of generosity involved moving the Morgans out of the Bottoms. "She said to my father, 'First we should build you a house, a proper rectory for you and your family. . . . *Your daughter needs a room of her own.*" Together the minister and the philanthropist spent months going over the plans, first for the rectory and then for a new church. "When Mrs. Johnson got to the point of building the church, she decided that Mr. McCarthy, who was a member of St. Mary's Episcopal Church, should be baptized there . . . for this purpose she said to my father, 'I think it would be nice if you had a pool' . . . so a big baptismal pool was built under the place where the choir usually sat with a floor over it that rolled back when it was being used for baptisms."

Margaret had a fondness for the white woman and carefully watched the way her father related to her. She deeply appreciated Mrs. Johnson's insistence that she needed a room of her own. By then she was almost nine years old and she yearned for her own private space. She also enjoyed Mrs. Johnson's generosity. "From time to time Mrs. Johnson would send me bananas. In those days we only had fruit that was not native to Vicksburg at Christmas time. So for her to send me bananas, on no special occasion, felt like a very lovely thing."

As Margaret watched her father and Mrs. Johnson, she learned important lessons about the art of asking and receiving. She learned that one could approach a rich patron without diminishing oneself. She neither saw her father as obsequious ("I thought he was courageous in his dealings with Fanny Johnson") nor regarded Mrs. Johnson as patronizing ("She did it graciously"). These were encounters based on caste and class differences, but they did not seem to be demeaning to Reverend Morgan. "I began to have an image of a white person who is respectful of my father. My father would ask for what he wanted. I think I began to take in this idea. . . . Here are people who have. . . . If you don't have what you need, you can ask for it." In asking respectfully (not begging or backing off), one had to begin with an assumption of human equality. People who had less were not necessarily less worthy.

Years later Margaret saw the bargain between the minister and the philanthropist as more complex. "I got the picture about the chauffeur, Mr. McCarthy, who looked white, with blondish, straight hair, and who was beloved by Fanny Johnson. I began to see that her generosity to my father was wrapped up in her fondness for her chauffeur . . . it took the edge off the *pure* idea of Fanny Johnson and my father." Years later, when Mr. McCarthy "absconded," "disappeared without a word"—abandoning his wife and three children and forsaking his job—Margaret began to question anew the complicated, murky relationships that might have inspired Mrs. Johnson's philanthropy.

The Morgans' new house was built on First North Street, between Jackson and Main streets. Within two years they had moved out of the Bottoms, to high ground, and were living amid middle-class and upper-middle-class blacks and whites. "Soon after we were there, First North was paved—thanks to Mrs. Fanny Johnson." From the all-black Bottoms, the Morgans moved into a section of Vicksburg "not segregated in the same way. . . . If you looked in a certain direction down Main Street . . . you could find T. J. Ewing, a lawyer who couldn't practice through the Mississippi State Bar so he had to work through a white lawyer. . . . There was a family who lived a few doors down who was very fair, extremely middle-class. The father, who worked in the post office, had three families but only one legal wife, and everyone knew this.... One of his sons from one of his 'other' families was in the administration of the colored Methodist Church, a sort of regional church person. His daughter was the first black woman in the city to get her doctorate. People who worked in the post office (including the mail carrier, Mr. Sumner Oliver, a very fair man who lived in a nice house) were middle-class.... This was very much a black middle-class area, but all you had to do was turn the corner on Jackson Street and people were all white, and further down on First North Street there were whites also."

From the back porch of the Morgans' new house Margaret could easily see the white family next door. "Their backyard abutted on our front and side yards.... Their house faced on Jackson Street and ours on First North." Elizabeth, the redheaded, freckle-faced girl who lived next door, was the same age as Margaret. When the Morgans first moved in, Elizabeth would come over to the Morgans' yard to play with Margaret—climbing the fig tree, chasing the chickens, and telling secrets. Then one day when the girls were about eleven, Elizabeth arrived with an announcement that was not surprising to either of them: "My mama says I can't play with you anymore 'cause you're a nigger.'" Her words were part of the Vicksburg script. After a certain point no one expected the redheaded girl to continue to play with the girl with the long black braids next door. (This was despite the fact that both of their mothers were redheads. "Her mother had brighter red hair than mine.") Margaret greeted the news quietly, at first astonished by the sudden change of status. "I had some background. I was not unaware of how things were in Vicksburg . . . but playing with Elizabeth had come naturally, and I think I was somewhat saddened.... But I don't remember questioning it. I don't even remember talking to my parents about it . . . I think I just kept it to myself." Elizabeth was a playmate but not a friend like the ones at the Vicksburg Industrial School where Margaret went, or like her friend, named Geneva, who lived on First North. "I had Negro children with whom I played," says Margaret as a way of explaining "the categories" of friends in her life and the expectation that the real, enduring friendships would be with other children of color.

The house at 906 First North was much finer than the gunshot gray rectory in the Bottoms. It had a large, gracious front porch with a swing, a rocking chair, and a bench for outdoor sitting to catch the cool night air. There were three bedrooms, a study, a living room, a dining room, and a kitchen. The back porch led out to a green backyard surrounded by a white picket fence, a lovely fig tree that produced juicy fruit, and a few chickens that produced enough eggs for breakfast. Unlike the house in the Bottoms, every detail of 906 First North is clear in Margaret's memory. As we talk, she draws the floor plan and marks in the furniture. "This is where the piano stood in the living room, so my mother who was cooking in the kitchen could lean out into the hall and check on me while I practiced. . . . This is the pantry, the shelves, the light. . . . This is where my mother made wine in bottles. This was during prohibition. . . . This is the corner in the dining room where the cabinet radio stood . . . I called it the 'courting corner' because later that was where Charles and I would sit and talk and talk. The sound from the radio would mask our voices. . . . This is where we sat at the kitchen table, Mama here, Papa here, Margaret here . . . Papa always had his eye on the sink because it was his job to do the dishes after the meal. . . . This is the couch in my room where I would play with my dolls, combing their hair . . . always blond hair . . . and here was my wonderful window where I could stand and listen to the bird sounds. . . . My mother would leave her door open, and I could look in from my room and see her getting dressed . . . always very slowly . . . lacing up her corset, then her stockings and slip." Each piece of furniture—the piano, the radio, the couch, the kitchen table—brings back a flood of related memories, as if drawing the rooms on paper connects her to the childhood patterns of everyday life on First North.

Sometimes the drawings pose new questions. Margaret places the furniture in her bedroom—the bed, the makeshift couch . . . "Is that all that was in my room? . . . *I had a bare room!*" The discovery seems shocking. She looks surprised, appalled at the barrenness. Then she unravels the memory. "My mother was not a good housekeeper. She could never throw anything away . . . she filled my room with what we called 'sally.' . . . 'Sally' was boxes of clothes for the needy. Since St. Mary's was considered to be a colored mission in the poor, be-nighted South, we would receive boxes of clothes from parishes mostly in the North. The sally would come to 906 First North in huge wooden crates. . . . But the people in our church really didn't need sally. . . . Half the time my mother wouldn't even look into these boxes. She would just stick them in my room . . . the boxes would pile up. My room wasn't bare, it was full of sally."

As Margaret describes their home to me, she not only uncovers surprises, but also underscores enduring images. The most prominent of these is once again the large photograph of Candy Man that hung above the couch in the living room. The picture, three feet by four feet, dominates the room. Candy Man, who was then nine or ten months old, is perched on a chair. He is wearing a white knit outfit— hat, sweater, shirt, and leggings. His short arms are stretched out on either side, and his tiny hands clasp the chair's arms. He looks like a serious, imperious little prince perched on his throne. He gazes down on everyone who enters the house. The facts of his short life are unclear to Margaret, but the feelings of his presence in their family, long after his death, are still intense. "He is more in my heart than in my head," says Margaret as she tries to piece together the few bits of information that she has about the baby boy. "I don't know where my brother was born. My mother could have gone to Richmond, to be with her mother. . . . He was born with a swelling on his head. I don't know the cause. Maybe it was some kind of a brain problem or defect of the skull . . . I think it was more than an injury from the forceps during birth . . . or maybe the illness had nothing to do with the swelling . . . maybe it was a cerebral anomaly." Margaret the physician searches for possible causes of her brother's death. But they are stabs in the dark, guesses in hindsight. Finally she lands on two facts. "He died at eleven months. He died in my grandmother's arms. While he was dying, she took him and opened and closed his arms, trying to resuscitate him."

Although his picture hung in the center of the living room and the sadness lingered in the family's life, Candy Man was rarely talked about. The silence was oppressive for Margaret, who lived in the shadow of this tiny but dominant figure. "My mother never talked about him. About that I was suspicious. My father would say, 'If the boy had lived he would have been a priest of the church' . . . or 'If he had lived he would have brought in some wood for the fur-nace.' . . . My grandmother talked about him a lot. He was much beloved by my grandmother, who would say to me, 'What a beautiful baby he was. He was fair and had golden curls.' "

Mom Margaret's litany of love and adoration for her dead grandson always made Margaret feel diminished. Such a deep longing for the fair golden boy made the brown girl feel less special. Sometimes she thought that her grandmother's rhapsody about Candy Man was designed to make her feel as if she would never quite measure up. Mom Margaret was a tease and enjoyed watching kids squirm with discomfort or embarrassment. Her worst teasing was reserved for Margaret's father, whom she would mimic mercilessly until her granddaughter couldn't bear it any longer. "This could make me cry," says Margaret, remembering the way her grandmother pushed her into despair. Mom Margaret would waddle across the floor, leaning way back with her stomach sticking out, and say to her granddaughter, "Look here, girl, this is the way your papa looks when he walks." As Margaret tried to hold back tears, her grandmother would sit down and rear back in peals of laughter. Just as she loved Candy Man for his whiteness, so she belittled her son-in-law for his blackness. Margaret, so thoroughly identified with her father, always felt the mimicry as a deep personal assault. "I think I always knew this had something to do with color . . . mine and my father's."

Putting Down Roots in Vicksburg

THE MINISTER'S CHILD

THE new St. Mary's Church, built through Mrs. Johnson's generosity, stood right next-door to the rectory. It was a handsome brick building, sturdier and more impressive than the old St. Mary's on Grove Street. Margaret spent a lot of time in the church. As her father's daughter, she was expected to be present at all of the services: special occasions such as baptisms, marriages, and funerals, as well as the regular Sunday services. By far the heaviest day was Sunday, with two morning services, evening Vespers, and a musical program in the afternoon for parishioners and guests. Margaret can remember fighting off the sleep that would hang over her like a massive weight during the long evening services. "When I was seven years old and in the choir, the bishop came at night and I was terrified lest I would fall asleep. I remember speaking to my father and he said, 'Well, you just look at me and that will make you stay awake.' I would sit there and stare at him . . . still terrified . . . and my eyes would close."

Margaret not only felt a responsibility to be present and stay awake in church, but also felt compelled to be vigilant and sensitive to her father's needs. She had special antennae to pick up her father's every move and motive. "I was very much aware of my father all the time. He would sing with the choir and his voice was very big—it was a nice voice. I was aware that it sounded bigger than anybody else's. There were the voices of the choir and then there was my father's bellowing of the hymns." One reason Margaret felt obligated to attend so fully to her father was that her mother seemed irresponsible toward his work. She sensed that her mother was expressing her anger through her absence and lateness at church. Margaret assumed a double burden. "I felt responsible for helping to carry the church on. . . . My mother was always late to the service and I felt self-conscious about that . . . I would surmise there were certain times when she didn't want to be there so that's why she was late. . . . But she tended to be late *everywhere* except school. She would always get to school on time."

The mystery and darkness of funerals were prominent in Margaret's young life. "Church meant funerals." These were compelling, seductive events that both intrigued and repelled her: "There was a lady named Mrs. Gerron who died soon after we arrived in Vicksburg . . . I remember being at her house where she was laid out and somebody giving us a large can in which she had stored her meat on the porch. There was meat in this can . . . I was very suspicious of that meat when my mother cooked it and thought, 'Oh dear, I wonder if it will make us sick!' There was something about Mrs. Gerron's death and eating her meat that made me very afraid."

Although funerals had a certain eerie appeal for Margaret, she grew weary of the contrived sadness, the forced tears, and the long rituals. She found it difficult to feign mourning when she felt no sadness inside. The dissonance between the exterior expressions that were appropriate to the occasion and her interior emptiness troubled her. "I think I had a difficult time being in the position as my father's daughter and seeing my father minister to people. He would be administering and responding in a *feeling sense* to people who were grieving. . . . I now recognize that this is part of my interest in catharsis, my interest in how you help people with their feelings . . . but as a young child I had difficulty playing a role when I didn't honestly have the feelings to go with it. . . . It was as if everyone was sad and I couldn't bring myself to be sad." As the Rector led the people in mourning and the parishioners swooned with grief, Margaret would suddenly feel like bursting out laughing. The sadder the ceremony, the more she wanted to explode. "I had to hold myself very tight . . . I would get all tied up with the idea of 'Suppose I laugh out loud. What would happen?' I think that having to go to *every* funeral must have made me angry, and this came out in my wanting desperately to laugh . . . which was something no one ever really knew." As she tells of her attempts to hold in her laughter, Margaret's expression again looks as if it is going to burst. Her eyes dart mischievously from side to side and there is a certain panic lurking in them as well.

Over sixty years later these funeral memories are still intriguing to Margaret. She connects them to her present interests, as well as to her special capacities in working with children. "My experience remembering how I felt then stands me in good stead in my work now." The child psychiatrist tries to understand the child's "feeling perspective"—a view that may be strikingly different from the adult view. Her ability to recapture her own potent feelings as a child—the urge to burst into laughter at deadly serious moments, the sense of overwhelming heaviness as her drooping eyelids want to give way to sleep—helps her connect with her young patients "to get the story directly from them."

Margaret speaks of children's feelings almost reverentially. She remembers how her grandmother Mom Margaret loved to tease children, to poke fun at them until the tears flowed, and she now regards that hard teasing as "meanness." The adults in her life did not have an empathetic regard of children, did not take children's feelings seriously or seek to understand their special perspective. Perhaps in her work as a psychoanalyst and psychotherapist, she has become the idealized person to whom Margaret the child would have longed to talk—someone who would understand the irrationality, the "unreasonable feelings"; someone you could trust to keep your secrets; someone who enjoyed the searching and wandering fantasies.

As an only child, Margaret spent long periods of time with no one to talk to but herself. "I walked to school, across town to the railroad tracks, up the railroad tracks to Cherry Street . . . a long way . . . at least three miles, probably more. . . . Thinking about everything under the sun." There were no brothers or sisters with whom she could test out her feelings; and there was no one to distract her from thought. Her mind turned back on itself and built elaborate, embellished narratives. Margaret knew of no grown-ups who would have been accepting or encouraging of the strange twists of her mind.

Some of Margaret's fantasies skirted the world of magic and spirits. In Vicksburg, she took piano lessons from a Mrs. Ewing, an olive-complexioned lady from Louisiana whose straight hair was pulled back in a tight bun at the nape of her neck. When Margaret heard that Mrs. Ewing was from Louisiana, "might even have been Creole," her imagination went to work. If she is a Creole, Margaret thought, she can deal with powders and potions . . . she can do magic things. One afternoon, when Margaret was taking a lesson, Mrs. Ewing got up from the piano bench and headed for the kitchen. She instructed her pupil to continue practicing her scales. Margaret strained to hear what Mrs. Ewing was doing back there. She could hear her stirring something; sifting, pouring, pounding, mixing. Margaret's playing stopped completely as she tried to decipher the kitchen noises. "She's making a potion!" Margaret said to herself with alarm. She kept provocative images to herself, to be revisited again and again on her long, solitary walks.

When Margaret was nine or ten years old, she and her parents drove out to the country to the funeral of a very young woman who had been disabled for most of her life. Her body was laid out in the living room. Margaret could remember visiting her when the woman was weak, crippled, and bedridden. This was not an old person whose death was expected. She was taken before her time, and Margaret felt a potent connection to the body lying still in the open coffin. "I can see the body in the living room, kids running in and out, the door slamming, people sitting in a circle crying, wailing, talking, eating, drinking." Before driving out to the country, Margaret had decided that she would become involved with the spirits. "This time I convinced myself that I would communicate with this young woman who had died." All her life, she had heard talk about ghosts and spirits. "It was always said that when people died, something about them remained." Margaret "planned" to experience the world beyond.

After the Reverend had delivered an impassioned funeral service, the Morgans headed back to Vicksburg in the dark of night. Margaret and her mother were seated in the back of a parishioner's car, with her father up in the front beside the driver. They were driving slowly along the winding dirt roads, the headlights sending a beacon through the cold night air. Margaret, who had been deep in her own thoughts, gazed out the front windshield. "I saw a small figure sitting on the radiator cap. It was the dead woman ... I was sure she was there with us ... I convinced myself (or did I?) ... I have a very good imagination." It was a freezing winter night, unusually cold for Mississippi, and the road was full of potholes covered with ice. As the car turned a curve on the narrow road, it hit one of the ice spots, jolted forward out of control, and spun around until it "turned half over." The passengers were shaken but uninjured. They climbed out slowly and tried to ease their panic. As Margaret slid out, she saw the dead woman's image again, still poised on the radiator cap. She turned to her mother and said quietly, "She's still there. I saw her." Mary knew right away whom Margaret meant and asked no questions. The mother took her daughter's vision seriously; and when Reverend Morgan was told, he too believed her without question. "We came to a *quiet understanding* that I had seen the spirit of this woman." Her parents simply "believed," yet did not want "to push the idea too far." As she retells the story, with its dramatic flavor, Margaret admits, "I don't know how much of this I concocted."

Although Margaret speaks of her vision that night as an open question, an intriguing possibility, for her mother the vision was confirmation of something she already had suspected. Mary was pretty certain that her daughter had special powers. She would say, "You were born in the hospital, so I don't know whether you had a caul over your face ... but I think you did." In southern as well as many other traditions, a caul is a sign that the baby will grow up to "see things." If Margaret had a caul, she would lead a life more "in touch with the spirits," and the vision of the small figure on the car radiator just served to confirm Mary's premonitions.

This early fascination with powders and potions, ghosts and spirits, and this dramatic communication with the dead woman, are not dismissed lightly by Margaret. Although she questions how much of such visions were the result of her rich fantasy life, she still harbors a "quiet" acceptance of some of these qualities in herself ("I remain open to the possibilities") and counts them as perhaps important to her present "trade."

Margaret's fantasies were reinforced by a black southern culture in which people believed in the afterlife and kept a healthy respect for "the spirits." But most of life didn't have this dramatic flavor.

Days followed along without the appearance of images and ghosts. On these regular days, Margaret was still surrounded by the Holy Spirit, "the idea of God as Spirit." Unlike "the spirits," God was decidedly without image. "I think I picked up from my father that God was not a figure ... I was puzzled a little about the picture of Jesus, but I recognized fairly early that Jesus would turn out to be the way the artist pictured him. ... There were occasional church calendars with Jesus as a brown man, and undertakers' fans, with Jesus, Mary, and the Baby, also as brown figures." In contrast, the Holy Spirit was invisible and all-surrounding. Margaret learned to feel this Spirit as a strong presence in her life. She prayed regularly and sought comfort and strength from this source. "My father taught me to read Psalm 27 ... 'The Lord is my light and salvation' ... 'be of good courage' is the way it ends. He taught me to read this Psalm just before my examinations. You had to study for exams, but you also read that Psalm. I had a sense of being in touch with the Spirit, Lord Jesus God ... and I expected a response." I ask whether she gave God credit if she did well on her exams, and Margaret says without a hint of remorse, "I think once I had done well I felt it was mine! I had done my part. I had invoked help."

The Spirit offered support when Margaret faced tough challenges. The Spirit also surveyed and scrutinized her moral decisions. "I had a pretty strict moral sense, as children brought up at that time did ... I had a keen sense of when I had been bad or when I might have had bad thoughts. I was not allowed to say 'lie,' because it was considered to be a bad word and I had some fears of telling a lie ... I prayed about the things I knew were wrong." Occasionally Margaret felt pushed to defy the heavy moral code. Her friends would offer her a challenge, tempt her into wrongdoing, and she would find that she couldn't resist them. She had a mischievous spirit that responded enthusiastically to dares, and sometimes she also felt the need to prove to her friends that she wasn't a prudish minister's daughter.

"When I was about eleven my friends decided that Clarence Middleton was my beau. ... One of my friends dared me to kiss him. There was a sense that Reverend Morgan's daughter wouldn't do this, and I was out to prove that I was a regular kid! ... Everyone lay in wait for the day that I was going to kiss Clarence ... so I kissed him . . . just walked up to him one day and 'pop.' He didn't know what had hit him! He had nothing to do with it whatsoever." Such mischief had heavy costs. It would feel exciting and challenging as Margaret responded to the dare. They won't believe this! I'll show them! But when it was over, the excitement would evaporate and the worries would begin. The burst of courage, the pleasure of her friends' utter amazement at the nerve of the minister's daughter, would be followed by haunting remorse. "I felt I had done something bad. . . . Maybe there was something I should pray about. I had kissed a boy . . . I had a lot of things I had to think of all by myself." Left alone with these concerns, Margaret could feel profoundly alone. She would guard her worries carefully. "That was my private life . . . that I had kissed a boy and that I had done something bad was *entirely* private. . . . The fact that I didn't have any siblings meant that I had a large private life. The things I thought were not acceptable to my parents; I just wouldn't tell them."

Being Reverend Morgan's daughter made Margaret feel different from her friends. When she carried her briefcase to school, some of the kids would call across the street, "Good day, Sister Missionary." She cringed at the image of "a Baptist church missionary lady," humorless, sullen, and gray. They knew she hated being called that, and they knew it would get a rise out of her. To prove that she was a "regular" kid, she would again do something dramatically mischievous, and then worry privately.

In Margaret's tendency toward solitude and secrets, she resembled her mother. But there were differences. Mary's solitude seemed to be related to her sense of being "alone"—too far from her mother and sisters, isolated and distant from those she loved the most. It was a solitude of sadness. Her daughter, also alone much of the time, seemed to relish the privacy. She grew up as an only child, the younger sister of a dead brother, and she usually enjoyed the endless hours of rumination. The only times when she felt the loneliness of exclusion was when her mother rejoined the Smith clan or when she developed intimate friendships with other women. When Mary formed these womanly relationships, the bonds were deep and solid. Margaret would listen to their talk and feel longing and jealousy.

The strongest friendship Mary Morgan had was with Mrs. Sadie

Merrick, the wife of the director of the colored YMCA in Vicksburg, who was quite a bit younger than Mary. They saw a great deal of each other, exchanged gossip, shared confidences, and "talked for hours and hours." Margaret resented the fact that her mother would talk about her to Mrs. Merrick. That seemed disloyal. "When I was about eleven, I remember hearing Sadie Merrick say to my mother, 'Don't you think Margaret is developing a little early?' At eleven I was about the same height as I am now, and I sure enough had the same bosoms. . . . My mother would discuss this with her, and of course there was no discussion whatsoever with me." The fragments of the ladies' talk disturbed Margaret and made her worry more about the already alarming subject of breasts. "I had to live through the horror of developing early. What had I done to get these bosoms!" On the other hand, who was Sadie Merrick to talk? She had a sister, about Margaret's age, actually named Titta Graves, who also had big breasts. (Titta was a nickname commonly given to younger sisters. It was supposed to "sound like 'sister' in baby talk." Everyone called poor Titta Graves by her nickname, and her best friend was another Titta, Titta Murray.) "I went down to visit Titta Graves in Port Gibson, a small town about fifty or sixty miles from Vicksburg. She was not too different in build from me, except she had friends who, unlike Titta, were cute and little, and there were boys who loved these cute and little girls. . . . I felt all the worse. I didn't want to have these big busts."

The visit to Port Gibson was full of troubling feelings and fantasies. "There was a cemetery near Titta Graves's house in which there were fig trees with luscious fruit. We used to go and pick them, and I wondered whether they were so luscious because they had something to do with the dead people. Then there were the boys who I wished liked me as much as the cute girls. I got the feeling they were teasing me about something." But there was no one for Margaret to talk to about these worries—no sisters, no friends, and certainly not her parents. "I had some feeling that being a minister's child put me a little off-limits with other people my age . . . whether that was true I don't know."

Mary Morgan's other close friend was Miss Annie Davis. Sadie Merrick was a Baptist, but Annie Davis, a single woman, was an

Episcopalian and a staunch member of St. Mary's. Miss Davis, a very large, "exceedingly black lady" would come to the Morgans' house, settle into a chair, and talk for hours. Margaret can remember her sitting in her mother's room while Mary got herself corseted and dressed, always a slow, laborious process. "They would leave the bedroom door open and I could see the two of them . . . my mother getting dressed and Annie Davis talking on and on. I didn't like that. I didn't trust that woman, and I always wondered whether my mother *really* liked her." Margaret watched this scene and felt her jealousy rise. Her feelings were heightened by Miss Davis's disdain for children. She would come into their house and ignore Margaret; or even worse, she would look down her nose at her with a haughty glare. Then she would enjoy intimate hours with the child's mother. "Miss Annie Davis had the attitude of a person who would laugh *at* a child, not *with* a child. I thought of her as devious."

One day, without notice, Miss Davis left for Chicago. A year later she returned to Vicksburg with a beautiful baby boy. The child was "of olive complexion and his mother rubbed him with oil and made him smooth and lovely." The townsfolk buzzed about Annie Davis's new baby; the grapevine spun an elaborate tale. Margaret can remember how enthusiastically the church women participated in the gossip. A schoolteacher who lived with a family around the corner couldn't contain her curiosity. The teacher had steatopygia, "a huge bottom that wags along behind you," and Margaret remembers how she looked from the rear as she mounted the steps to her house. One day, just after Annie Davis returned from Chicago, the nosy teacher waddled down the steps and spoke to Margaret, who was passing below on the sidewalk. "Hello, Margaret." Her greeting had a quality that made the girl know she was about to gossip. "Why hello, ma'am. (I was very respectful)." "Margaret, I hear that Annie Davis is back." She knew that Annie Davis and Mary Morgan were fast friends, and she hoped to get the juicy news from Mary's daughter. "How long was Annie Davis away?" she inquired with raised eyebrows, sniffing out the details. Margaret's response was quick and sure: "You know that's her adopted baby." Even though Margaret didn't like Annie Davis and was "a little jealous that she was so close" to her mother, she would not tolerate the teacher's wrongheaded gossip. "I was mostly saying to her, 'I know what you're asking.'"

So Margaret's sense of being set apart from the community as the minister's child encourged her to speak out. Her independence and perception of her role made her both private and outspoken. These qualities sometimes made adults regard her as unusual, maybe even threatening. "I remember standing out in front of the church listening to my mother talking with this lady with a French name. I made some comment, and this lady said to my mother, 'Don't you think Margaret is a little *peculiar*, Mrs. Morgan?'" The lady was not used to children speaking up, and she didn't like it. "I was saying something a little out of the way . . . making some comment she thought I had no business making." To Mary Morgan's credit, she never joined in the adult suspicion of Margaret. She would listen sweetly to the parishioner's talk—as a good minister's wife should—but she would not try to quiet her daughter. "That was the great thing about my mother. She never seemed to get upset about things like that."

Margaret remembers the parishioners' gossip about her rides in the car with James Buck when she was about thirteen. James was fifteen, the son of an indulgent father who "gave him everything, including a car." James would ask Margaret to go for spins in his car, and Margaret would accept enthusiastically. "I thought it was the greatest fun in the world to ride in that car." The neighbors were amazed that Margaret would go riding with a boy—this was simply not appropriate for a girl from a respectable family—and they were shocked that her mother would allow it. Mary Morgan began to receive telephone calls. "I saw Margaret riding in James's car." Again, Mary received the news pleasantly, let the callers know that she was aware of the car rides, and then chose not to talk to her daughter about it. The mother trusted her daughter's judgment, allowed her much more freedom than most Vicksburg mothers, and may have even enjoyed her daughter's daring spirit. "In my early adolescence," says Margaret firmly, "I would dare to do things that other girls wouldn't. I never had a wish to offend by doing something terrible . . . I was just going about my life responding to challenges."

Although her mother allowed Margaret to move beyond the limits imposed on most of the adolescent girls they knew, the impulse "to dare" came from her father. Sandy Morgan's temperament allowed him to reach out to people, ask for what he wanted, and move about town with minimal inhibition. His daughter, temperamentally identified with her father, incorporated his style and took it a step further. "I even dared speak to white people. My father had some worry about that." Margaret's boldness was also a response to her father's litany about his dead son. "If the boy had lived he would have been a priest of the church; he would have brought in the wood; if he had lived he would have done this, and that, and all sorts of marvelous things. . . ." Margaret heard all this as a pointed challenge. The ministry was not possible for her; women could not be ordained as Episcopal priests. But she could take the place of her brother in other ways. She could be outgoing, ambitious, and strong. She could be the son that her wonderful father had lost. "I sort of tried to be what my brother would have been."

When Mary Morgan married Sandy, she followed him to the godforsaken black charges of the Deep South on one condition: that she would be able to visit her mother and sisters every other summer. Mary could not bear to leave the Smith women unless she could be assured of regular reunions with them. Sandy Morgan willingly agreed. He was wise enough to know that his wife needed the journeys north. Her health, their marriage, depended on them. Margaret remembers their restorative nature. "Those trips were very important, particularly since my mother's tendency toward depression was clearly related to her separation from her mother."

Several weeks before Mary and Margaret were scheduled to leave for New York, Sandy Morgan would approach his next-door neighbor who was the manager of the ticket office at the railroad station. He would wait until he saw the father of redheaded Elizabeth outside in his backyard, and he would approach the fence between their houses. "My wife is going to New York," Reverend Morgan would say to the railroad manager, who had grown used to the unusual request. "That was at a time in Vicksburg when many middle-class Negroes would go on vacation to Chicago but never to New York, so we felt very special," remembers Margaret. The station manager would arrange for the Morgans to get the first available reservations.

"It was a *great* accomplishment to get the tickets, and they were very long, with individual stubs to be detached at different stops along the way."

The first leg of the journey was Jackson, Mississippi, fifty miles away. From Vicksburg to Chicago, they would have to travel in a segregated coach; Negroes were not allowed in the Pullman cars. Mary and Margaret waited expectantly for the Cairo, Illinois, stop at the Mason-Dixon line, when they would be able to switch to better accommodations. "On the black coaches when we'd hear the call 'Cairo,' everyone would brighten up." It isn't that the separation between whites and coloreds would suddenly disappear—there was still a green curtain behind which the Negroes had to sit in the dining car—but the Cairo call rang out promise and hope. Mary and Margaret could then move to their reservations in the Pullman car, where they usually shared a berth but occasionally were able to spread out to the upper one. The trip to New York took a little over three days, and Margaret remembers it as a wonderful adventure and a great extravagance. "This was all very expensive for us. You have to remember that at this time my father was earning eighty-five dollars a month." The journey's excitement sometimes consumed the young girl and she would feel sickness coming on. "I can remember my mother grabbing my dress off and I was sick in my slip."

During the winter before their New York trip, mother and daughter would go downtown to buy fabric. Mrs. McClarren, the dressmaker, would spend months sewing their wardrobe—a collection of classically tailored blue and brown dresses. These would be accompanied by gloves, hats, and shoes bought at Barron's store, where the Morgans had a charge account. The clothes were packed carefully in large trunks that held more than enough clothes for their three-month stay in New York. Margaret enjoyed the preparations, but she yearned for a more colorful wardrobe. Each time Mary insisted that the dark materials would look better next to Margaret's brown skin; the bright colors would stand out and make her appear darker. And each time Margaret would be disappointed; she knew that the colors would look good on her. On one shopping tour, Margaret's begging finally got to Mary and she softened for a moment. Margaret had spotted a bright orange dress and she fell in love with it. She had to have it. "The dress was on sale—that is the *only* reason I had a prayer of convincing my mother." She tried the dress on; it looked wonderful, and Mary conceded reluctantly. "But that gorgeous dress was never worn ... It just hung in the closet. ... My mother never let me wear it."

When their train arrived in New York, the reunions were intense and tearful. "Mom Margaret would be waiting for her child Mary to whom she was devoted ... they wept and embraced." Margaret watched her mother's growing excitement as the train brought them closer. Mary was not a demonstrative woman, but her daughter knew her well enough to see the sadness slide from her face. She knew that her mother felt happiest in the entangled circle of Smith women; a circle that sometimes made young Margaret feel excluded.

With her mother, Mary was making up for lost time. Way down there in Mississippi she felt left out of the Smith family circle; she felt jealous of her siblings who lived close to the mother source. So when she arrived for the summer, Mary made energetic attempts to redefine her place in the family, to make sure that she recaptured her mother's attentions. Margaret, envious of the love being drawn away from her, watched her mother's pursuit of Mom Margaret and felt a deep anxiety. "I was very conscious of what was going on. You see, my mother used to grieve about not being with her mother. During the two years she was not with her mother, it was as if she was left out, as far as Mom Margaret was concerned. Her sisters had her mother ... I was worried about my mother. ... If your mother is worried about her mother, then she is removed from you."

Mary was competing with powerful siblings. Her youngest sister, Hazel, had come to New York with Mom Margaret as an adolescent and had stuck close by her mother's side until she married Uncle Jimmy in her mid-thirties. But even then, Hazel never strayed far. She always remained within shouting distance—in an apartment in the same building or in a place close enough so she could see her mother several times a week. Aunt Ninnie, the oldest, had decided on pure maternal devotion. She would live with her mother until her death, care for her with devotion and loyalty, and never abandon her for marriage until after Mom Margaret took her last dying breath. Ninnie's all-consuming attachment made her tense and rigid. With

Harvey Brown, her suitor of thirty years who had followed her from Richmond, Ninnie gritted her teeth and endured. There is a wonderful photograph of Margaret with her grandmother, her mother, and her aunts out on one of their favorite daylong excursions in the countryside. They have packed a picnic lunch and piled into Aunt Hazel's shiny Buick. Their faces are smiling and relaxed—all except Aunt Ninnie's—in one of the rare times when the family conflicts eased. Margaret enjoys looking at the happy photo. "All of these people are capable of being good humored and having lots of fun. . . . Everybody is feeling pretty loose except Aunt Ninnie, who is looking pretty tight. . . ."

No matter how much Ninnie loved her mother, she never captured her heart the way Andrew did. Poor sick Andrew, a lonely figure making desperate noises, stole Mom Margaret's love from his faithful sisters. As Ninnie gave up her life for Mom Margaret, her mother turned toward her son. Mom Margaret felt remorse and guilt about Andrew. She wept for him and worried endlessly. "The sisters lived with an awareness that Mom Margaret had this grieving preoccupation . . . look what he does to Mama!" For Mary, who came so far to receive some of her mother's love, there were powerful competitors: Hazel, who stayed so close; Ninnie, who was forever, grimly faithful; and Andrew, who owned Mom Margaret's heart.

Margaret's first memories of her visits to New York stretch back to when she was five. "The Smiths were living at 2409 Seventh Avenue between 140th and 141st Street in a 'railroad' apartment on Seventh Avenue." At the upper reaches of Harlem, the apartment was in a section of the city that "Negroes" had recently inhabited. They were pushing the boundaries of Harlem, breaking the color bar, moving in, and redefining it as their own. "These were nice houses, very well kept. There were gardens in the center of the street." For the little girl from the rural South—the Morgans were on the move from Widewater, Virginia, to Mound Bayou, Mississippi, when Margaret was five—Harlem seemed large and stately and full of action. Margaret didn't get to be part of the action. She was rarely out in the street, but she could get a nice view of the city scene from the dining-room window. "What I remember mostly were the parades on Sundays." She watched the Cuban children who lived next door playing on the stoop and jumping rope. "I used to think I would get a Spanish accent from listening so hard to these kids." She could also hear the shouting and singing coming from the little church next door, much more raucous and spirited than the services in her father's church. But Margaret was mostly engaged by what was happening inside the house, and she watched that action very closely. She watched the Smith sisters jockey for position, and she listened to Andrew's desperate rantings through the frosted-glass door that separated his tiny room at the end of the long railroad flat.

This was the summer that Margaret was struck down by a terrible pneumonia. A few weeks after they arrived in New York she became very ill and was "not expected to live." The illness revived horrible memories of Candy Man's death as the Smith ladies circled the sick child and prayed for her life. Margaret's fever soared, and she spent days and days in a fuzzy, delirious state. "I can remember the room I was in—an inside room without windows. I can remember what must have been the end of the illness. My grandmother bound red onions to my feet, which were supposed to draw the fever out . . . the fever was 'drawn out' and I got better." In the fever's haze, Margaret could feel the hovering women, the cool wet rags on her forehead, the spoons of warm soup down her raw throat, and the heavy worrying. Would she live? "I have this vague memory of people moving around me, and my mother hovering over. *So she really cares!*" Margaret's voice rises in amazement. This mother, about whose love she felt so uncertain, was there *with her*, circling her sickbed, concerned and wanting her to survive.

Margaret's discovery, while desperately sick, that her mother really cared reappeared in a powerful dream that first came to her when she was nine years old. The same dream has come back to her many times over the past sixty years. In the dream, the Morgans are living on First North Street in Vicksburg. Margaret has died and is laid out in the front living room. The coffin is on the large table directly opposite Candy Man's picture. Margaret, the dreamer, hears of the young girl's death. "I decided as a neighbor to go and pay my respects to Mrs. Morgan. I had my speech ready. I opened the front gate, walked down the path, up the porch steps, and rang the doorbell. Mrs. Morgan came to the door and I can remember the intensity with which I was looking at her. I said, 'Mrs. Morgan, I hear that Margaret died, I'm so sorry.'. . . and then I looked at her and I looked at her. *I wanted to see if she was really sad* . . . I can remember the *yearning* of looking at her face."

Margaret's longing for an unquestioned love was related to fears that her mother might one day leave her—not just depart, but that she would be seduced by another man. "There was always this question of whether a man would take my mother away." One evening, when she was ten years old, Margaret accompanied her mother to a revival meeting at the Jackson Street Baptist Church. The preacher was an "old gentleman friend" of Mary's from Richmond. He had come to Vicksburg to preach at the revival meeting, and mother and daughter sat in the crowded pew listening to his spirited and elegant delivery. "My mother had inhibitions, but she also was a very dramatic soul." As Mary sat there devouring every word from the preacher's mouth, something within her stirred, and Margaret watched with horror as "her bosom began heaving." "I thought, oh no, is she going to shout?" Panic struck the daughter as the mother grew more and more intensely enthralled. Margaret's mind began to race. "What is going to happen? What about my beautiful, wonderful father? . . . What will happen to me? This is dreadful!"

Margaret stuck close to her mother as they greeted the preacher after the service. She wanted to make sure that her mother wouldn't run away with this man and abandon her. Thankfully, Mary had resumed her stately decorum and Margaret felt greatly relieved. "I was in such great pain during all of this." Fears of a parent abandoning reason were deeply etched in the young child, and she remembers this in her work with children today. "What is important to the child in any situation is that the parent remain in control. When parents seem to lose control, *all* is lost as far as the child is concerned."

Harlem

IN THE COMPANY OF WOMEN

C ANDY MAN's death inspired Margaret's pursuit of medicine. When she was nine or ten years old, the dream took shape and visited her daily: "I want to be a doctor in order to save a child like my brother from death." The events of his death, retold again and again, and the sorrow that consumed her family would become sustaining motivations for years to come as Margaret faced the hard work, discipline, and struggle of becoming a physician. As a young determined child, she was also compelled by the irrational wish to do something that would secure her parents' love and devotion. "I wanted to prevent his death for my mother and father. I thought, if I had been able to do that, look how they would have *loved* me. . . ." Her wish to "save babies" and gain her parents' undying affection also grew out of competition with her dead brother, the boy with the golden curls who was perfect in every way. "The words that come to my mind," Margaret says with a slight hint of embarrassment, "are, I wasn't fair [light-skinned]—like Candy Man and Mother Mary—but I knew what I wanted and I thought I could do it."

On her long solitary walks in Vicksburg, she had decided to go to New York to live. She never doubted that she would go. She never worried that her parents might not give her permission. She had decided to become a doctor, so she needed a good sound education. She had to go north to get it. "This was not coming from my parents, but it was coming from *me* . . . I wanted to go to New York because I wanted to go to a better school . . . so I could be a doctor . . . so I would be able to save babies!" Once she had the plan firmly in her head, thanks to all the time she spent alone, plotting and dreaming, it was not difficult to convince her parents. Despite all their problems, they always seemed to regard their daughter with respect. "My mother and father immediately took me seriously . . . they said, 'Margaret wants to go.' "

So off to New York she went, staying north after one of her every-other-year summer visits with her mother. After three years of high school in Vicksburg, she moved to New York to live with her aunts and attend Wadleigh High, one of the two classical high schools in New York for young women (the other being Hunter High). She was fourteen and committed to the idea of pursuing her schooling in New York, even though she recognized how difficult it would be to live with Mom Margaret and the aunts. "I thought, 'I don't need to let them bother me.' " She thought she could manage to separate herself from their restrictions. Having never raised children themselves, the aunts were impatient and overprotective. Their apprehensions were heightened by what they perceived to be the special dangers of being responsible for a girl. "They thought to take a *girl* to live with you was a tremendous responsibility . . . she might get pregnant!"

The aunts took their protective role very seriously. Among their campaigns was the continuing insistence that Margaret wear a bra. They were still intent upon "*containing* the adolescent female." "They were probably right," admits Margaret with a smile. "I remember wearing a knit suit that was clinging around my breasts . . . and I remember the clerk in the grocery store taking a long look at me . . . I *was* aware of my breasts." In the seductive streets of Harlem, any conscientious adult would feel concerned about a budding fourteen-year-old, and even as an adolescent Margaret could appreciate the Smith ladies' devotion to safety. But some of their restraints felt thoroughly unnecessary. She ached for more independence and missed the freedoms of Vicksburg, where she roamed the city alone. When the aunts became unbearably intrusive, Margaret would fight back. "They wanted to know where I was at *all* times. Aunt Ninnie told me to post a schedule so that they'd be able to track my every move. I got mad! I made an elaborate calendar on a big sheet of paper—

overdoing it—and put it up in the kitchen. Aunt Ninnie knew I was making fun of their restrictions, and she was not amused."

Not always trusting that she was adhering to the schedule posted in the kitchen, the aunts would shadow her. "I remember that Aunt Hazel followed me, by car, to see whether I was going where I said I was going . . . was that my fantasy? . . . No, that was *real* . . . I took rides on top of a double-decker bus to Washington Square just to get away. . . . They could be tough, Aunt Hazel and Aunt Ninnie. They didn't think of any dangers out there [in the city], only dangers in *me*!"

Margaret's determination, and what she later saw as the self-centeredness that comes with being an only child, helped her stand up to her aunts' and grandmother's overprotective intrusions. These qualities also kept her from noticing some of the complexities in the life around her. As an analyst, decades later, she is amazed that when she went to live with her grandmother, Aunt Ninnie, and Uncle Andrew in New York, she never once thought about whom she might be displacing as she took over the front bedroom looking over the garden. (Aunt Hazel and her husband, Uncle Jimmy, lived in a separate apartment upstairs on the fifth floor.) "Grandmother and Aunt Ninnie had a room together. I *never* thought about who might have been put out because I moved in. Whose room *did* I have?" Was it Andrew's, who had a cot to sleep on in the dining room? Was it Ninnie's, who was forced to share a double bed with her mother because her niece had decided to come to New York? It shocks Margaret that she never asked these questions at fourteen; and she is even more surprised that they only occur to her as she relives the events more than five decades later.

Margaret managed to escape the tough, intrusive aunts who only knew this way to love her. She was ingenious in taking advantage of her most limited freedoms. "I used to walk to school, from 149th Street, where we lived in the Dunbar Apartments, to 115th Street and save ten cents . . . and I used to meet Mary Seabrook on the way." Mary Ellen Seabrook was Margaret's best friend. They both went to Wadleigh High School and were the same age, their birthdays separated by one day. They would walk arm-in-arm down Seventh Avenue, talking and giggling and inventing amusement. "We shared fantasies and we'd do crazy things. . . . Once we were walking along and we said that the next couple that would come along, we'd go up to the man, grab his arms, look deep into his eyes, and say, 'Hello, I haven't seen you in so long' . . . and we did it, to a perfect stranger. . . . Then we'd break off laughing." Sometimes Mary and Margaret would be joined by a third friend who was in the class below them at Wadleigh and who lived close to the Seabrooks. As they paraded to school together, they would call themselves "The Three Musketeers . . . Muskie, Tuskie, and Tear."

Not only was Mary Seabrook a wonderful soulmate, she also had a loving family who became very important to Margaret. When Margaret recalls her relationship with the Seabrooks, tears come to her eyes. "I loved to go there because it was so *peaceful* and they *loved* me. . . . They loved me as Mary's friend. . . . It was like going home." It probably felt more like home—or at least idealized notions of the way a family should feel—than Margaret's life at the Dunbar Apartments. Margaret felt surrounded by overprotectiveness, by the strange ways of Andrew, by the anger and jealousy the aunts felt about their mother's preoccupation with Andrew. The aunts' house did not have the loving, warm quality of the Seabrooks'. Their love was expressed through admonition, protection, and guilt, not through the tender expression of affection.

The Seabrooks lived on 139th Street, on the walking route from the aunts' apartment to Wadleigh High School. Margaret would stop and pick up Mary every morning and walk home with her in the afternoons. She was not allowed to stop at the Seabrooks' after school because the aunts insisted that she return directly home. In fact, Hazel and Ninnie were not aware that their niece was walking the thirty-five blocks to and from school rather than spend ten cents on bus fare. Margaret was secretly saving her money to buy a violin. Her violin teacher had said that she played well enough to deserve a fine instrument, so she was storing every penny away. She also preferred to walk. She welcomed the time and space to be alone and daydream. And once Mary Seabrook joined her, there was fun and adventure.

Margaret was allowed to visit the Seabrooks on weekends and holidays. Their home was considered "safe" by the aunts, and she went there often and most happily. "They lived in an old apartment house, and their place was tiny and immaculate.... It was so small, just *stuffed* with things." Mary Ellen's maternal grandmother, Mamie Palmer, a lively, energetic woman, shined the pots until you could use the bottoms like mirrors. Mrs. Palmer ran this household with discipline and caring. Her daughter, Mary's mother, had an illness that sometimes incapacitated her, and she was treated gently by her family. Despite her infirmity, she always welcomed Margaret graciously, beaming her soft energy like a flickering candle. Mary's father, Mr. Seabrook, "was lovely and kind.... He would come in from work and head to the kitchen for his food, which would be promptly placed in front of him by his wife.... I see him sitting by himself with his plate propped on the tub tops, eating huge piles of rice." In the Seabrook household, tiny and stuffed as it was, Margaret felt warmly welcomed and surrounded by family love. "They were *all* nice to me ... I would eat there ... like going home," she says again to underscore the safety and abundance of this modest home.

There were other homes where Margaret was allowed to visit. Olivia Pleasants, also a classmate at Wadleigh, was a whiz in math and science. Their friendship was neither as intense nor as gleeful as Margaret's was with Mary Seabrook. As a matter of fact, Margaret remembers her as sad. Her sadness was understandable. Olivia's mother had died when she was very young; her father was a very busy physician, and she was primarily responsible for raising her younger brother and running the household. "She was the mother of the family. I would not go to her house to play. I'd watch her work ... I can just remember walking into the house and it being so *dark* ... just dark. I have no other memory except the darkness."

Eunice Mattis, a third "bosom buddy," was one of several children who were orphaned when the youngest ones were still dependent. With the sudden death of their father and mother, Eunice's older sisters became the parents and providers. Margaret watched with awe as this family of children raised one another. Eunice, one of the youngest, studied her lessons, shopped for food, helped to prepare the family's meals, and cleaned their small apartment—all with a cheerful, undaunted determination. And Margaret watched Eunice and her siblings reach out to their church—a small, proud congregation of Plymouth Brethren—for clothing, for food, for all manner of sustenance when their young family needed it. Eunice seemed very satistfied, both maintained and nourished by her family.

When Margaret thinks of Olivia's sadness and the company they kept in the dark house while she watched her friend do the chores, and when she thinks of Eunice and her siblings bravely raising each other, she realizes how much her adolescence in New York was a time of reaching out to people. These friendships were new to Margaret, and she is surprised, as she remembers these first years in New York, at how much her world expanded. Part of this "reaching out" was a wish to escape the long tentacles of her aunts. It was a relief to have places to go that were permissible by their standards. But there was also a yearning for friendship. There was loneliness in Vicksburg as an only child, as the youngest in her class, as an achiever with a mind of her own, and as the Reverend's daughter, "Sister Missionary." All those things set her apart, and even as a child, Margaret would occasionally worry about the "sinfulness" of her self-centered ways. Harlem offered the chance for being close to friends— linking arms and walking forward together.

For both Margaret and the aunts there was a clear distinction between the "good girls"—like Mary, Olivia, and Eunice—and the "fast girls." They were intriguing, but clearly dangerous. Margaret knew that she must be responsible to herself and her dreams, and that meant forming friendships with girls who shared her style and values. Margaret pictures the "other kind" of girls at Wadleigh High, who walked with worldly struts, who occasionally ventured into jazzier sections of Harlem, who dated boys, knew how to flirt, and thought that studious girls like Margaret were utterly prudish. "They liked *boys* . . . I remember one of them even talked to me about girls who liked *girls*. . . ." Margaret listened with quiet fascination, knowing they were from another world.

Margaret felt the same curiosity about Erma Mayo whose family her grandmother and aunts had known in Richmond. Three generations of Mayos had moved to a brownstone in Harlem not far from the Dunbar Apartments. Uncle Walter, who lived on the first floor, was a musician who loved to play his pipe organ. Any time of day or night, you could pass by and hear the smooth melodies. "Music is such sweet melody," Walter would croon. On the second floor lived Grannison Mayo and his wife, both enthusiastic alcoholics. They would lean out their window and shout friendly greetings to passersby. And on the third floor lived Baby Lee Mayo, who was Erma's mother. She was separated from her husband and raising her daughter with the help of this lively and eclectic clan. Erma, a classmate at Wadleigh, was to Margaret's mind the "other kind" of girl. She watched Erma from afar. Erma had nothing to do with Margaret, who must have seemed childish and overearnest to her.

The Mayo girl got herself pregnant in high school, and her pregnancy caused a huge crisis in the aunts' house. "I had to be talked to about that," says Margaret, who felt as though she had been held responsible for this dire event. "Her getting pregnant was an *amazing tragedy* in my house. Aunt Ninnie screamed, 'You see what happens to girls!'" Erma stopped school and had her baby; and Margaret watched as if this were a stranger's story. "Years passed. She had a nice boy . . . met a man . . . finally married, then separated." The progress of Erma's life was so different from her own, and the differences felt strange and disorienting. "Seeing Erma and her son . . . going on with my life, she with hers. . . . It seemed amazing that life went on such a different path." This "woman of the world" had created a life foreign to Margaret, who was finishing high school, going off to college, moving on to medical school, marrying and having children—all in the right order. But over the years, as she watched Erma's life, Margaret saw that it was not tragic or doomed or over just because she had committed this "terrible act" of getting pregnant. Her life moved on, and she made something of it.

Margaret's move from Mississippi to New York was primarily motivated by her determination to pursue a better education. A good high school education would lead to a better college, which would be the ticket to medical school. The local black colleges in the South, Toogaloo and Alcorn, didn't seem special enough places to her. But Margaret was also ready to leave Vicksburg. The friction between her parents had grown more disturbing to her. "I wanted to be away from home, away from watching the interchange between my mother and father." She knew, even then, that leaving Vicksburg would not be a clean escape—that she would not be moving to a household free of trouble and anxiety. Her summers spent in New York with her aunts and grandmother had given her more than a glimpse of the drama she would find there. But they were not her parents. They did not form a tight triangle like the Vicksburg Morgans, and she expected to be able to keep a comfortable distance.

The Morgan triangle was an intense one and difficult to break. When she was only nine, Margaret had a dream that prefigured her escape to New York. In the dream, she and her mother are in New York. Both are dressed in their elegant city finery. On Margaret's head is a wide straw hat with alternate black and white stripes and a streamer down the back. Mary is also decked out in a wide hat. They are about to take a trip on an elevated train. They climb the steps to the train platform and start to board the train together. There is a space between the platform and the train, and Margaret experiences a moment's trepidation as she steps cautiously from one to the other. As she leaps the short distance from the platform onto the open coach at the end of the train, she suddenly realizes that her mother is no longer behind her. Mary has not managed to jump onto the train. Margaret looks down, and there is her mother in the street below. She is sitting on a spike at the center of a turnstile, but she doesn't seem scared or uncomfortable. She is just sitting there, looking up at Margaret on the platform. Looking down at her mother, Margaret experiences surprise but no guilt or remorse. She says, "Oh!", but that is all she utters.

I listen to my mother, now sixty years older, retell the vivid details of the dream—the way her bonnet looked, the anxiety about moving from the platform to the open coach, the mother perched on the spike down in the street below—and I ask her for an interpretation. She seems poised between Margaret, the nine-year-old dreamer, and the seventy-two year-old analyst reinterpreting memories of the child's dream; she then decides to look at the dream squarely and boldly, as analyst. After all, the child's view is no longer available to her. She says, "We were wearing similar hats . . . both *womankind*. . . . I'd say that the elevated steps we used to get onto the train . . . well, steps most often have sexual meaning . . . I got rid of her. . . . It was not my fault. She fell . . . the nature of what she fell on . . . could be a male organ. She didn't seem to be in any pain. . . . *She was out of the way and I was on my way....* It was a competitive dream...there was an Electra component....Despite her suspicions about my father's philandering, he was still mine...and she was out of the way."

Well before she left for New York, Margaret remembers wanting to push out the boundaries of the family triangle. "When I was about five, I desperately wanted a brother or sister." A living sibling would have to be better company than a competitive, idealized dead brother. "My mother had told me that babies came in airplanes. I would be playing inside the house and hear an airplane overhead, and I would go rushing outside to see if the baby had arrived...but of course I was *ambivalent* about whether I really wanted a sibling or not."

When Margaret turned six, her mother suddenly changed her story. The little girl would no longer rush out to search the sky for approaching airplanes. The new story about babies, although true, was frightening and confusing. "When my mother told me where babies really come from, I lost interest.... At the same time, she was also giving me the whole story about sex and telling me what I mustn't let boys do...she *warned* me.... It became something I didn't want to have anything to do with.... It was also then that she told me about menstruation." Babies, sex, menstruation, all became part of a potent warning. The "truth" about where babies came from certainly cured Margaret of wanting a brother or a sister. Along with the other accompanying messages, it had made her want to stay away from anything having to do with bodies and blood. Was the injury that she got from Orville Mosley's broken truck that made her bleed around her vagina...was that related to menstruation? She must keep that a secret.

In the Morgan family you had to be careful not to tell too much or express too much. Margaret can remember falling down the hard stone steps of the church when she was very young. Quickly she jumped up from the fall, as if she were unhurt, and began to laugh cheerfully. She thought her mother was watching her, and she was determined not to cry. But when she looked up, Mary was nowhere to be seen. Her mother had not seen the fall; so Margaret began to wail. She broke the family rules of restraint and cried like a child.

Margaret's parents were intrusive in many ways, but they gave their daughter an enormous amount of autonomy in making decisions about her life. In some respects, Margaret had the power of an adult in her family—a power that gave her more space and autonomy than most children her age but also a great deal more responsibility. She remembers the summer of her fourteenth year when she announced her decision to go to school in New York. "I thought it might affect the college, then the medical school, that I would go to . . . and I was right. I remember feeling a sense of responsibility, because if I made the decision I had to live with it."

Living in New York meant seeing her parents every other summer. More frequent trips would be too costly. She communicated with her parents through letters, but she often felt a deep longing to see them. This loneliness was the price she paid for her single-minded pursuit. "I sometimes missed them very much . . . but I didn't feel neglected, because this was of my own doing. I was making my own way, creating my own world." Nevertheless, there were moments when Margaret wished for the protection and limits that might have been there if she were living with her parents.

Margaret was permitted by her parents to choose and develop relationships with boyfriends. Here again, they trusted her judgment to make a wise choice and expected that she would select a young man who deserved her attentions. While the aunts worried and hovered and traced Margaret's every move, Mary was trying to assure them that their concerns were unnecessary. "When they [the aunts] complained to Mother, she didn't respond and get upset. She would say to them, 'She'll be all right. Don't worry about her.' " Margaret is still amazed by the latitude her parents offered, especially in relation to the young men in her life. "I did what I wanted to. I *handled* it."

Although the aunts spent enormous energy containing and protecting their female adolescent charge, even they could not shield her from all life's dangers. Among the only activities that her mother prohibited were sitting in the sun ("turning black") and swimming ("possibly drowning"). When Margaret arrived in New York, she decided to challenge her mother's second prohibition; she was determined to learn to swim. When the aunts agreed to her plan, she was surprised and relieved. And when Aunt Hazel decided to join her in taking swimming lessons, she was simply astonished. Each week Aunt Hazel and Margaret would go to the public bathhouse ("an ordinary, heterosexual place to swim . . . a great place filled with children") to take swimming lessons together. Aunt Hazel, having lived with her fear of the water for much longer, was even more determined to master swimming than her niece.

One day, after one of their lessons, Margaret was swimming on her own in the shallow part of the pool, practicing her breathing and perfecting her strokes, moving cautiously from one edge of the pool to the other. When she would get tired, she'd simply stand up in the shallow water and rest. Swimming brought on high anxiety, and she paused often to calm her nerves. On this afternoon, the pool was crowded with people and the lifeguard had her hands full keeping track of the bobbing bodies. As Margaret continued to practice, she moved imperceptibly out into the deeper waters. The next time she got tired and needed to stand, she discovered her feet could not touch the bottom and she panicked—a panic that would not let her call out, a panic that made her go blank and silent. "When I couldn't stand up, I put my head back under and held my breath . . . that is the last I recall."

Someone noticed Margaret's body deep under the water and yelled to the lifeguard, "Look, there is someone lying on the bottom." The lifeguard acted quickly; she dived into the water, dragged Margaret's limp, heavy body out of the pool, and proceeded to administer artificial respiration. As Margaret came to, she saw the lifeguard hovering anxiously over her and noticed the circle of people looking on in horror. "My first words were to the lifeguard: 'Oh, I'm so sorry you had to get wet.' " Her first utterance was an apology! Margaret shakes her head in disbelief. "Why didn't I scream for help? I just quit. I did *nothing*. . . . This sounds very bad to me now!"

That night Margaret lay in her bed, terrified, as her mind rehearsed the day's near calamity. Hazel, who had felt helpless and frightened at the pool's edge, hovered close by, bringing hot tea and wet cloths to wipe Margaret's brow. With all of Aunt Hazel's determined efforts and extreme caution, she knew then that she could not protect Margaret from all life's dangers. After all, she had been with her niece at the pool. She had not let Margaret out of her sight . . . and still, she had almost died.

Early in her life, Margaret had stood out as a successful student—

the kind of child that teachers grab onto in order to make them feel effective and competent. As the daughter of a "fierce" and determined teacher, she learned the student role early: the discipline and skills required to accomplish a task, and the social interactions that sustain good student-teacher relationships. She talked before she learned to walk and began to read at three. This early learning was reinforced and rewarded throughout her schooling. By the time she had finished the Vicksburg Industrial School at twelve and moved on to Magnolia High School, her reputation as a star student was well established. She was at least two years younger than all of her classmates—hardworking and innocent.

Mr. Bowman, the math teacher and principal of Magnolia High, had a special fondness for Margaret, and she had much respect for him. "He enjoyed my open-faced innocence, but mostly he enjoyed the way I could do math. . . . He was a stern taskmaster in class and called us by our last names. 'Morgan, go to the board.' He asked me to do it when no one else knew how. I was the person of last resort . . . I knew my math." Margaret felt the same kind of skill and confidence in English. She and her English teacher, Miss Cox, developed a respectful admiration for one another. Although Mr. Bowman and Miss Cox were favorite teachers for whom Margaret felt great admiration, there was always a respectful, well-defined distance between teacher and student. "You weren't *friends* with teachers." There were no intimacies expressed or confusions about the limits of the relationship. "I liked Miss Cox very much. I think she liked me . . . I was, in a sense, a *positively aggressive* student. I knew the answers and I spoke out."

The positive relationships Margaret established with her teachers carried over to her reputation among her classmates. She managed to be successful without flaunting her achievements, without lording it over others. She does not remember resentment. She remembers, instead, a generosity from her older classmates, their tenderness toward a child in their midst. "Kids were kind to me and treated me as younger. I was young and I was smart, and nobody seemed to mind that. I didn't get in anybody's space. I didn't try to be the teacher's pet . . . I *earned* the response that I got, but I didn't flash it, or live above anybody."

Even though Mr. Bowman, her principal and favorite teacher, discouraged Margaret from leaving Magnolia High before her senior year, and cautioned her parents that this was an unwise decision, Margaret's plan prevailed. Her aunts had asked acquaintances who knew the educational scene in the city to recommend the best school for their achieving niece. Wadleigh was chosen over Hunter because its location, on 114th–115th streets between Seventh and Eighth avenues, made it closer to Harlem. There was no question that she would attend a girls' school. The aunts viewed coeducation with dread and suspicion.

In order to be admitted to Wadleigh, prospective students had to take entrance examinations—both achievement tests and departmental exams. For the fourteen-year-old-girl from Mississippi, the achievement tests were an ordeal—a strange format for testing knowledge at a baffling, accelerated pace. She did poorly on the achievement tests (a pattern that would continue through college). "I was not geared to rapid test taking. I expected to sit there and think about it. I remember them taking the test away before I ever got started." The contrast in style and pace between the teaching methods in her black school in the Deep South and in the classical, academic high school in the urban Northeast must have contributed to Margaret's frustrations and low scores on the standardized tests. But her depressed scores did not simply reflect the differences in cultural style and educational expectations. Margaret's intelligence does not lie in the quick, discrete response, in the immediate recall of fact. Her mind works more slowly as it considers various perspectives, considers competing interpretations, and puts pieces together. She asks questions that may have no answer. She attends to information that is broader than the narrow constructs of traditional academic discourse. She is not a rapid speaker, but uses carefully chosen words. These intellectual and temperamental tendencies did not make her a good candidate for the standardized tests.

In contrast to the difficult and baffling standardized tests, Margaret did very well on the departmental examinations that were also required. She soared in English and mathematics, the subjects in which she had been well trained in Vicksburg. For the English examination, she was required to write a composition about "My First Job." Margaret chose to write about a job she had been hired for at five, when in the lazy hot summer heat of Mississippi, her father said that he would give her a penny for every fly that she killed. Not only was the composition literate and grammatically correct, but it also revealed Margaret's love of story telling, her interest in turning ordinary experiences into memorable events. The English teachers were impressed with the essay and awarded her full credit for four years of high school English, exempting her from taking more at Wadleigh. She had similar success with her mathematics test and was given permission to take intermediate algebra at Wadleigh. It was on the basis of the skills and talents she displayed on the departmental exams that Margaret was admitted to Wadleigh. After three years at Magnolia High, it was determined that she needed a year and a half more credits to graduate from Wadleigh. "By the time they added up my credits, I had eighteen months of school left . . . but I decided to take two years and graduate with my class, which meant I lost a year."

But Margaret lost no time in distinguishing herself as an achieving student at Wadleigh. After her first year there, she was named to the honor society, called Arista, which gave her a special, privileged place in the school. The Aristas wore blue and gold banners across their chests and special pins. They patrolled halls and stood at the doors during school assemblies to watch over the orderly procession of their fellow students. In this girls' academic high school, scholarly achievement was rewarded publicly and revered by both faculty and students.

A central figure at Wadleigh was Miss Anna Pearl MacVay, who was the dean and Margaret's Greek tutor. A classicist by training, Dean MacVay "looked like someone in a Latin or Greek book." She piled her silky white hair on top of her head, and her carriage was tall and regal. Every signal she sent off seemed to convey her high standards for achievement and conduct and her impatience at even the slightest evidence of procrastination or laziness. Several times a week Margaret would read Greek with the dean in her small office on the first floor. Her power was overwhelming and unquestioned by Margaret, who was swept up in the tide of high expectations. "She came across as a no-nonsense lady. . . . She ran my life. . . . I felt very small with her . . . read my Greek and did what I was supposed to do. Her eyes were upon me and I felt responsible." There were only a few Greek students in the school, and they all met singly in tutorials with Dean MacVay; but it was Margaret who seemed to be at the very center of her stern gaze. "She kept her eyes on me." MacVay organized her academic schedule, made sure that all of her requirements were fulfilled, scrutinized her applications for Regents examinations and educational fellowships, and decided to which colleges she should apply. Their relationship was intense but pragmatic. "I knew she cared, but she didn't show affection or warmth.... She wanted to see that a capable young woman was directed into the right paths."

MacVay's special contact with Margaret was echoed in Margaret's relationships with many of the teachers at Wadleigh. They, too, saw her talent and dedication and made decisions about what was best for her. "The teachers at Wadleigh saw that I was a good student and very much involved.... I remember my biology teacher saying, 'You *will* belong to the Biology Club.' ... In Wadleigh, they put the screws on you if they thought you were capable ... particularly if you were Negro ... there were not many of us who functioned at that level ... once you presented yourself, you were moved forward. I accepted all this ... these forces were quite apart from family, which exerted its own kind of influence."

Not only was Margaret "accepting" of the plan laid out for her by the dean and her teachers, and not only did she see the convergence of her own dreams and their activities on her behalf, but she also saw the whole arrangement as "normal." "I had the feeling that is what happened when you came to New York. I didn't feel super-special." The "normal" educational encounters led to extraordinary achievements—achievements that were not magical but that grew out of deep commitment and daily, grinding, hard work. On graduation day, "the Negro girl from Mississippi" walked off with the top prizes in Greek and Latin and was admitted to Cornell University on a full academic scholarship, the *only* black undergraduate in arts and sciences at the time.

Although Wadleigh had a predominantly white student body, there was a strong black presence there. With "maybe as much as a third of us [Negro girls] in each class," Margaret never felt like a lonely

The Reverend Sandy Alonzo Morgan,
Vicksburg, Mississippi, ca. 1924

Mary Elizabeth Smith Morgan,
ca. 1924

"Mrs. Ewing's Class," Vicksburg Industrial School, Vicksburg, Mississippi, ca. 1925
Margaret, front row, second from right

Margaret and her mother,
New York, summer, 1928

This was the only context I lived in. But these ladies in New York were *minority* people. There were very few Negro teachers in the high schools of New York and almost no Negro principals . . . they had gotten to where they were because they were *unusual*. . . . When they put the finger on you, they were saying, 'You have an opportunity!' " So in his capacity as "heavy uncle," Reverend Johnson provided the meeting place and made connections. He remembered Sandy Morgan's solemn request, "I put my daughter in your hands," and he took it to heart.

Most of the women who influenced Margaret were teachers—master teachers with commanding reputations in the community. Their encouragement cast a light over Margaret's life. Just knowing them seemed to make dreams come alive. With these dreams set on medicine, Margaret was particularly overjoyed to meet Dr. Mae Chinn, a leading physician in Harlem. She, too, reached out to the girl from Mississippi and was generous in her encouragement and praise. Her presence and stature in the community made Dr. Chinn seem very large. "As I remember these women, they seem *larger than life* . . . when I saw Mae Chinn just a few years ago, I was amazed that she was shorter than I am!"

All these women conveyed their expectations through praise and admonition, but mostly by example; by the way they conducted themselves, communicated their thoughts, and pursued their goals; by their striking combination of personal ambition and community responsibility. Margaret revered them and wanted to emulate them in her own life. But she was already aware of one way in which their lives did not match the one she wanted to live. All these ladies were unmarried, spinsters who believed that it was impossible to marry and have a career. If you had professional ambitions, you had to be single-minded and absolute in your dedication to your work and live completely the role of your profession. Being a dedicated teacher in Harlem was a life, not a job. It meant teaching generations of children in the classroom, but it also meant standing as a symbol of knowledge, grace, and truth in the community, and reaching out to youngsters who had the capacity to follow in your footsteps. The demands were both professional and deeply personal. These women were mothering Harlem. After giving so bountifully to the community, they may have had no more energy for nurturing a family of their own. And the complications of sustaining a marriage might have inhibited the clear-headed and clean dedication to standards that these ladies felt so deeply. "The idea of being married was *contradictory* to having a career. The ladies would say, 'I hope you don't get interested in *boys!*' . . . All eyes were upon you. 'If you're going to be a doctor, you have to give yourself to it completely' . . . For them the contradictions were clear between being married and having a professional life."

Margaret was troubled by this message. She regarded the women with awe and great respect, but even in her adolescent reverence she could not accept celibacy as part of her life view. The message, of course, was piercingly reinforced by the aunts, whose doubting barbs actually spurred Margaret on. "Oh, you'll never become a doctor. You'll get married and that will be the end of that." The aunts' skepticism felt more discouraging than the teacher-spinsters' warnings; but both seemed at odds with the vision Margaret had already formed of a life filled with work and love, career and marriage— dedication and commitment to both worlds. She responded to the aunts' words with quiet anger and determination to show them that they were wrong about her. She would not be discouraged from her dream. She *would* become a doctor. One day they would eat their words. The advice of her professional mentors, however, left her confused and puzzled. After all, they were worldly and sophisticated women who knew the demands of a career and were directing her out of their sense of commitment to *her* goals. Maybe they were right. Maybe a career required the single-minded pursuit. "I was at least *ambivalent* about the marriage/career question . . . I had a lot of different things going in my head."

Happily, Margaret did not yet have to test her ambivalence, or face the challenge her aunts presented, because her life in New York was filled almost exclusively with women. She went to a girls' high school and had close and satisfying friendships with a warm circle of classmates. Margaret did not think much about boys. Each day was spent with her friends Mary, Eunice, and Olivia, in school, in church, on adventures in the city. And, of course, the aunts prohibited any contact with boys. They were suspicious at the least mention of the male species. One day, when Margaret came home talking about a West Indian boy she had met at a club meeting hosted by one of her classmates, Aunt Ninnie hit the roof. This young man, whoever he was, was not to be trusted and not to be seen again. He was probably one of those West Indians with wives and children back home in the Islands. He would lure you in, tempt you with his smooth talk, take advantage of your innocence, and then abandon you. Aunt Ninnie's ragings went on and on. It seemed easier and wiser to live a life free of males than it was to listen to the endless rantings of her aunts.

Besides Reverend Johnson, "who took my upbringing seriously," there were only two "other men" who were part of Margaret's life in Harlem. Andrew, the wounded and sick son of Grandmother, lived in the same apartment. "He *occupied space* in Aunt Ninnie's house," says Margaret simply. The simple words cover over complex feelings. This tortured man consumed a great deal of psychic space in the family, even though his movements were mostly limited to the dining room, where he slept on a cot and stood peering out the window for hours at a time. His hallucinations and loud talk confused and annoyed Margaret, who knew nothing about mental illness and thought it was his fault. While Margaret was irritated and disturbed by Andrew's uncontrolled rantings, Aunt Ninnie harbored a seething anger toward him. After all, she had chosen to be the good and devoted daughter of Grandmother. If she married her patient man-friend, Harvey, her mother would be furious and she would no longer be the "good" child. Aunt Ninnie did not so much resent Andrew for the square feet he occupied in the dining room, or even his hallucinatory screaming and rantings. What enraged Aunt Ninnie more than anything was her mother's deep preoccupation with her troubled son. Even though Ninnie gave all of herself to her mother, waited to marry Harvey, still her mother's worries were focused on Andrew. Andrew did more than simply occupy space; he consumed their mother's attention and love. Margaret danced around the edges of this fight for Grandmother's affections, but she couldn't help siding with Aunt Ninnie and incorporating some of her rage at Andrew.

The other man in Margaret's life was Uncle Jimmy, Aunt Hazel's husband, who lived upstairs on the fifth floor of the Dunbar Apartments. Uncle Jimmy was rarely home, because he had a job working in the dining car on the railroad. But when he returned home, Margaret was always glad to see him. A big, dark-brown-skinned man, Uncle Jimmy would give her a warm smile and a big hug. Their relationship was easy and comforting. "I liked him and he liked me. He was content. He *made* things; always busy doing. You could just hang around him. He loved to cook and would use these huge bowls to bake cakes. He baked several at a time, big gestures, enjoying himself thoroughly . . . and he'd say, 'Give me the baking powder, Margaret' . . . and I was there. I didn't feel in the way. . . . Yes, I was glad when he came home." Their affection for one another began early and seemed very different from the strained relationships Margaret had with the aunts. When Aunt Hazel was first dating Uncle Jimmy, Margaret was five or six years old. Margaret would be told he was coming to call and she would get all dressed up in a fancy dress, hair newly plaited, face scrubbed clean. "I would arrange myself in a chair and sit waiting for him. Then he would come, and I would always be so surprised that he was coming to see *Hazel* and not me." Margaret laughs lightly at the memory of the disappointed child, a memory that echoes her fond feeling for this big comfortable man.

Dean Anna Pearl MacVay had carefully orchestrated Margaret's applications to college, making sure she took the appropriate tests, signed the correct forms, and followed "the right paths." Dean MacVay had selected three schools for Margaret: Hunter College in New York City, because it would be tuition free; Smith College, because it was an elite sister school in the dignified tradition of Wadleigh High; and Cornell University, because it had a fine reputation as a large, coeducational institution. Margaret knew little about these places. She had not visited them nor heard anything about their academic merits or social life; but she never thought to question Dean MacVay's judgment. "I went where I was told." When she received acceptances from all three places, she felt pleasure, but no surprise. After all she had dutifully followed "the right paths." Hunter, a city school, seemed least attractive to both Margaret and the dean, and was quickly eliminated from the list. Smith did not offer Margaret the full tuition scholarship that Cornell did, so Cornell was chosen. Knowing the dean's preference for the female environment of Smith, Margaret felt relieved by Cornell's generosity. Since she needed every bit of the scholarship, she had to choose Cornell—the place where she had secretly hoped to go because there would be boys, men, the "male species." After two years in the company of women at school and at home, she was eager for the possibility of male companionship.

Ithaca

THE EXOTIC TOKEN

I N the fall of 1932, Margaret arrived at the Ithaca train station with nine dollars in her pocket. Standing at the station with her suitcase in her hand, she took in the strange landscape. "My Lord, where is this?" she whispered to herself. Her sense of adventure took over. "That's how I handled my fears." She hailed a taxi and told the driver to take her to Cornell. Her rising anticipation matched the terrain of Ithaca as the taxi climbed up to the university. The driver found the small house on campus that housed the office of the dean of women. Margaret was wearing a suit that had been made for the occasion by her mother's seamstress in Vicksburg: steel gray, with shoulder pads and a fitted waist. She carried a black purse, with matching shoes, but did not wear the gray gloves that would have completed the outfit. Her thick black braids, gleaming almost blue in the bright afternoon sun, were wrapped into buns on either side of her head, a concession to the adult image she was trying out. By the time she paid the driver, Margaret had depleted her nine-dollar supply considerably.

Dean Fitch welcomed her and told her where to register for courses. Margaret was the only black undergraduate on the arts and sciences campus. Where would she live? No blacks were allowed in the dormitory, of course. Dean Fitch at first recommended a place in town where she had sent other black students in the past—"a nice place on the hill" where she said the "Negro graduate students enjoyed" staying. But with so few dollars in her pocket, Margaret told the dean that she would have to find a place where she could work for room and board. (Several months later, Margaret found that the "nice place on the hill" was a house of ill repute. She peered in the window and saw a "house full of couches." It was a place that slept during the day and came alive at night with sounds of dancing, laughter, and carousing. "I discovered from people in town that it was a questionable place.") After consulting her files, Dean Fitch found a family in town who wanted "help." She wrote their address on a card and sent Margaret on her way. It was a long walk to 209 Hudson Street, the Dillons' house. "Sure enough, they said fine, I could come and live with them."

Margaret's rendition of this tale is told with spare restraint. She does not mention fear, or loneliness, or anger at being suddenly thrust into the servant role. I listen, disbelieving, struck by the sharp contrasts between my mother's solitary arrival at Cornell in the fall of 1932 and my landing at Swarthmore thirty years later. I arrived at college surrounded by family and things: books, posters, bedspreads, record player, musical instruments, and clothes. The trip from home to school was a staged journey full of family stories, acknowledgment of transition and anticipation, long embraces, and tears. It was only after my mother and father, handsome in their proud-parent roles and "full of nachas," had unpacked the car, carried piles of stuff to the dormitory room, walked slowly around the beautiful campus greeting other eager families, and attended the President's tea—it was only then that they reluctantly released me and took off for home. Watching the car round the corner and out of sight, I felt suddenly alone, on my own. I burst out laughing as the tears slid down my cheeks. I'm on my own! As I listen to Margaret's story—arriving at Cornell without fanfare, without money, without another soul—I suddenly feel the privileges and abundance of my generation. I experience again my mother's uncomplaining courage, a courage that transformed loneliness into adventure.

"The Dillons seemed to like the fact that I was Negro," says Margaret—her way of saying that it was easier for the Dillons to feel comfortable with "colored help" than with a white Cornell student. Mrs. Dillon insisted that Margaret step quickly into the servant position when she was home and not confuse her student and servant lives. Margaret wore a uniform, waited on table, and ate separately in the kitchen. "Mrs. Dillon was more rigid than her husband. She wanted me in my place. She seemed pleased that I was a Cornell student but aware that I was Negro." The days were filled with classes and housework. Margaret would leave for classes each morning and return home to do the Dillons' ironing, washing, and housecleaning. She would also be asked to take care of their four-year-old grandniece, who was often around in the afternoons. Once, when Margaret was soaking in the bathtub, the little girl walked into the bathroom and exclaimed with wonder, "Ooh, Margie is brown all over!" The Dillons' adolescent son and daughter were rarely part of Margaret's life. "Occasionally, they would ask, 'Margaret, have you seen my so-and-so?'" Mr. Dillon, a real estate man and part-time songwriter, was a benign and distant presence. In any case, Margaret had no real wish to get close to the Dillons. This was a job, and she had neither the energy nor the interest to try to become a part of the family.

Margaret lived and slept in the attic, a room that was not insulated and became ice cold in Ithaca's winters. The Dillons provided her with a heater that barely took the chill off the frigid air. After dinner, Margaret would finish the dishes and climb the stairs to the attic. "When it was time to get into that cold bed, I went," says Margaret with a visible shiver. She would bring the heater closer and closer to her bed as she tried to find warmth under the cold sheets. One night, in an act of desperation, she brought the heater into bed with her. Soon there was a smell of scorching linen. Her reflexes were quick enough to save herself from being burned, but the sheets were singed, terrifying evidence the next morning of how close she had come to disaster.

Soon the aunts came to the rescue. In the winter of Margaret's first year, Aunt Ninnie and Aunt Hazel drove up to Ithaca to visit her. They found a place to stay in town and stayed for a few days. With them they brought a magnificent raccoon coat, the most beautiful coat Margaret had ever seen, a wonderfully extravagant present. The coat finally made it bearable to sleep in the Dillons' attic. Margaret would pull the heater close—not too close—pile the blankets on, and top it all off with the raccoon coat, before slipping between the icy sheets. Underneath this heavy mound, she would finally find a safe warmth. Each winter night she would give thanks to the aunts for the fur coat.

When the aunts went to Ithaca, they took something else of great importance to Margaret: a new trust and support. In Harlem, they had constantly doubted Margaret's intentions and undermined her dreams. "You'll never become a doctor—you'll get married," they would warn if she even seemed to be *thinking* about boys. But when they went to Cornell and saw their niece diligently working and studying, they seemed, for the first time, to take her seriously. "When they saw me at Cornell, they were heartened.... They thought I might really go to medical school after all." Along with the lovely, comforting coat, the aunts imparted a vote of confidence in Margaret's dream.

After two years of living at the Dillons', Margaret got tired of the cold attic. She found a larger, warmer room with the Burnhams, a Cornell faculty family who lived on the other side of town. Although her room was more comfortable and she enjoyed looking out of their living room window at one of Ithaca's lakes, life in the Burnham household was anything but peaceful. Mrs. Burnham, a flighty, anxious woman, fought frequently with her husband and carried on a lively affair with the doctor next door. Both Mr. and Mrs. Burnham found parenting hard and had troubled relationships with their only child, an eight-year-old boy, who became Margaret's ally. Margaret can remember her strong identification with this boy, who felt attacked by his parents. "We respected each other a great deal ... my room was right next to the boy's room.... We had each other." Work was harder at the Burnhams' than it had been at the Dillons', and Margaret was tired when she finally went to bed each night. She was "the maid," and Mrs. Burnham communicated the distance and distrust that often accompany servant-employer relationships. "In the evening, I'd wait on the table. After I finished serving the family, I'd bring my plate to the table and *she* would serve it ... and that was all I got! I'd eat my meager plateful in the kitchen.... She kept account of every bit of food ... except the peanut butter. So I ate a lot of peanut butter."

After a year at the Burnhams', Margaret was able to "retire" from room and board. She was sorry to abandon the Burnham boy for whom she had become a nurturant and kindly figure, but she was thrilled to leave the family bickering and the stingy cupboard. Mostly, she was relieved to live her own life free of the demands and inhibitions that come with serving others. With poise and dignity she had accepted her three years of work at the Dillons' and the Burnhams'. But to be free of this servitude in her senior year felt wonderfully liberating. Margaret was able to do this because she found a job working for a histologist on the agriculture campus at Cornell. The professor had positions for National Youth Act workers, and Margaret joined his research team as a technician. Mostly she remembers the frigid working conditions. "I made tissue slides and worked in the cold-storage room." This cold did not feel unfriendly, however. The job allowed her autonomy and privacy, and the technical skills held the fascination and exactitude of the laboratory work that she knew she would find in medical school.

"It was a great year," says Margaret, beaming in retrospect. "It was free and easy." She even remembers how she looked: adventurous and exotic. "I had my raccoon coat and I wore my hair in braids . . . people thought I was an Indian." Her exotic look brought her to the attention of the International Club, and she was invited to one of their elegant dinner parties. "Do you come from a foreign country?" asked her dinner partner, intrigued by this appealing brown girl with Indian braids. "Yes," she said with pleasure and mischief. "I'm from Mississippi."

The raccoon coat hung in the closet of Margaret's room at Mrs. Jones's house. Mrs. Hattie Jones, an institution in the Negro community of Ithaca, had a large comfortable house and a generous heart. Married to a big-time gambler, Mrs. Jones enjoyed a luxurious lifestyle. Her handsome young chauffeur squired her around town in a shiny car, and she wore wonderful, dramatic costumes. Not only did she treat herself to good living; she also felt a responsibility for "young Negroes coming up" and rented out rooms in her big house to generations of black university students. "We paid very little for the room . . . this was Mrs. Jones's philanthropy. . . . And she made luscious meals for us . . . the dinners cost twenty-five cents." Each morning Margaret would wash, get dressed, and come down the stairs with her box of corn flakes. She would have the corn flakes "with Mrs. Jones's milk" and soon leave for her classes and her chilly work. At noon she would savor her lunch—always the same—a Mr. Goodbar candy bar that she ate thankfully and ritualistically and called "Monsieur Bon Bon." By day's end, she was headed back to Mrs. Jones's, now hungry enough for a huge dinner. Mrs. Jones was famous for making folks "feel like home." She'd cook deep-fried pork chops smothered in onions with homemade applesauce, collard greens, and buttered corn bread. Or she would fix fried chicken and cover the rice with a thick gravy. The dinners were topped off with delectable desserts: sweet potato pie, coconut cake, or a bowl of ice cream. After dinner, Margaret would find the peace and solitude of her room. The routine began again the next day. It was a routine that gave order, purpose, and certainty to Margaret's days, and it was a routine that had its simple pleasures. She enjoyed her own private room in Mrs. Jones's house, without the demands and humiliation of domestic work, and felt the time drawing closer and closer when she would be going to medical school.

Although her senior year at Cornell had its quiet joys, Margaret's memories of her four years in Ithaca are neither full nor pleasurable. "I have sparse memories of Cornell." Together we have discussed why the memories were so meager, the details so hard to retrieve. Perhaps it was the austerity of the first few years, or perhaps life was so difficult and lonely that the memories have faded out of self-protection. In any case, the most vivid pictures are somber: waiting on tables, stealing peanut butter, bitter cold nights in the attic, and staying out of the way of family conflict. Her memories of university life itself—classes, professors, even friends—are dim. Trying to understand these lost recollections, Margaret explains, "I was struggling. I did my work. I made few connections."

The closer Margaret got to medical school, the more interesting and rewarding was her academic life. The first couple of years of liberal arts courses were occasionally engaging, but the time often felt wasted, or at least remote from her dream of becoming a physician. During her freshman year, Dr. Short (one of the few professors whose name she remembers, because it fit him) taught her poetry. She remembers the small class, and his rounded back, which made his already short frame seem even more diminutive. His intellectual, nonemotional tone seemed to clash with the poetry's intention. Solid geometry—a subject for which Margaret had been "excellently prepared" by Mr. Bowman, her mathematics teacher and principal at Vicksburg's Magnolia High—was easy, and she "did well but didn't enjoy it much."

An experience in Introduction to Sociology, taught by a Professor Woodward, remains fresh in her mind. "I went to the large lectures, listening carefully, taking notes . . . I did the reading . . . I also thought about things quite a bit. . . . When the time came, I took the midterm exam and got a C . . . I was amazed by the grade. I went to talk to Professor Woodward, and he looked over the exam and said, 'I gave you the appropriate grade.' " His voice was kindly and his manner undefensive. Margaret wanted to pursue the matter further. She took out her notebook and saw the discrepancies between his lecture notes and her responses on the exam. The differences did not seem to surprise or disturb her as she exclaimed with an innocence that amazed the professor, "But I disagree with what you said. I know that is *your* interpretation, but I don't see it that way." His response was pleasant but firm: "Miss Morgan, you don't disagree in Introduction to Sociology." Margaret smiles at the memory of her innocence and fearlessness, and at the professor's bemusement.

She had probably understood correctly that sociology was an interpretive discipline that invited rumination and critical thinking. It was supposed to be different from exercises in mathematics, for example, where she relished the discrete, sure answers and enjoyed the exacting methods and procedures. But sociology made her "think about things," and turn the ideas over in her own mind. She was "amazed" that this was seen as inappropriate by her professor. The conference with Woodward was "all very pleasant," but it left a mark of dismay and disappointment on the eager, hardworking freshman.

During her first year at Cornell, she took and endured other courses, such as Introduction to Psychology and Ancient History ("I was real surprised at how much work there was in Ancient History . . . I struggled"). A part of her felt as though she were marking time. One course that engaged her intellect and imagination was Organic Chemistry. Her face suddenly lights up as she remembers this bright spot in her class schedule. "I was *excited* by chemistry . . . as the premed courses came along the next year I thought, *'This is why I am here.'*" Comparative Anatomy, in her sophomore year, held the same magic: "I felt I was getting into the good stuff!" And even the introductory course in physics, which Margaret "never latched onto" and for which she earned a disappointing C, attracted her interest in her senior year when it reappeared in the guise of Medical Physics. By all academic measures, Medical Physics was a much more demanding and difficult course, but Margaret "did amazingly well." "It was the motivation . . . its relationship to medicine," says Margaret with certainty. Margaret's overall memories are of a bland diet of liberal arts requirements, enhanced by exciting premed courses. In these courses that anticipated her medical career, Margaret threw herself into the material with high energy and commitment.

Margaret's life at Cornell paled in comparison to the vitality and enthusiasm that she had felt at Wadleigh High. At Cornell, she did not feel special as a student; at Wadleigh, she had been "the chosen one," admired and respected by her teachers. At Cornell, she often felt at sea, without direction or purpose. At Wadleigh, she had been kept on course by the fierce and caring direction of the dean who had guided her with a firm hand: "I did what I was told to do." At Cornell, she never felt like a high-achieving student, even though she had a fine academic record. At Wadleigh, she had been a member of the honor society and was decorated with ribbons and medals for her superior record. In college, she had to go it alone, remote from caring and concerned teachers ("I mostly just did my academic work, then my domestic work for room and board"). In high school, she had been at the center of her teachers' gaze ("Their eyes were upon me; I felt responsible").

There were no mentors for Margaret in Ithaca. The "Negro ladies" in Harlem—Dr. Mae Chinn, Miss Lucille Spence, and Miss Melva Price—who had offered Margaret great encouragement and support were no longer there. Their proud, determined images were etched in her mind, but she was not able to sit and talk with them, sip tea in their well-appointed parlors, watch the way they moved through the world, or listen to their uncompromising admonitions. She missed the warm embrace of Harlem. There was nothing to take its place in Ithaca. Mrs. Hattie Jones was generous to Margaret, as she was to all of the young students whom she helped out. But Mrs. Jones was not like the Harlem ladies. Her relationship to Margaret was part of a kindly but distant philanthropy. She provided room and board, not guidance and support. She was not particularly invested in Margaret's ambitions; the Harlem ladies saw themselves mirrored in Margaret's dreams.

Margaret also missed her high-school friends. She missed the intimacies and adventures she had shared with Mary Seabrook and the warm, trusting friendship with Eunice Mattis. As the only black undergraduate when she arrived at Cornell in 1932, Margaret felt a dramatic loss and gnawing loneliness. She did manage to make a few friends, but not with the same closeness and commitment that she felt with Mary or Eunice or Olivia.

At Cornell, she grew closest to Babette Kurtz, whom she met at the freshman tea given by the dean of women. "We both had hats on and we became good friends." Babette was from a Jewish family in New York, and Margaret enjoyed the obvious contrasts in their personality and style. "Babette was talkative and plump." As one of their first acts of friendship, Babette and Margaret decided to take a dance class together. Margaret laughs at the memory of their dance class. "It was totally impossible for Babette. She would say, 'Margaret, you stand in front of me and I'll follow.' " The friendship with Babette spread to her family, and Margaret would sometimes travel to New York and visit with the Kurtzes during holidays. She liked Babette's sisters and parents and enjoyed their intensely close, highly verbal household. Babette introduced Margaret to some of her other friends who were at Cornell from New York, widening her circle of acquaintances. "These were all Jewish girls . . . Betty Silver, Lee Schwartz." Margaret would sometimes spend time in their dormitories, where she was not permitted to live but was allowed to visit. Occasionally, they would talk, even joke, about Margaret's exclusion from the living quarters. But they never talked about the distance between them that they must have all felt, particularly Margaret, who would return from the companionship of the dormitory to her solitary life as household servant.

In the fall of 1933, Sarah Thomas arrived at Cornell from Binghamton, New York, the second black student on the arts and sciences campus. A friendship developed between Margaret and Sarah, but at first it had the forced quality that often accompanies the relationship of two tokens—a sense that they were supposed to be companions, that their brown skins should necessarily bind them together. "Sarah and I were friendly," says Margaret, trying to capture her mixed feelings, of pleasure in the other girl's presence and resentment at the assumption that they should become bosom buddies. "With only two undergraduate Negro women on the whole campus, people expected us to be together. . . . We were fairly good friends, but we felt sort of pushed together."

Their friendship became more than a necessity when they worked together the summer after Margaret's sophomore year, at Quaker Lake, a resort community not far from Sarah's home. Sarah had found jobs for both of them with the same family in a large household. Although the work was demanding and strenuous ("We did everything: planned meals, cooked, cleaned. We managed the household"), the setting was beautiful and their companionship made the work feel lighter. Margaret remembers their long walks through the woods after they had finished their chores, swimming in the cool lake, and the lovely sense of freedom that came with these simple adventures. She also remembers how the remote setting and common work brought them closer together. "It was sort of isolated up there. . . . I picture us waiting by the mailbox for letters from home . . . at least we had each other."

Margaret and Sarah returned from Quaker Lake with a friendship bolstered by memories of hard work, laughter, and shared adventure. No longer defined by others' expectations, the bond between them was their own. Sarah's family became part of this deepening friendship and made Margaret feel welcome. Theirs was another household of women. Sarah's father had died early in her childhood, and her mother and two sisters lived together in a way that both intrigued and attracted Margaret. Margaret can picture Mrs. Thomas, Sarah's mother, who had not left her house for many years. She sent her daughters off into the world, with doses of support and reassurance, but she remained home, keeping the place spotless. "This was the first time I had seen someone wrapping rags around a dust mop."

Mrs. Thomas welcomed her daughters' friends. "She was gracious to us, making us feel welcome." In her junior year, Sarah married, and once again their friendship was transformed. The adventurous, laughing companionship of Quaker Lake developed into a respectful and caring but more distant relationship.

On her first summer home from college, Margaret met a young man named Charles Lawrence. A student at Morehouse College in Atlanta, Charles was also nineteen. Hazel Harrison, a renowned concert pianist, had been scheduled to come to Vicksburg to give a concert that summer. When artists and entertainers came to perform in Vicksburg, it was customary for the local talent to give recitals during the intermission. Charles Lawrence, known for his fine trumpet playing, was asked to play during the intermission of Hazel Harrison's concert. He agreed but needed an accompanist. Having heard through the grapevine that Margaret Morgan was in town for the summer, and that she played the piano, he decided to call and ask her to play with him.

"Margaret Morgan being 'in town' was a big thing for the Negro community," says Margaret with no hint of immodesty. She is merely stating the fact of her visibility and reputation in this town. She had gone off and "made good" and now came home to share some of her accomplishments with the folks who had believed in her and helped raise her.

Margaret saw herself as "privileged" in Vicksburg. For me, over fifty years later, it is hard to understand her feelings of abundance and well-being in this segregated town in the Deep South. My own feelings are influenced by what she has told me: this is the town where, on a street corner nearby, just a few years before, Negroes were lynched on a tree by angry white mobs; where the white neighbor girl Elizabeth, whom she had played with in both their yards for years, told her all of a sudden that "my mother says I can't play with you 'cause you're a nigger"; where the boundaries between whites and coloreds were so deeply ingrained in the community psyche that they were rarely challenged as inappropriate. Despite all of these ugly realities—that seemed normal and ordinary, not particularly malignant—Margaret felt privileged. (She continues to use this word as a way of conveying her plentiful experience as a child and adolescent in Vicksburg.)

The sense of privilege came from her father's respectable position in the community; from her journeys to New York with her mother every other summer; from the large trunks they took with them on the train, filled with clothes tailored by their seamstress; from her reputation as a star student at Magnolia High. The privilege may have also been attached to her dream. To plan to be a doctor was, after all, a *privilege*. Such a plan, so consciously made and fiercely pursued, grew from the experience of a plentiful life, not from feelings of deprivation or longing. Margaret tries to explain this crucial distinction to her daughter, raised thirty years later in the Northeast. For her, feelings of privilege had flourished alongside the parallel reality of a castelike, oppressive, depriving society.

One of Margaret's worlds—the black community—felt abundant and rewarding. The other—the white world—was recognized as dehumanizing but experienced as largely irrelevant. The white world of Vicksburg was not one that Margaret would have chosen to enter. She did not feel the daily assaults of exclusion because she did not want to be part of it. Although momentarily stunned by the words of her redheaded friend next door, she did not feel particularly injured. She had known a day would arrive when the white picket fence would become a boundary, and she had long since protected herself from rejection by defining the friendship in superficial terms. "She was not my *real* friend . . . she couldn't really hurt me." Because of her sense of belonging to an admiring and supportive community, Margaret looked forward to coming home to Vicksburg each summer.

Charles's call, asking her if she would be willing to accompany him when he played during Miss Harrison's intermission, pleased Margaret but was not a total surprise. Although she acted as if he were a perfect stranger, she had heard of him, even admired him from a distance. A few weeks earlier, Margaret had been down at the YMCA visiting her mother's close friend Sadie Merrick. Mrs. Merrick was the wife of the director of the colored YMCA where Charles's father was the student coordinator. They were walking across the balcony above the gymnasium, when Margaret looked down and spotted a handsome young stranger with a tennis racket, practicing his serve against the wooden backboard. In the most casual tone, she asked Mrs. Merrick about him. "Oh, that's Charles Lawrence," said Mrs. Merrick, sensing Margaret's interest, ". . . and he has got a girlfriend . . . one of the Dillard girls." So Margaret knew who was calling and quickly accepted Charles's invitation to join him in the concert.

"I invited him to come up . . . and we practiced *a lot*," Margaret recalls with pleasure and excitement still flickering across her face. "*All* the time, we practiced and practiced. Afterwards we would sit and talk in the dining room, which was slightly off to one side of the house . . . we'd put the radio on as a kind of sound barrier." My mother gives a mischievous smile. "We practiced and practiced, then performed . . . then went right on practicing afterward. . . . Then we hit on the idea of giving another concert." Since the Hazel Harrison concert no longer provided the excuse for getting together, Margaret and Charles planned another. This time they would be the star performers, requiring even more practice, of course. The concert would help them raise money for their education. It was a perfect plan, upright and honorable from every perspective and designed to guarantee them a summer's worth of time together. The concert, scheduled for summer's end in Vicksburg, included Charles on the trumpet accompanied by Margaret on the piano; Margaret playing solo piano; and Margaret playing the violin with Mrs. Lucille Ewing, her old piano teacher, accompanying her.

Whether or not the concert was a great artistic success, it was not economically rewarding. But Charles and Margaret had loved the practice, the talk, the time together, so much that they decided to take the concert "on the road." Greenville, Mississippi, a couple of hundred miles from Vicksburg, was their next, and final, stop. They drove to Greenville with Charles and Margaret next to the driver in the front seat, and Mrs. Ewing and Mrs. Morgan in the back. The two ladies watched their every move. "If my head would fall over toward Charles, Mrs. Ewing would say from the backseat, 'Oooh!' "

When Margaret remembers the summer of 1933, she refers to it fondly as the "Summer of Discovering Charles Lawrence." Their long conversations on the porch swing in the damp evening air, or

Margaret wearing her Greek-Prize Medal from Wadleigh High School, New York, 1932

Margaret at her graduation from Wadleigh High School, New York, 1932

Margaret during her freshman year at Cornell, wearing the raccoon coat, 1933

Theater group at the colored YMCA, Vicksburg, Mississippi, 1934.
Led by Letitia (seated, middle, to the right of the woman in plaid dress) and Charles
Lawrence, Sr. (front row, left). Charles's sister Ann is third from the left in the back row
(in white blouse). His sister Lois is sixth from the left in the back row, above and to the
left of her mother, Letitia. Margaret is to the left of Lois.

Margaret in the anatomy laboratory, Columbia University School of Medicine, 1936

in the dining room, their voices masked by the parlor radio, fueled their growing relationship. As Margaret tells it, their conversations cast them into the roles in which they each felt most comfortable: Margaret as receptive listener and Charles as enthusiastic raconteur. But recognizing that her view of herself as quiet and Charles as talkative may not match Charles's memories of that summer of discovery, she says with a smile, "*From my angle* . . . you, of course, will have to ask Charles, who will certainly have a different perspective. . . . From my angle, I did a lot of listening. I've always known how to ask the right question to get people talking. . . . Charles enjoyed talking, and I enjoyed listening."

Margaret knows that Charles will tell a different story. She also knows that I will be suspicious of her version, because the characterization of Margaret as quiet has always been the source of family jokes and teasing. While the world sees Margaret as quiet, serene, thoroughly receptive, her family *knows* her as an energetic talker. She is not loud or garrulous, but at the family dinner table she clearly holds her own with lively and detailed stories. Her tales are long and skillfully dramatized, sometimes even accompanied by tears running slowly down her cheek. Only her family and her close friends are treated to these winding tales. She is rarely the storyteller in public. So the world gets a view that is at odds with our insiders' perspective.

The public image lives on, however, and is partly, perhaps mostly, true. I have many memories of Margaret at a large social gathering, attentively listening to someone's stories. I see her approach a small child, drop to her knees to be at eye level with him, and begin the conversation with an inquiry, ready to listen, however rambling or incoherent the reply, intent upon understanding. I especially remember walks with her—just the two of us—inspired by her concern for something happening in my life. "Sal, you want to take a walk around the circle?" Often we would stop along the way, on some big rocks on the side of the road, where she would sit and listen. And, of course, she makes her living listening, as a psychoanalyst. Although we laugh when she teasingly claims "I am the quiet one," we know that quiet is a very large part of her and that listening is her first way of engaging people.

Margaret's attraction to Charles was immediate, from the moment she looked down upon him from the YMCA balcony. "I thought he was unbelievably handsome. . . . I can see him leaving my house and walking along the fence . . . broad shoulders, very straight, a lot of energy. . . . I can see him in his maroon Morehouse sweater." It was his vitality that made him seem particularly appealing. When he came to visit he brought a lively and infectious energy. "I thought he was very happy, and very interested in many things." As Margaret listened, Charles ruminated about his emerging commitments to pacifism and socialism. As Margaret listened, Charles discussed Shakespeare and DuBois. She was intrigued by this worldliness, and by his determination to communicate to her what he was thinking about. "He had so much to talk about. . . . He knew so much more about what was going on in the world. . . . He was much more broadly educated."

Listening to this Morehouse man made Margaret aware of the stark differences between their college experiences. Here she was at a first-rate, large, cosmopolitan university, feeling shut off not only from the world of ideas and political ferment but also from the larger society and the special plight of American Negroes. And there he was, at a small Negro college in Atlanta, being introduced to new and bold ideas, being pushed to consider alternative perspectives, changing and growing. Here she was at Cornell feeling isolated and alone in the pursuit of her dream. There he was at Morehouse, surrounded by interested and supportive professors, embraced by the warmth and camaraderie of his peers, and rewarded with visibility and honor for his scholastic achievements. Margaret still marvels at the contrasts. "Charles met people at Morehouse . . . people who were *important*. . . . You would have thought that I would have been exposed to more at Cornell but at this small Negro college they were much more aware of what was going on in the world. I never met people at Cornell who were educated in the same sense Charles was."

Not only did Margaret recognize the contrasts in their college experiences, she also felt the great differences between Charles and other boyfriends she had had before. Since her graduation from high school, Margaret had had several suitors. Summers in Vicksburg were expected to be the time for blossoming romance among the college-age set, and Margaret had enjoyed these first experiences of male company. She had also met a couple of young Negro men at Cornell who had been smitten by her. But the pleasure of these romances was usually quickly eroded by the young man's wish to get serious too quickly. Too soon they would want to make the relationship permanent, and Margaret would feel a troubling claustrophobia. "It was scary to me that young men asked me to marry them . . . very often I found myself being apprehensive. The proposal always seemed to come too soon. . . . In those days, this was the way a man said 'I want a close relationship with you.' I would say, 'Really, I'm not interested in getting married,' and they would feel so *offended*." Margaret's apprehension was partly related to the young men's haste. They were so eager to lure her in and tie the knot that they seemed to forget about attending to the relationship. It all felt so rushed and premature when they would abruptly propose. But a deeper fear lay in Margaret's concern that these suitors would stand in the way of her dream. "I had been brought up not to trust them . . . I worried that they'd get in the way of my becoming a doctor . . . I was out to prove everyone wrong who said 'You're not going to become a doctor. You'll get married and have a hundred children.' "

But with Charles there was never this sense of distrust and panic. Never did she experience the claustrophobia, the worry that he would block her from what she wanted to do. The opposite happened, in fact. Their wonderful, intense conversations gently convinced her of his support. Their commitment to one another seemed to emerge without being forced; the bonds developed quickly. "Very soon I loved him and wanted to be related forever after." The connections between them were fueled by talking, listening, and a deep respect for each other's dreams. Margaret loved Charles's sense of purpose and vision, but she also loved the way he admired and seriously attended to hers. Instead of fearing that he would block her path, she saw him there beside her offering his witness and support. I ask, "How did Dad feel about your dream to pursue medicine?" Margaret replies, without hesitation, "He immediately *joined* it."

By the end of the summer Charles and Margaret were "talking about marriage." The marriage plans were almost immediately linked to work pursuits. Together they dreamed of a project that would combine their respective professional roles, a clinic and community center in Vicksburg. Margaret, as a doctor, would provide health services to the Negro community; and Charles, as a sociologist, would combine social inquiry and social action. As Margaret describes their young vision, the excitement of it is still written on her face. "By the time we were talking about marriage, we were creating a plan for the community center.... It was going to be located down at the old Vicksburg Industrial School ... we could see it in our minds!" The plan appealed not only to their sense of a common adventure but also to deeper commitments.

Margaret had been away from Mississippi since she was fourteen. She felt the pull from her parents, and she felt the need to give something back to the community that had nurtured her. "I had been away a long time ... perhaps I should be coming back to Mississippi ... and coming back with my husband.... This was the chance for the reincarnation of Candy Man ... at least from my parents' point of view." Margaret was still haunted by the old fantasy that might be realized if she practiced medicine in Vicksburg. "I continued to believe, at some level, if I had been a physician there I might have saved Candy Man's life and made my mother happy forever.... Here was my chance."

For Charles, the vision was shaped by different forces but also related to family commitments. His work at the planned community center would continue a Lawrence family tradition of social service and social action. His parents, both teachers, had moved from Boston to Utica, Mississippi, a few months after Charles's birth to be part of the brave efforts of social reform in the rural South. By now this background in social service, valued deeply by his parents, had been enriched and elaborated on by his experience at Morehouse College. The plan he had made with Margaret combined the enduring family values and the newly emerging ideological and intellectual justifications learned at college.

As she describes their vision and their motivations, Margaret contrasts the Lawrences and the Morgans. "Charles's parents, particularly his mother, Letitia, were more socially minded than my parents. My parents were involved in the concrete life of the community ... my father with the church and the school, my mother with her teaching. . . . For my mother, her teaching was a great caring kind of thing. She *had* to teach those children; they *had* to learn. Each child was of great concern. . . . Letitia, on the other hand, was out there doing social work sorts of things. As an educational supervisor, she traveled around and spoke a lot. . . . She was "Mrs. Lawrence" *out there*."

The contrast between Mary, concrete, caring, and very private, and Letitia, extroverted, assertive, and socially active, reminds Margaret of the ways in which she resembles her mother. This comes, perhaps, as a surprise. She usually feels identified with her father, but here she sees Mary's imprint on her way of being in the world. "I was like my mother . . . I still am to a certain extent. I've always been thoroughly involved in my work and the relationships involved there. I am not really an administrative type, out there representing an institution. I am concrete, active . . . I most enjoy teaching by working, and I've not wanted to be far from that . . . maybe I have been a little frightened of not *doing*."

As she speaks about the concrete, caring nature of her work, the wish to engage people directly, Margaret's hands make the motions of a gardener. I see her there planting her violet and gold pansies in the dark soil, enjoying the cool earth, the hard work, and the promise of growth and flowering. I also see her kneading whole wheat dough for "Maggie bread," enjoying pounding and turning, these age-old motions of nurturance. These same hands enjoy making a sloppy, runny finger painting with one of her young patients. She is showing him—"Go ahead, you can make a mess!"—and making big, sweeping motions that let the paint dribble down her arms and down onto the floor. "I teach by working," she says so emphatically that I know she wants me to see it as one of the qualities that defines her. "I haven't wanted to be far from that."

These qualities are also among the ways that she is so different from my father, a difference that at first caused her some pain when she judged "his way" to be better. Gradually she came to value her own way and feel at home with her natural inclinations. She is like her mother in her direct, quiet caring, and Charles is like his mother in his outspoken, analytic, aggressive pursuit of the world. He is "out there."

As their long conversations continued, and in retrospect, Margaret could also sense differences in the way they spoke. She used images and metaphors to capture the experience and the feeling that went with it. Charles's language was exacting and economical, almost as if he was reading a text. For him, words had a set, clean-cut meaning; for her, many refracted images and associations were conveyed. In the early days of their relationship, Margaret regarded Charles's language and style with awe and some envy, wishing she could be so certain, so outgoing. Now she has made peace with the contrasts and also learned along the way some of Charles's skills that might be helpful to her. "I had to learn, as time went on, how to be onstage, outgoing . . . this did not come naturally."

Compared to the house Margaret grew up in, Charles's home reverberated with noise and laughter. Both decibel level and emotions ran high. The Lawrences' relationships seemed charged with love and humor and an intensity that could exclude non–family members. Sitting in their living room during family exchanges, Margaret would feel invisible. "They were very involved with one another . . . you could visit them and no one would know you were there. . . ." Margaret had never experienced such high family energy, nor been surrounded by so many people. The Morgans were much more circumspect and restrained. They would smile at pleasant conversation, but Margaret had never heard the raucous laughter, the teasing, and the intense discussions that she found at the Lawrences'. They were a bigger family—with four children—but their bigness seemed to be exaggerated by the quality of their relationships, robust and full. When Margaret visited, which happened only rarely ("It was not expected of a girl in Vicksburg to spend a lot of time with her boyfriend's family"), she would feel the reticence and awkwardness of one who is entering slightly foreign territory. She searched for cues on how to behave, how to participate, and what to say; but she mostly remained safely silent, enjoying the family drama.

The Lawrences, however, immediately admired Margaret's quiet and discrete presence. They were drawn to her nature, which seemed to allow her to sit on the family's periphery and still be felt at the center. Mother Letitia (whom Margaret later called "Mama Lettie"), an outspoken and judgmental woman, saw the young woman's dignity and decorum and thought her own daughters, Lois and Ann, should be exposed to these fine qualities. The first summer of Margaret and Charles's romance, Letitia figured out a way to introduce her daughters to the good influence of Margaret. She asked Margaret if she would be willing to give them piano lessons, and made it clear that musical training was less important than the chance for the girls to be around a young woman of such high caliber. "They were in high school and I was a college girl at Cornell ... Mama Lettie was interested in their getting to know me and being identified with me." Margaret does not remember any great success in the musical training during those few months; neither did she notice the identification and patterning that Mrs. Lawrence had hoped for. She does remember, however, feeling pleased at being held up as a standard for young womanly conduct. She knew that was a sign that Mrs. Lawrence thought she was worthy of her son's attentions.

Both mothers gave readings at community events, and their contrasting style embodied the differences between the two families. Margaret can reenact these readings. She makes the theatrical gestures that accompanied her mother's dramatic readings. Her voice rises from a soft, mysterious whisper to a crescendo and then onto another emotional extreme; and the memories of Mary—shy and often withdrawn—throwing her full energy into this melodrama bring smiles and tears to Margaret's face. "Mother's dramatic readings were *very* emotional. She used to recite with music ... 'The Lost Chord' ... I can see her now: 'Seated one day at the organ' ... [Margaret swoons in exaggerated imitation] ... the music rolling, her chest heaving ... I can still see the cover of the tan and maroon sheet music she used. ... Another one she loved to do was 'My little blue-eyed Luisa, I love her so well.' " Mrs. Morgan was known in Vicksburg for these "readings," which she offered at church gatherings or at functions held at the YMCA.

Letitia also did readings, but they were very different from Mary's and likely to be performed in other settings. She would visit prisons or hospitals or speak at political meetings and recite stirring poetry in order to illuminate her messages about equality and social justice. Letitia joined art and social commentary. There was no swoon in her voice, no crescendos, no music. Her manner was strong, straight-forward, and determined. "Letitia was apt to do Paul Laurence Dunbar, a Negro poet. . . . Her material had racial themes. . . ."

While Margaret was vividly aware of these family contrasts, and found them both appealing and a little frightening, she also soon recognized that she and Charles held similar places in their families. Charles, as oldest child, and Margaret, as only child, had each been given an unusual amount of autonomy and responsibility. In many ways, they were both treated as adults. "Charles was the oldest, very bright, and he was highly respected by his parents. They were devoted to him. . . . He was almost a *third* parent. . . . He was extremely close to his mother, and she would often confide in him. . . . Charles began driving at the age of eight . . . and the summer after his thirteenth birthday, he drove his mother and siblings from Mississippi to Boston. . . . You have expectations of children, and they live up to them. . . . *Charles was the outstanding person in the family*." Charles's special place of prominence and power was not unlike Margaret's experience in her own family, and she believes this was one source of their deep understanding of one another. Each could perceive and respect the other's power because they were each embued with it themselves. "Both of us were autonomous people. Our parents stood back from us and said, 'Oh, that is what you're going to do' . . . we were each expected to be responsible for ourselves."

Besides the laughter and intense relationships that drew Margaret to the Lawrences, she was also attracted by their physical beauty. They were a handsome family. Margaret's memory of them comes around—as it so often does—to their color. Skin color, such a pow-erful piece of the black community experience, had exaggerated meaning in Margaret's family, where her mother "looked like white" and her father, with whom she was so deeply identified, was dark-brown-skinned. Margaret, medium-brown-skinned, was seen by many folks in Vicksburg as "light-skinned," a perception that reflected their mixed response to her "good hair," high intelligence, attractive ap-pearance, and fine family. But with a mother who "looked like white" and a dead brother whose "fair skin and golden curls" were tearfully remembered as Christlike qualities, Margaret never saw herself as "light-skinned." She could never match the beauty of Candy Man, whose baby picture looked down on her every day from its prominent place above the living-room couch. She, with brown skin, was inextricably identified with her father in a way that kept her wondering about her mother's love. So skin color meant a lot to Margaret, maybe more than to other Negroes in Vicksburg to whom it meant a great deal.

When I ask her what else stands out about the Lawrences in her memories, Margaret pauses, then says in a measured, careful way, "I think it was important to me that this was a predominantly fair-skinned family. . . . I was very sensitive to this issue because of my grandmother's relationship to my father . . . she didn't want any of her daughters to marry black men. She'd say, 'Don't marry a black man. That is *bad*.' . . . and they *all* did. My grandmother would make fun of my father . . . and that caused me such pain."

While it was significant to Margaret that the Lawrences were fair-skinned, it was important that Charles was not the fairest of them all. "I guess Charles was the darkest. . . . Charles was who he was in the family, but he had the 'worst hair' . . . Lois was relatively fair and had 'good hair' . . . Geoff *definitely* had 'good hair' . . . there were jokes about hair in the family, but it was a serious issue." There was some relief in Charles's brownness. Although lighter than hers, his color was browner than that of the others in his family, which somehow allowed them to be closer. But even now, after almost fifty years of marriage, Margaret raises a poignant question never asked. "I often wonder how it felt for Charles to choose a girl darker than his family. . . . These things meant a great deal . . . I know *I* had some feeling that I had done well to marry lighter."

I listen to all this talk about color and try to connect to the feelings behind it, try to understand how it could be that such a question was not asked in a relationship where intimate talk and honest exchange were the rule. I have the sensation of hearing the words and connecting to them cerebrally but not feeling them in my gut. I have been raised in a family that has tried not to pass on the deep emotions and divisiveness attached to skin color, and I have incorporated only the most superficial understanding of what my mother is really talking about. In my mind's eye, I can see the subtle color wheel of "like white," fair, light-skinned, light-browned-skinned, and so on, and can begin to understand the ways the skin color changes depending upon the context. My feelings about these distinctions are nowhere near as charged as my mother's. I find myself wondering whether she feels more strongly about this than others do (colored folks from the Deep South growing up about the same time as she did), or whether she is simply more in touch with how she feels. I strongly suspect that it is the latter—that the subject of skin color and hair texture, so central to black folks' valuing of one another and the subject of jokes that mask deep pain, is something Margaret is relatively undefensive and open about. Not only can she recall her late adolescent views of how skin color affected the people in her life, she can also recall the feelings attached to those perceptions—feelings that most other people would probably not admit out loud. "When I was an adolescent, I thought that it was my father's *fault* that I was darker."

The Boston Man from Utica, Mississippi

*I*N Margaret's first memories of Charles, he is playing the trumpet. She can see him in his Morehouse sweater, tall, broad-shouldered, his muscled forearms making soft ripples in the wool. His large powerful hands almost make the trumpet look small. The left hand holds the horn, while the right fingers seem to dance over the keys. They practice for hours, Margaret at the piano and Charles standing beside her, their eyes often meeting.

Charles had learned to play the horn from his father, Charles Sr., a handsome, light-skinned man who was a "great trumpeter." The first time his mother, Letitia Harris, noticed Charles Lawrence, Sr., he was at a school party, playing the trumpet. Letitia had traveled down to Alabama from Boston to teach at Snow Hill Normal and Industrial Institute, a struggling rural school for the "colored" children in the region. She was twenty-one, a lovely, vibrant young woman. When she arrived at Snow Hill, the staff gave her a welcoming party and Charles Sr. brought along his trumpet. After dinner, Charles, who was the school's bandmaster, entertained everyone with a wonderful assortment of show tunes, Negro spirituals, and jazz and classical selections. This restrained and dignified young man came alive in his music. He could make the horn do anything, from smooth syrupy blues to baroque intricacy. The guests were appreciative—especially the woman from Boston who had come south to teach English and "domestic sciences" to the country children. Charles, who had been at Snow Hill for only a year, teaching music (he also played the violin) and tailoring and coaching athletics, noticed the attractive northern teacher and they soon began a proper courtship. By the end of the school term, Charles and Letitia were married. A couple of months later they left the South and traveled back to Boston to find work and start a family. For Charles, Boston was a strange and forbidding place; for Letitia, it was home.

Since she was two and a half, when her mother had died in childbirth, Letitia and her older sister, Julia, had lived with their Aunt Kate and Uncle Bob on Western Avenue in Cambridge, Massachusetts. They had been "virtually adopted" by Kate and Bob Brown, a childless couple who raised the girls as their own. The Browns lived a disciplined and active life in Boston, enjoying the status and comforts available to the "old Boston colored society." For fifty years, Uncle Bob, a proud dark-skinned man, and a witty story-teller, worked as a Pullman porter on the Boston-Maine Railroad. He was a member of the Twelfth Baptist Church on Shawmut Avenue, where for many years he was deacon, trustee, and treasurer. Aunt Kate, a fair-skinned woman, was much more restrained than her fun-loving husband. Although she had no formal vocation, she was a committed community person, volunteering in hospitals and old folks' homes, raising money for the church, and enjoying the sisterhood of the Eastern Stars, a colored sorority. "Who constitutes the black bourgeoisie depends upon the historical period you are referring to," says my father, the sociologist, "for that time, the Browns were part of it. . . . Uncle Bob owned his own home, owned his own car, and summered on the Cape."

Letitia, a child of this "colored society," stood tall, walked with dignity, dressed carefully, and let her tongue linger over the long Boston vowels. She never lost her Boston accent; it became a symbolic part of her identity, following her to the Deep South, where she lived most of her life. Letitia's mother had had three children: a boy, also named Charles, who was twelve or thirteen years older, and Julia, who was just a few years older than Letitia. When their mother died, Charles, by then a late adolescent, struck off on his own to New York City, where he led an independent and industrious life, married well and raised a family, worked for the post office, and became a proficient student of French literature. Letitia, a strong-willed and indomitable girl, lived in the shadow of her sister's beauty. It was decided very early that Julia was "the pretty one," and she cherished the role with a kind of arrogance that only beautiful people can get away with. Letitia used to tell a story about Julia as a young adolescent. She and Julia were out together and met an old family friend. "Julia, you get prettier and prettier all the time," the woman beamed, and then she turned to Letitia and said, "You're not half as ugly as you used to be." My father used to tell us this story as a lesson on "how not to treat siblings." "There was nothing to validate that [the friend's observation of Letitia] in terms of my mother's appearance. . . . She was a very attractive woman . . . she was vivacious, intelligent . . . and carried herself with great dignity." Then, as if this has the most meaning to her son, he says, "She was always friendly with all sorts and conditions of people." Julia may have been prettier in the way that colored society cared about, but Letitia's beauty went deeper.

When the Browns headed to Cape Cod for the summer, Letitia and Julia would travel to Charles City County, Virginia, where their father and grandfather still lived, and where their family had deep roots. These roots, although securely planted in Virginia for several generations, had been replanted in turn from Boston, where the family legend begins prior to the American Revolution. As Charles tells it, his mother's family was first represented in the United States by a couple of men who were called "Brown" probably because of their color. They were blacksmiths and they lived in Boston. The Brown brothers married two Scotch-Irish women ("The fact that their ancestry was identifiable suggests that they were fairly recent immigrants") and moved to Virginia, where they settled in a coastal region called Charles City County. The small, close-knit community became a haven for "free people of color," former slaves, and American Indians who had settled in the region. "They had a limited number of people with whom they could marry. . . . They intermarried a good deal . . . cousins married cousins." Tom Cotman, Letitia's maternal grandfather and Aunt Kate's father, is the oldest relative whom Charles can remember. He was shown "the pass" that legitimized his great-grandfather's free status, which he had to carry on his person to prove he had "the right to be walking around."

Tom Cotman, called "Pappy Tom," was a man of diverse talents.

By trade he was a farmer who had been a landholder in Charles City County long before the Civil War. By ambition, he was a politician, an active Republican who held county patronage offices. But perhaps the skill for which Pappy Tom was the best known was his finesse as the local dentist. "He was the county tooth puller. . . . If somebody came with an infected tooth, well, he'd pull his tractor over to the side and take his pliers out of his toolbox and pull their teeth." Charles II enjoys this "living legend" and grins. "Of course, there was no great reputation for the infection that followed that procedure."

When Letitia and Julia returned to Charles City County each summer, they would stay with their grandfather, Pappy Tom, and be drawn back into the southern, rural culture. At the center of the Charles City community stood Elam Baptist Church. Since everyone in Charles City was "related," the family and congregation were the same. Everyone gathered there for all kinds of family and community functions. The babies were baptized at Elam; the young people were married there; and the old people were buried there. When the Brown men had first migrated south around the time of the American Revolution, they had joined the Old Guilfield Baptist Church in Richmond, but soon after established a mission in their own Charles City County. It was a struggling mission with a handful of parishioners, but it belonged to the community ("all the land about the church was owned by the Brown family . . . and they deeded part of the land over to the church") and it became their spiritual focus. As the community grew, with mixtures of Indians and "Coloreds," the church grew and flourished. "In those days, because of the Black codes, the slave codes, when colored people met or worshiped they had to have a white person present . . . a white pastor. . . . Even though they had their own leadership, they had to have a white pastor present . . . they used to pay him a dollar a day . . . a lot of money in those days." After the Civil War, a white presence was no longer required and Samuel Brown became the "first regularly elected, ordained colored pastor of Elam." As Charles II recounts the history of the Elam Baptist Church, he stresses that the church was more than a religious center. It symbolized the strength, pride, and dignity of this extended family. It represented the interlocking of political activity and spiritual commitment. The simple white-wooden frame structure, lovingly built and carefully tended, expressed the solid, unpretentious quality of these hardworking rural folk.

Charles Sr. also had deep roots in the church. The Reverend Job Lawrence, Charles's father, was a well-educated, ambitious Presbyterian minister who had graduated from Maryville College in Tennessee and gone to divinity school at Howard University in Washington, D.C. In those days Maryville College practiced "coeducation. . . . That is, blacks and whites together. The coeds were the coloreds." Job Lawrence had been born into slavery, to a slave mother and her master in eastern Tennessee, near Knoxville. The legend on this side of the family is shorter, less detailed, gathered from various sources. Charles II is careful to point out the missing links and the discrepancies. I ask my father, who relishes history and is a famous tracer of roots, why the story is not more complete. (My friends who have met him often tell me that my dad's intense curiosity and generous questions have encouraged them to tell their whole story. In no time, they are telling him about their parents, their grandparents, who they were, where they lived, how they lived, and Dad is the appreciative listener, asking *and* remembering.) "Why don't you have your dad's version?" I ask incredulously. There is a long silence, then a shadow of sadness that lingers on his face. "I guess I never got him to tell me." His resigned words seem to speak of the respectful distance, the silence between them—the shyness of both men that never permitted the son to ask the probing questions that come naturally to him.

But even the fragments are intriguing. "Apparently it was common knowledge that Job was the son of a master named Wallace. . . . When Wallace, my great-grandfather, lost everything he had in gambling, he sold my grandfather Job and his mother to his brother. He gave Job a silver dollar, and earned his undying enmity." The jaw of Charles II tightens as he speaks these bitter words. After the Civil War, Job found a job working as a houseboy for a man named Lawrence who was a paint entrepreneur. The Lawrence family "was very good to him," and he decided to take their name as his own.

Missouri Ann, a pretty white woman, became Job's wife after he became a "free man." The couple met when Job was enrolled as a student at Maryville College. "Missouri Ann was apparently the illegitimate granddaughter of the president of Maryville." Charles II tells this tale cautiously, knowing that it has probably been embellished and dramatized as it has been passed across the generations. He uses words like "apparently" or "it is said that" to warn me not to fasten on this legend as literal truth. "The legend is that there were two brothers who were leading politicians in Tennessee; one of them was Missouri Ann's father.... The president of Maryville had a daughter, and she had an illegitimate child out of an affair with the promising young politician. The child was Missouri Ann." The president's family was deeply embarrassed by their daughter's promiscuous behavior and the child it produced, and the politician worried that the public humiliation might compromise his career. The baby was secretly given away to Grandmother Wallace [no relation to Job's father and master], a kindly old slave lady who raised Missouri Ann as her own.

From birth, this white girl was raised "colored" and was therefore honored and pleased to marry Job, the handsome, industrious "coed" who proposed to her. Many years later, when Job and Missouri Ann already had several children, a fancy horse-drawn carriage drew up to their front door. "The carriage belonged to the governor, who wanted his daughter, Missouri Ann, to come and live with him." The young politician, who had fathered the illegitimate child, had realized his ambition to become governor of Tennessee. When he descended the steps of the gilded carriage and offered his daughter the chance to "come home," Missouri Ann looked at him in horror and her children grew quiet and still as stones. She hid her bitterness behind a simple response. She *was* home. She knew of no other home. These people were her family. "She said she was happily married and she would not go." Missouri Ann walked into her house with her back to the governor's carriage as it drove away.

Job and Missouri Ann had nine children, and Charles Sr. was the third youngest. The parents cared deeply about education and spent all of Job's meager minister's salary on their children's schooling. "All of the children had some taste of boarding school; several of them finished high school, which was more than high school in today's terms. They also finished with some sort of trade." When Charles was fifteen, Missouri Ann died and Job decided to send his son to Tuskegee Institute in Alabama, a military school that would provide discipline and structure for the young adolescent. "My father was said to be a man of not always governable temper," says Charles II with a broad smile. At Tuskegee he showed "great talent in playing the cornet" in the concert band. One day, when he didn't respond immediately to a directive, the concertmaster threw the baton at Charles. With his quick reflexes, Charles managed to catch the baton and hurl it back at the concertmaster. Students had been expelled from Tuskegee for lesser offenses, but Charles "apparently got away with it."

Soon after arriving at Tuskegee, Charles became the office boy of Booker T. Washington, the Institute's Principal and founder. Washington noticed the boy's diligence and talent and may have even been attracted by his willfulness. If his explosive energy could be channeled in productive directions, the young man had a promising future ahead of him. Perhaps the man and boy were drawn to one another by their physical likeness. "Both of them were half-white." Whatever the reasons for their mutual admiration, Washington had a strong influence on his young charge, "both personally and ideologically." Charles watched closely as Booker T. Washington negotiated deals, pursued money sources, made political pronouncements, and secured his place as the most influential Negro of the period. "By the time my father finished Tuskegee in 1911, Booker T. Washington was at the height of his political power. . . . He never held any office, but he was a trusted adviser to Teddy Roosevelt and President Taft. It was said that if there were political plums to be given out to the Negro community, they were always checked first with Booker T. Washington. Because of his power, the ideal of an industrial education—Washington's goal for Negroes—had to be espoused even by liberal arts colleges." Charles watched Washington closely and admired his style and philosophy. As his office boy, he learned the skills of quiet observation and restrained discretion; he even managed to govern his temper. Theirs was a relationship of admiration but not intimacy. "Washington didn't think of my father as a son," but he did care about the young man's future. When Charles graduated from Tuskegee at the age of nineteen, Washington made the appropriate contacts. It was Booker T. Washington who recommended him to Mr. Edwards, the principal of Snow Hill Normal and Industrial Institute, the place where Charles and Letitia met.

The young couple stayed at Snow Hill Normal for only a year after Letitia's arrival. The young woman from Boston had gone to Alabama with the best intentions; she wanted to bring light and culture to the rural "colored folk" of the region. But even with all her energy and goodwill, she quickly grew weary of the harsh conditions, the meager resources, the struggles of teaching overworked farm children. She missed her friends and family in Boston. Letitia pleaded with her new husband to return to Boston, and he agreed to try living in her city. The couple found a small apartment in Cambridge, and Uncle Bob found Charles a job working as a Pullman porter on the Boston-Maine line. For Uncle Bob, the Pullman porter job came naturally. He could quietly tolerate the white folks' commands and abuse. He counted on his humor to win them over and keep him going. Uncle Bob could even manage to find dignity in his work. But Charles found the obsequiousness necessary for the job intolerable. He simply couldn't play the part, and "he didn't look the part. . . . People weren't used to having white Pullman porters . . . and most people thought he was white."

By the time their first child, Charles II, was born—on May 2, 1915, two years, to the day, after their marriage—Charles Sr. "had determined that being a Pullman porter was not for him." With a wife and new baby, he needed work and welcomed the visit of Mr. Henry William Holtzclaw, the principal of Utica Normal and Industrial Institute in Mississippi, who had come north on a recruiting trip. He had obtained Charles Lawrence's name from Booker T. Washington. Holtzclaw, whose school was largely financed by northern philanthropy, had come to Boston to woo potential donors and to recruit young teachers. The principal had a vitality and commitment that appealed to Charles and Letitia, and they were drawn by his zealous message—the chance to participate in building an educated Negro community in the Deep South. "In returning south, I think they had a good bit of the service motive . . . a kind of missionary zeal. . . . They were young and wanted to do important work, social action, community building." Letitia bid farewell to Boston reluctantly and promised herself that she would always keep her Boston identity and connection. She would go to the South, give to the South, but never become truly southern.

When the Lawrences moved to Utica Institute, Charles was six months old. Three other children followed: Geoffrey eighteen months later, and Lois and Ann, who were five and seven years younger than Charles. Even though the children's ages were fairly evenly distributed, Charles always stood out as much older than his siblings. There was Charles and there were "the children." Charles's precocity was legendary in Utica. Very soon his parents treated him like an adult, with all the respect and responsibility that are implied by adult status. And very soon he wore the adult mantle with pride and seriousness. As a young adult, Charles reminisced about the special place he was given in his family, a place he seemed to incorporate, even relish.

"My parents and I were very good friends, from my earliest recollections. Although I would never have taken the liberty to 'get fresh' with either of them, I was always treated by them as a contemporary. For this reason, I firmly believe that I felt no sense of deprivation at the arrival of my siblings. . . . My relationship to them was that of an ancient brother. (As I look back on it, I must have been a terrible pill for them!) My only entry into their play was usually as a peacemaker in a fight. (I usually was successful in bringing them to friendly enough terms to 'gang up' on me for interfering.)"

Charles Sr. had gone to Utica to teach music and tailoring. He had learned the latter trade while a student at Tuskegee. During his fifteen years on the staff of Utica Institute, he became dean of boys, bookkeeper, and treasurer; none of these jobs involved giving up an old one. He was an industrious and multitalented man, whose endowments and skills evoked admiration and awe in his son. To the small boy, it almost seemed as if there were nothing his father couldn't do if he put his mind to it. "In those days Pop was a good singer and an excellent trumpet player. He was easily the best-dressed man in our rural community, and next to the school principal was the most widely traveled. In my extreme youth, I practically worshiped him as a demigod, trying desperately to emulate him. I therefore learned to play the trumpet at eight and learned to keep books. Out of loyalty I tried to learn tailoring; with the needle I was inept. . . . I identified with my father, but never thought I could reach him. . . . He was a paragon." Charles II pauses as he searches for the "ancient feelings" he had toward his father, and then says softly—as if he fears he will sound disloyal—"I think he was my favorite parent."

If Charles's father was unreachable, his mother was close and omnipresent. Letitia made her large presence felt. She had increased in size with the pregnancy of each child and had become impressively plump. "She was a big woman, literally and figuratively, weighing well over two hundred and fifty pounds." Letitia presided in the middle of the family, issuing commands, making pronouncements, telling jokes, and laughing heartily. As she sat there, people came to her, seeking counsel or solace, asking forgiveness, and wanting to learn. Letitia had the power to make people feel big and confident or little and insecure. "My mother tended to dominate any situation in which she found herself—and to do so without apparent effort. . . . She had the ability to make people who served her in whatever capacity feel that she was doing them a favor."

Although Charles had great admiration for his father and wanted to follow in his footsteps, he was drawn into his mother's fierce orbit, probably more closely than any of his siblings. As he reached for his father, he was absorbed by his mother. As he yearned to be like "Pop," people immediately identified him as "the spit and image" of his mother. In Charles, even as a young boy, people saw Letitia's vitality and power. In Charles, they saw his mother's keen intelligence, her love for ideas, her passion for words and books. In Charles, they saw Letitia's ability to influence, to orchestrate, to energize groups of people. Charles also had Letitia's features. "I looked more like my mother, and I think many people thought my intellectual bent was more from my mother's side than my father's. My father was a very practical man, so he didn't spend a lot of time studying; my mother read a great deal."

Letitia filled their house with books, which Charles in turn consumed with enthusiasm and interest. Reading was his greatest pleasure. He could open the pages of a book and find his way out of the deadening parochialisms of Utica. Their home library had over five hundred volumes ("an impressive collection for a family of our status"), and Letitia was a member of the Book-of-the-Month Club ("or its equivalent of the day"). Charles would wait anxiously for the new books to arrive and then devour them in a marathon sitting. Their shelves were also filled with encyclopedias, a set of Shakespeare, and periodicals to which his mother subscribed: *The Ladies' Home Journal*, *Cosmopolitan*, *The Forum*, *Crisis*, and *The Chicago Defender*—a collection of readings that included light, popular fare, political analysis, black cultural and social news, and reports of daily events by a large city paper. After Charles had read everything he could lay his hands on at home, he would go over to the Utica Institute Library and poke through the shelves until he found a book he had not yet read. By thirteen, he was reading the library's copies of *The Nation* and *The New Republic*, and was engaged by the political discourse he found there.

Charles remembers the miraculous moment of learning how to read. He was about to leave the first grade, just before being "double promoted" to the third grade along with Narcelle Stamps and Helen Walker. "Up until that time I read from memory, having had passages read to me." One evening as he lay on his bed, gazing at a book before falling off to sleep, quite suddenly Charles discovered he could unlock the secret code and read for himself. Charles's face brightens as he relives the powerful moment. "It was like magic to me! I hadn't known how to read and suddenly I did . . . I had leapt across a great chasm." Once this door had been unlocked, Charles read voraciously. At night his parents had to make him close the book "he had his head in" and turn off the lights. During the day, he had to be prodded to put down his book and do his chores. His reading led to wonderful reveries. "If I had the option to read and daydream, or else do my chores, I was likely to be doing the former until I discovered that I had no choice but to do the latter."

Charles was also precocious in his choices of what to read. By age ten, he was wading through the plays of Shakespeare with the support and guidance of Miss Luddington, a retired schoolmarm from Wisconsin who had come to Utica to teach in her old age. She developed a great fondness for Charles, who responded enthusiastically to intellectual challenge. They would sit for hours discussing drama and poetry, she always pushing him to seek new interpretations. Their mutual attraction also had a moralistic and temperamental basis. "Miss Luddington was a midwestern antitobacconist, prohibitionist, and prude; but so was I at the time."

When he mentions his relationship to Miss Luddington, Charles is reminded of how, during childhood, reading became his vehicle for stature and prominence in the Utica community. One Sunday evening at the chapel service, Mr. Holtzclaw, the principal, issued a challenge to all the students. With great fanfare he announced that he would give a five-dollar prize to the first student who came forward to give a report on a book that at the time of the announcement he or she had not already read. Most of the youngsters did not even listen to the announcement; they knew they had no chance of winning the money. A few others attended to Mr. Holtzclaw's challenge and tried to think of a short, easy book that might be quickly scanned. But everyone knew that Charles, Utica's star student, would take the offer seriously and have the best chance of claiming the prize.

On the following Sunday, in chapel, eight-year-old Charles stood in front of his peers and teachers and offered a comprehensive report on Booker T. Washington's *Up from Slavery*. He told the assembled group "much more than they wanted to know." The audience listened dutifully to young Charles with a combination of admiration and keen annoyance. At seventy, Charles reflects on his motives, first sadly then humorously. "I was a very conforming child, very anxious to please my parents . . . highly moralistic, and I mean that in a slightly pejorative sense." Reading, digesting, and reporting on this "grown-up" book was an enormous task for a third grader. "This did nothing to undermine my reputation as an intellectual and a prude, both of which I was."

Charles's chapel presentation of Washington's book marked the beginning of a distinguished oratorical career. Not only did Charles love reading, he also enjoyed the theater of words spoken out loud. Oratory was a fine southern tradition; Letitia was known for her masterful and strong speeches, and Charles naturally followed in these cultural and familial footsteps. In Utica, there were two major oratorical contests, and Charles began competing in them as a young adolescent. After hours of rumination, he would choose a topic with dramatic and ideological potential—one that could be persuasively "argued," not merely presented—and then spend days in the library devouring books on the topic and outlining the central themes. Facts would be translated into drama and practiced over and over, to the mirror, to the cotton fields, to blank walls . . . and finally to his parents, who listened with critical and discerning ears. "Both of my parents would coach me, giving me suggestions and criticisms." Finally, the day of the contest would arrive, the speech smooth and memorized, the young man carefully suited up. By the time Charles delivered his oration, the anxiety had eased into a strong self-confidence. "I was the local orator," he says simply. "In the course of time I won all the prizes."

At its height, Utica Normal and Industrial Institute had about five hundred students, ranging in age from five to fifty years, and thirty-five or forty teachers. Utica had a day school and a night school. The great majority of students were boarders who lived in dormitories that grew shabby from inattention and lack of resources. Most of the students came from poor and working-class families in the surrounding countryside, and they would first enroll in the night school in order to continue their labors in the fields. By evening they would arrive at class bone weary and try desperately to keep their eyes open. Most of the teachers at Utica were recent graduates of Tuskegee Institute, Talladega College, or Alcorn College; they taught both an academic subject and a trade. Even as a little boy, Charles never thought of the Utica campus as large. It was a comfortable place for children to roam, small in scale and unpretentious. Ginn Hall was a large brick building with administrative offices on the first floor, classrooms and the auditorium (called "the chapel") on the second floor, and boys' dormitory rooms on the third. Washington Hall was a four-story frame building that served as the girls' dormitory. An assortment of smaller buildings housed the trade shops, including the printing office and the tailor shop that Charles's father managed.

While the buildings felt ordinary to the young boy, the surrounding countryside seemed grand in the way it stretched for miles beyond the campus. It is this land that Charles still speaks of with awe and affection. The studious boy, who seemed always to have his head in a book, did notice the rural Mississippi terrain and grew to love it.

His large hands make arcs in the air as he describes the contours of Utica's land. "Utica Institute was located in both Hines and Copiah counties. Copiah County was to the south of Hines County. Hines County was by and large verdant. It had rich soil, a lot of bottom soil. Copiah County was largely hills and in general was a poorer county economically. At one point Utica owned eighteen hundred acres of land, much of it in Hines County, and it began at White Oak Creek (a little creek about a mile from the campus). The creek was a great source of gravel. The land which represented the northern boundary of Utica's land went all the way back up to the county line, approximately a mile north of White Oak Creek."

When he pictures the landscape, Charles sees the strong and proud image of Mr. McAdney. "Running north from the creek a mile or so was Mr. Pleasant McAdney's plantation." For a "colored" man, Mr. McAdney had a lot of status in Utica. He was admired for his large parcel of land that he farmed with great efficiency and care, for the fair way he treated the sharecroppers who chopped his cotton, and for his ability to make white folks "show him respect." Charles remembers the way Mr. McAdney would dress when he went to town to do business: clean neatly pressed overalls, a jacket, and a collar and tie. And he recalls the way he moved about in town: with a firm stride, and eyes that took in everything but rarely gave away what he was thinking or feeling. For young Charles, Mr. McAdney stood as a symbol of survival in the rural South. Watching him was a lesson in maintaining nobility and self-respect against entrenched and malignant racism. The boy watched carefully, to the point of incorporating some of Mr. McAdney's ways into his own repertoire of survival. "Mr. McAdney was a remarkable man; he was an extraordinary balance of accommodation and dignity. When he had business transactions in town with Mr. Simmons, the president of the bank and a leading local merchant, he'd put on his pressed overalls and he'd go in to talk.... As I said, Mr. McAdney was an accommodating man and he'd go in the back door.... There was something about Mr. McAdney which served as a warning to the white power structure that they could not trespass personally with him."

Mr. McAdney had "high regard" for Charles's parents. He liked their style and generosity, the dignity and restraint that they had imported from Boston. In a neighborly way, he felt moved to help them raise their boys. For several summers, when Charles and his brother Geoffrey were still in elementary school, Mr. McAdney would put them to work on his plantation chopping cotton. "We'd pick cotton, and he gave us a penny a pound and a huge midday dinner . . . beef and chicken, corn, beans, rice, and peach or potato pie." Given the boys' skill at chopping cotton, Charles thinks they were probably overpaid, but he recognizes that Mr. McAdney's purpose was not to hire the most productive laborers. "Mr. McAdney saw this as really helping to raise us, teaching us the discipline of hard work. . . . He never missed the chance to give advice . . . advice along the lines of the Protestant ethic. If you worked hard and saved your money, you would succeed in the world and people would respect you . . . which was true of Mr. McAdney, who had almost unlimited credit in that community."

As Charles and Geoffrey lifted their hoes and gathered their bales, Mr. McAdney's voice could be heard burning its way through the thick Mississippi heat: more effort, tougher muscles, sweat harder. Around the dinner table, where the boys sat down only after washing their hands, McAdney's admonitions would mix with the delicious aromas of the hot food. The heavy, daily doses of "the Protestant ethic" were not always welcomed by young Charles (who already had his own deeply implanted urges to please adults), but they were never forgotten. They added to the already weighty seriousness that Charles lugged around with him.

When the Lawrences first arrived in Utica, they moved into one of the faculty houses across the road from the campus and lived there for several years, until the institutional surrounding felt like home. Everyone in the family was overjoyed when the Patterson house, a place on the hill not far from the school, became vacant and they could piece together the resources to buy it. This was their first house on "our own land," and Letitia lovingly named it Hillcrest. Charles remembers how this house became a lively place of welcome and nurturance for the school community. "The younger faculty persons gravitated to my mother for lively conversation and to my father for his musical taste and talent. We owned a phonograph and a rather extensive collection of records for that time and place, a collection that embraced the field from Mamie Smith's blues to Enrico Caruso. My mother was an excellent cook and a willing one. Dignitaries who visited the institute would always manage to have a meal at our home. In this way, I met George Washington Carver, Robert R. Moten—visiting artists and lecturers who brought a fresh breath of the outside world to our environment, which was otherwise circumscribed by caste and poverty."

The house on the hill was not only a cultural and social oasis but also one of the rare Negro homes in the region where white folks crossed the threshold, where "coloreds" and whites would break bread together. "One of the odd things about our home—for our community—was that white persons were often entertained. Many of the benefactors of Utica were New Englanders, and these people felt most at home when visiting with my mother. We children always ate at the family table—even when we had distinguished guests; and I felt no sense of racial difference in my extreme youth, although I lived in the heart of Mississippi."

Charles remembers Hillcrest as an asylum from the dreary southern rural scene, as a place of retreat from the callous and malicious white power structure. The wonderful memories of good food, laughter, and music have imprinted the house in Charles's mind. Unlike most recollections, in which the physical details have long since faded, Charles can envision Hillcrest perfectly. "The house was wood-framed, made of pine . . . built all on one level. You entered the living room and there was a fireplace directly in front of you. In the back of the living room was a dining room. As you came out of the dining room on the left was a breakfast room and next to that a kitchen. . . . Off to the right of the living room was an entrance to my parents' bedroom. There was a fireplace in their bedroom with the same chimney. Just in back of their bedroom was my sisters' bedroom, which also had a fireplace. So there were three fireplaces, and I don't think they had separate flues . . . then in back of the girls' bedroom there was a bathroom, which worked when the water was on; and in back of the bathroom was Geoffrey's and my room. Our room had no heat. It wasn't really necessary." My father seems to dwell on the fireplaces, rather than furniture or pictures or books, for reasons he goes on to explain.

When Charles was thirteen, he got pneumonia during the Christmas holidays and became dangerously ill. "Nobody had heard of sulphur drugs or penicillin for pneumonia." As his condition grew worse, he was moved into the girls' bedroom so he could be more directly warmed by the fire's heat. Fires blazed in all the fireplaces so that the house would be toasty for the sick boy. Charles remembers the terror of disorientation brought on by the high fever and the sweat that poured down his body as the fires burned inside him and all around. "I was given toddies with liquor in it to 'help bring on the crisis.' You looked forward to the crisis as a time that would tell whether you were going to make it or not. I remember drinking sweet toddies and becoming delirious." Everyone was relieved when "the temperature broke" and Charles seemed safely on the road to recovery.

On the Sunday morning following the first sign of his return to health, a horrible tragedy occurred. Letitia was standing in the living room by the fireplace wearing a dress that she had just picked up at the cleaner's. She reached toward the mantel to get a book, and the flames leapt up and licked the edges of her dress. The fire began to inch its way up her skirt, moving toward her torso and arms. At the sound of her desperate cries, Charles Sr. came running and managed to subdue the flames that were beginning to cover his wife by wrapping her in a blanket. But the flames had leapt from the dress to the wooden walls, where they spread with terrifying speed. With fires burning for weeks in the winter, "the house was like a matchbox, ready to explode into flames." Mama Lettie's first move was to go and collect her firstborn son from his sickbed. Charles's description is stark and painful: "Mother came to my bed to get me. She walked me out to the car, and we sat there and watched our house burn down." The flames rose up, and Hillcrest, with all the family's possessions, burned to the ground. "All we had left was our car" from which they watched the horrifying event. All four children escaped injury, but Letitia and Charles Sr. were covered with burns.

With his pneumonia still raging, Charles was taken to the school infirmary, while the rest of the family spent the night at the Holtzclaws' house. From his bed, Charles could peer out of the window and see a narrow slice of the Holtzclaws' yard. That night he felt more alone than ever, twisting and turning, in and out of horrible, burning nightmares. Early the next morning his father arrived at his bedside, and Charles could hardly bear the sight of him. He was all bandaged up, moving slowly, and trying to talk in a calm voice. He brought frightening news. He and Mama Lettie had been badly burned and would have to go to the hospital in Vicksburg for a few weeks to get medical attention.

Charles Sr. urged his son not to worry, to concentrate on getting well himself; but pain was written all over his face, and the news felt terrifying to the boy. Charles felt scared for his parents. How injured were they? Would they survive? Would the burns leave terrible scars? How long would they have to stay in the hospital? His mind raced with desperate questions, but he remained silent as his father walked away, forcing his aching body, trying to hide the pain. Once he was alone, Charles's terror quickened. He felt abandoned by his parents just when he needed them most. But it was worse than that. If his parents were gone and he was sick in bed, "who would care for the children?" After all, it was his job to protect his younger siblings, and he could hardly raise his head up from the pillow. From his bed, he looked out of the window, fighting back the tears, and watched the hearse (which served as the school's ambulance) take his bandaged parents off to the hospital in Vicksburg. Charles's voice grows somber as he relives the departure of the black hearse.

Charles remained in the infirmary for a couple of weeks and successfully fought off the pneumonia. "The children" came to see him every day, their faces long and their eyes waiting, impatient for their big brother's recovery. As soon as Charles was released from the infirmary, he arranged for someone to drive all of them to visit their parents in the hospital. All dressed up, they drove the fifty miles in stony silence, and found their mother and father in the "colored wing" of the Street Sanatorium. Charles shakes his head in disgust at the memory. "The 'colored wing' was really some beds over the garage in the hospital." He remembers the awful feeling of seeing his parents "all bandaged up" in these crude and dirty conditions, and also how furious he felt at the way they were being treated by the hospital staff. "My mother's hands were all bandaged up. The nurse would come in and just put the food in front of her, and my father would have to get out of his bed and feed her. . . . I remember recognizing the injustice of it all."

Despite the awful experience of seeing his parents humiliated, it was good having the family back together again. The visit lasted for hours, as Charles sat quietly between his parents' beds reading a book and "the children" played noisily at their feet. Charles, at thirteen, the studious, responsible son; and Geoffrey, Lois, and Ann, then eleven and a half, eight, and six, enjoying frivolous games. Letitia was soothed by the children's voices as she dozed in and out of sleep. "I remember my father leaned over and told me that this was the first time my mother had been able to sleep peacefully since arriving at the hospital." It was decades later, when Letitia was on her death-bed—with cancer, barely able to speak to the attending physician—that Charles discovered another piece of the Street Sanatorium trag-edy. At the time of the Hillcrest fire, she had had a miscarriage and was recovering from burns *and* the loss of her fifth child.

The Hillcrest fire was not the only one at Utica. Earlier, the main buildings had been leveled by fire. In 1926, Ginn Hall, the largest building, had been consumed by flame and the community grieved the death of two boys who could find no escape from the blaze. "It was a great blow to the school," recalls Charles of the incident that seemed to leave a bloody scar on the small school. The sadness lingered on without resolution or relief "and hung over everyone like heavy guilt." There was some suspicion that it was caused by arson, but no charges were ever brought against anyone. Then two years later, Washington Hall, the girls' dormitory, met the same fate. But this time, two girls from the school were indicted for arson, and all eyes were focused on the trial that became the centerpiece of local life for several weeks. "It was common knowledge that some of the boys visited some of the girls at night. A couple of the girls had been recently expelled from school for having boys in their room . . . and they had been heard to make threats of what they would do if they were expelled."

Although the ravages of these fires pain Charles even today, the most terrible part of the memory is the trial in which Charles Sr. became the scapegoat both of the racist, rednecked lawyers who were

Job and Missouri Ann Lawrence with their children;
Charles, Sr., front row, second from right, with bare feet

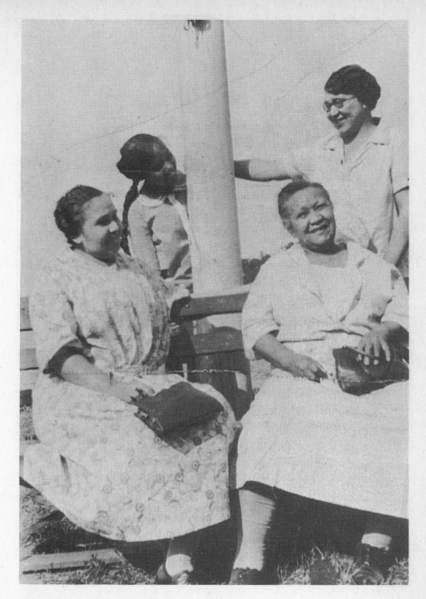

"The Smith ladies" on an outing, New York, 1928
FROM LEFT: Aunt Ninnie, Margaret, Mom Margaret, Mary

James Frasier, "Uncle Jimmy," at a beach
on Long Island,
ca. 1931

Andrew John Smith, Jr.
"Uncle Andrew,"
New York, ca. 1930

token and never felt the burden of having to "represent the race." And there were certainly enough blacks to be able to see variations among them—variations in color, style, intelligence, and achievement.

All of the teachers at Wadleigh were white, however, and almost all were female. The lack of black teachers there was a striking contrast to Magnolia High, where all of Margaret's teachers were black . . . in fact, all shades and conditions of black. "Miss Alma Cox was fair, from Louisiana, and looked 'like white.' Miss Temple, the history teacher, was a tall, ample black woman who looked like a picture from a Negro history book. She had a noble look and good posture." The Negro teachers in Vicksburg seemed like an ordinary collection of people: some great, some dedicated, some mediocre, some lazy. In Harlem (although not at Wadleigh), Margaret met black teachers who *all* seemed special and powerful. Only a handful of blacks were permitted to teach in the city's high schools, and Margaret came to know a few of them. It is hard to trace how she made their acquaintance. Once again, there were "forces" in Harlem that brought together these outstanding teachers and this dedicated student.

One such force was the Reverend John Johnson, an Episcopal minister who was the pastor of St. Martin's Church in Harlem. When Margaret was about to travel north to school, her father had written to his fellow minister and asked him to watch over his daughter while she was in the city. Reverend Johnson took on the role of "heavy uncle," "keeping an eye" on Margaret and "asking the appropriate questions." He had a kind of "delegated authority" that Margaret respected and took seriously but never felt dominated by. His church was a haven for her. Perhaps the part of Johnson's avuncular role that he took most seriously was the forging of networks between professional Negroes and Harlem's talented youngsters. He saw a gifted, ambitious child, and he wanted to link her with an adult who would serve as an example. In contemporary lingo, he searched for "mentors" for up-and-coming youngsters. With Reverend Morgan's request that he watch out for his daughter, and Margaret's big dreams of a medical career, Johnson saw great potential for matchmaking.

Margaret was introduced to Miss Melva Price, a "tall, *grand*, very dignified lady" with coal black skin and short cropped hair. She lived on prestigious Sugar Hill and taught classics at a New York City high school. "She would invite me to her house for tea. We would sit in her well-appointed apartment. She would make you feel like a lady." Miss Lucille Spence, a teacher of high-school English, smaller and daintier than Miss Price but no less dignified, also became a key figure during Margaret's adolescence. It is hard for Margaret to remember how she was introduced to these "ladies." (As she talks about these remarkable women, Margaret refers to them as ladies in order to convey their glowing femininity, their impeccable manners, and their absolutely correct decorum. "They were definitely called ladies back then, not women.") She has vague recollections of how the relationships were formed but vivid feelings about the importance of these women in her life. Meeting Miss Spence is somehow connected to a Good Friday service at St. Martin's. "The old church had been a white Episcopal church, which had been destroyed by fire. . . . By the time I joined St. Martin's, we worshiped in the second floor of the parish house while the nave was being rebuilt. I remember a Good Friday service that lasted three hours. A visiting minister was preaching the "Seven Last Words of Christ." As each "word" was spoken, the priest directed the people to walk up and put their sins in the tomb. It was very impressive to me, the drama of having people actually walking up to be relieved of their sins . . . somehow I relate Lucille Spence to this drama. . . . Maybe I was invited to her house after the service."

Margaret felt *chosen*, supported, and challenged by these impressive women. "These Negro ladies had a tremendous effect on me. . . . They were learned, with a concern for you as a person. . . . Somehow, if you were a good student, you managed to meet these Negro teachers. . . . They *looked* for promising Negro girls . . . there was a strong feeling like that in Harlem." Such women had a great sense of responsibility to the next generation in this black community, and they sought out and nurtured talent through personal connection. Once chosen by them, a girl felt a heavy responsibility. "The ladies were so *consciously* concerned about Negro girls in an otherwise white environment. I had grown up with Negro teachers in Vicksburg.

The Harris Family
FROM LEFT: Letitia, Charles, Sandy (father), and Julia

Letitia Harris, ca. 1908

Charles and Letitia Lawrence and their children, ca. 1923
FROM LEFT: Charles Sr., Charles II, Lois, Ann, Letitia, and Geoffrey

defending the girls *and* the local prosecutors who were indicting them. This was a big county trial; arson was a capital offense punishable by hanging, and the drama pitted blacks against blacks. It had all the makings of riveting theater. As chief disciplinarian and dean of the school, Charles Sr. became the Institute's major spokesperson. "My father was brought in to testify ... you can imagine what a dilemma he was in. The girls had hired a black lawyer from Jackson who in turn hired two white trial lawyers. ... The school authorities were not in sympathy with the county prosecutors, but they had no choice but to speak from their side."

When Charles Sr., handsome, dignified, and fair-skinned, took the stand, the defending lawyers mocked him. "Who are you? ... Are you a Jew?" they asked with a sneer, hating this "white-looking man" who they knew was "colored." Charles Sr. replied evenly, "No, I am not Jewish. I am a Negro." "He calls himself colored," the lawyers ridiculed. "It is slick niggers like Lawrence who go around getting people to send their daughters to 'college' when these girls should really be back at home on the farms ... yes, slick niggers like Lawrence lead these girls into trouble." Charles II never saw the terrible mockery of his father. It was awful enough to hear about it secondhand. "I remember my mother, who was at the trial, coming home and just weeping, talking about how my father had been maligned. ... It is still painful for me to think of the awful position my father was forced into. ... What the defending lawyers did was to appeal to the worst instincts of the all-white jury made up of rednecks. ... They quite openly inverted all of the values for which Utica stood at its best and for which Mr. Holtzclaw had labored so hard, and portrayed them as venal and bad." As his rage rises, Charles's throat tightens. He hates to be reminded of the ways in which Holtzclaw and his parents labored to build an institution that offered Negroes the chance for education and dignity, only to have their work brutally distorted by the malicious public testimony of the lawyers. He hates even more to be reminded of how his father suffered in the courtroom crossfire. "Some of my older friends, who were at the trial, would tease me, 'Lawrence, are you a Jew?'" Then they would fall out laughing while Charles tried to ignore their haunting calls.

In the end, the girls were acquitted and Charles's parents felt bitter relief. "There was even a certain admiration for the way in which the rednecked lawyers had succeeded in saving these girls from being convicted; but at the same time they did it by playing on all the prejudices that a white, rednecked jury in Copiah County had in 1927." Charles doesn't forget the small tragedy that was almost overshadowed by the big drama. "I believe the only mortality in the Washington Hall fire was our dog, Max. He followed my father into the building and didn't get out."

Charles rarely refers to childhood sorrow. The arson trial is a painful exception. An earlier experience also still troubles him to this day. When Charles was about ten, his parents bought a small general store not far from the school. It was called Lawrence and Lawrence Merchandise, and Letitia managed the place with the assistance of a part-time clerk. Being the only store for miles, they stocked all kinds of things: "staples, cheese, and crackers, sardines, potted meats, even oysters in season." One day when Charles was working in the store alone a boy named Hicks came in, and Charles got the unsettling feeling that he was looking to make trouble. The Hickses, a poor white family, lived up the road from Utica Institute, and the sons were crude and surly. When the boy sauntered in and asked for ice cream, young Charles served him quickly and hoped that he would keep moving. Instead, he slowly licked the ice cream and invented some mischief. When Mama Lettie returned to the store, the Hicks boy told her that Charles had served him ice cream and licked the dipper after scooping it out of the container.

Letitia's response still hurts in her son more than sixty years later. The years have made the facts fuzzy. Charles cannot remember whether he actually licked the spoon or not, but the facts seemed irrelevant at the time (and still do). What was important was that his mother took the word of the Hicks boy. "When he told my mother, she *believed* him ... even if I had lied, I was crushed that she believed him. . . . I remember being humiliated. The fact that she believed this white boy crushed me very badly." The punishment for Charles's alleged misdeed did not begin to compare to the humiliation of his mother's choice to side with the white boy.

My father never told me this story until we began work on this book. He was puzzled by how it seemed to come "out of the blue." In fact, I had never even heard of Lawrence and Lawrence Merchandise, which for a time had been a thriving country store that "extended credit to people from miles around." ("Of course, as times got harder, long before the Depression in the rural South, the store's business began to decline.") "Maybe," says Charles slowly, "I never mentioned the store to you because of its connection to the incident." The words he uses to express his feelings about "the incident" are as passionate as he ever gets: "This . . . crushed me very badly." Clearly, the pain of this event was related to Charles's deep attachment to his mother. He was identified with her, loved her deeply, and wanted to be the dutiful son who would make her proud. So doing something for which his mother felt anger or shame was letting her down and was jeopardizing his prized status as the "good son." But the sadness attached to this incident may have been related to something deeper than losing a notch in his standing as the dutiful son. He must also have been devastated by his mother's compromising her loyalty to him for "this white boy." How could she believe the Hicks boy, even if Charles might have lied? She was *his* mother and he deserved her devotion, particularly in relation to a hostile, untrusting cracker community.

Charles's parents insisted that their children experience the discipline and responsibilities of honest work and that they contribute a small share to the family's resources. By the time he was six or seven years old, Charles was chopping cotton at the McAdney plantation. A couple of years later he was clerking in the store, which felt less like a job than it did "an extension of his household chores." Compared to the heavy hand and constant demands of his mother, Mr. McAdney's orders almost felt like gentle persuasion. By age twelve, Charles was working in the offices of Utica Institute as special assistant to the principal—typing letters on an "early electric typewriter," running off memoranda on the duplicator ("a predecessor to the ditto machine"), and tending the campus switchboard. But it wasn't until the summer of his thirteenth year that Charles felt he had a "real job" in the real world, a man's world. "I went to work in the box factory in town. I earned two dollars a day along with everybody else—old men and young—but I was certainly the youngest one there."

Each morning Charles would rise before the rest of the family, throw on his work clothes, fix a filling breakfast for himself, and wait for the carpool of men who were traveling the five miles to the factory in town. He had heard about the box factory job "through the grapevine" and had arranged for the interview, brief and to the point. "How old are you? . . . Can you drive a car? . . . Have you done day laboring work?" Charles worried that his young age might be a disadvantage, but the foreman, who was looking for "strong men," took a hard look at his forearms, his chest, and his hands and hired him on the spot. For the first few weeks, Charles was assigned the muscle-building job of sorting the lumber and piling it up for processing. When the foreman spotted the young boy's industry, he gave him a promotion to the less grueling job of driving a truck. The truck was a Model T Ford, and Charles smiles with the memory of how he struggled with this dilapidated machine. "I learned to drive when I was about eight and was probably driving into town regularly by the time I was ten . . . but this factory truck was a challenge! The radius rod, that ties onto the steering mechanism, had a mind of its own, so you could never be sure which way it was going to turn. It was a pretty torn-up vehicle." Every two weeks Charles took home two dollars a day for five and a half days of work. "They held back what you made from Thursday through Saturday in order to make you come in on Monday."

Charles did not need the incentive. It wasn't that he so much enjoyed the sweating work or the grinding, boring pace of factory life. What he liked was learning about a new world, different from the somewhat protective sphere of Utica Institute. At Utica he was someone prized for the family he came from and revered for his intellectual talents. The status brought rewards and burdens. At the box factory he was "the kid" among eighteen-, twenty-, twenty-five-, and thirty-year-olds—the lowest on the totem pole, learning how to manage the tough scene. "I was in a lower, working-class man's world that summer, a world in which no sentence was undecorated by expletives and very often the nouns in the sentence were expletives." Charles negotiated a peripheral position on the edges of "the men's world." "They treated me as if they didn't think I really belonged there, but they didn't treat me with contempt. . . . They wouldn't offer me a chew of their tobacco (I did try it at least once and it was more than I wanted), but I got along with them." When Charles describes his "summer of initiation," it is clear that the chance to leave the institute and work in the factory had great value for the thirteen-year-old boy. It was the chance to taste the rewards of "real money," the chance to jockey for position in the male world, the chance to enter a culture where his family status had little meaning. "It was an important experience in my life," says Charles as he reflects on how his adolescent views of the box factory had echoes in his adult intellectual pursuits and social commitments.

Charles had hoped that the money he earned at the box factory would help to pay his tuition at Tuskegee Institute. "That was the year I had my mind set on going to Tuskegee Prep School. My parents were all set to send me. They had even bought me the trunk, but then we decided at the last minute that I was too young to go off to school, or too young for them to want me to go off." Not going to Tuskegee, his father's alma mater, was a distinct disappointment. He had dreamed of leaving tiny Utica for a larger, more prominent school, and he wanted to follow in "Pop's" footsteps. But when his mother decided against his going, he could feel the pain his departure would bring to her and he knew better than to try to change her mind. "Once you go off to school, you're gone . . . gone," she said. So Charles remained at Utica for high school and now is thankful for the decision. "I've often thought how different my life would have been if I had gone. . . . I would have been socialized into a military point of view. I probably would have made a very fine cadet and officer and been one of the colored generals during the Second World War! Or I might have been one of the fly boys who didn't get back. . . . But I was saved from that fate."

In high school Charles continued to soar as a musician and star scholar. By the time he was a senior, he had become bandleader and choir director, and Utica was enjoying some of its most ambitious musical programs. He was the school's valedictorian, with an overall average of 97, but even through his adolescent eyes he saw that many of the courses did not offer challenge, that many of the teachers were incompetent or lazy, and that his fellow students rarely offered much competition. "It was my good fortune to get the best teachers that Utica afforded. Fulton Holtzclaw, the principal's son, was our dean and a good historian. I learned a good deal of history and particularly began to be interested in Negro history because of his teaching. . . . Mr. Ben Williams was the math teacher, and he had a great reputation. . . . But, for the most part, there was a bare skeleton of a high-school faculty. . . . I'm sure my high-school average was inflated by the poor grades of my contemporaries."

Athletics—one of the areas in which his father was most distinguished—was not one of Charles's strengths. "I didn't go out for baseball because I could never throw. I was said to throw like a washerwoman, and that was an insult to washerwomen." While he did go out for football, his memories are wry and blunt: "I played quarterback on a not-very-good team. Fortunately, in those days quarterback was not synonymous with passing; they were the field generals calling the plays. I'd get players to the huddle, call the signals, and tell them what they meant."

By 1931, Charles's senior year at Utica, Charles Sr. was forced to look for another job. It was the middle of the Depression, and the school had reached its nadir, barely managing with a drastically depleted faculty, a declining student body, and crumbling buildings. "Utica was barely able to pay its employees every other week or so, and then just a piddling five dollars. . . . My father had to find a job that promised regular pay." When the position of "boys' work and athletic director" opened up at the colored YMCA in Vicksburg, all of the Lawrences moved there except Charles, who remained behind to complete his final year at Utica. By that time, he was a quasi-staffperson at Utica, enjoying, and being burdened by, adult roles. "That was a full year, and I was in a peculiar position because I had charge of the band and choir, drove the mail route, did the bookkeeping for the college, played football in season, and went to school."

Compared to his heavy duties at Utica, the promise of college loomed like a wonderful relief. By his eighteenth birthday Charles was hungry for a new environment, a more complicated and intel-

lectually demanding place. Morehouse College, a school of fine reputation in Atlanta, Georgia, gave "all male valedictorians one year's
tuition scholarship (forty dollars per semester), renewable provided
you stayed on the honor roll"; and Charles gladly accepted their offer.
In September 1932, Charles packed his clothes in a heavy leather
Gladstone bag loaned by his father and hung his suits and coats in
a wardrobe trunk bought for the occasion. Carrying his precious
trumpet in its case, he waved goodbye to his family as the train pulled
out of the station.

Part of the endowment that Charles brought with him as he set
off for Morehouse College was a deep, and already long-lived, religious commitment. At Utica, religion had stood at the center of school
life. The chapel was a large auditorium on the second floor of rebuilt
Ginn Hall, and every day it was filled with students and staff, singing
hymns, listening to sermons, and bowing their heads in prayer. Every
weekday morning began with chapel; there were several prayer meetings in the evenings; and on Sunday there were services both morning
and evening. The Sunday morning service was the most elaborate,
beginning with a parade around the campus. "The cadets [the title
given to boy students at Utica, reflecting the trace of militarism found
in most of the Negro schools in the South] and girls would line up
behind the band." Charles often led the procession with his golden
cornet. Once a year, Utica celebrated Religious Emphasis week with
daily homilies from a famous city preacher invited to the school to
give spellbinding, inspiring oratory to the rural folk. All of this
religious fervor went on at Utica despite the fact that Mr. Holtzclaw,
the principal, was an agnostic. Actually, he called himself a Univer-
salist, and each year he would shake the rafters of the small chapel
with an irreverent speech that he provocatively titled "Why There
Is No Hell." Each year the assembled congregation would listen to
the Holtzclaw harangue in stunned silence, the old-timers having
memorized the familiar arguments and the newcomers experiencing
shock. "It shook people up. Folks were horrified!" grins Charles,
who remembers being intrigued by Holtzclaw's attack on some basic
fundamentalist Christian tenets. He also recalls puzzling over the
quite comfortable coexistence of Holtzclaw's Universalism and the
good old-time Baptist theology that permeated the school.

The chapel services at Utica Institute did not represent the extent of the Lawrences' Sunday worship. When Charles was about seven years old, his mother began attending St. Peter's Baptist Church, where the Sunday service would begin at 12:30 or 1:00 P.M. Since the Utica service started at 11:00 A.M. and ended a little after noon, she was able to make it to St. Peter's in time for the morning procession. Charles joined Letitia most Sundays, and not long after he began attending St. Peter's, at the age of eight, he decided to join the church. Like most of Charles's life moves, the decision to be baptized at St. Peter's seems precocious—a young child making adultlike commitments. When I ask him about this, Charles measures his words very carefully: "Some might have said, 'There goes Charles Lawrence, again precocious in his religious choices as he is in everything else.' . . . I was not hypocritical. . . . It would be an exaggeration to say I had a conversion experience . . . but it is fair to say that I felt comfortable committing myself to being a good Christian."

On the Sunday morning young Charles decided to join the church, he sat still and attentive in the front row, on the mourner's bench, and let the Spirit wash over him. The opening prayers and petitions, the swooning hymns, the clerk's announcements, all seemed a fuzzy blur as the boy readied himself to be received by Christ. "The doors of the church are open," bellowed the deacon as the newly committed approached the altar and presented themselves. Deacon Griffin, a tall dark man, bent over Charles and "interviewed" him about his faith. Being satisfied that the boy truly "believed" and was "pure in heart," Deacon Griffin announced to the whole church in round and ceremonial tones, "Brother Charles Lawrence wants to become a member . . . in the profession of faith . . . Brother Peter, I move we accept Brother Charles for baptism so that he can become a full-bodied member of this church."

Some weeks later, on a brutally hot summer day, the baptism took place by the side of a pond, "actually a wide place in the creek." Charles was fully immersed. The baptism was preceded by a rousing revival meeting that is memorable to Charles less for its spiritual energy than for the preacher's faux pas. At the last minute, the pastor of St. Peter's could not attend the revival meeting, so "a less than literate man came to do the baptism. He preached about Gideon—

Gideon testing his soldiers." Charles grins as he comes to the punch line I've heard numerous times before. "The preacher said at one point, 'Gideon didn't know anything about military *tictacs*.'"

Charles Lawrence's baptism was a ceremonial occasion that linked him to his heritage and to his future. In his commitment there were echoes of his ancestry on both sides: of Elam Baptist Church in Charles City, Virginia, where Letitia had worshiped with all her extended family; of Grandfather Job, the Calvinist Presbyterian minister who raised all of his nine children to be believers. The baptism in the creek anticipated a life that would be guided by religious commitments, in which matters of spirit would be inextricably related to social change and political activism, in which God's love would be regarded as the basis for human relationship and intimacy. At eight, sitting on the mourner's bench at St. Peter's, Charles certainly didn't recognize the weight of his family history, but his ease and certainty in committing himself to be a "good Christian" must have been supported by this long, unquestioned religious tradition.

By the time Charles left for college, he had begun to give new shape to the old family patterns. He had his own questions and doubts, and at Morehouse he was drawn into an environment that freely mixed education, social, and religious convictions. Chapel was held daily, Monday through Friday, and on Sunday morning and Tuesday evening. Attendance was required; roll was taken and demerits given for absences. Although the daily gatherings were called "chapel," they were more than ritualized, religious occasions. With a student body of three hundred, chapel was a gathering place for the entire community. "We grumbled at going to compulsory chapel, but it built a high sense of morale in the student body." Every Tuesday morning Dr. John Hope, the first "colored president" of Morehouse, would speak; and at Tuesday evening chapel Dr. Archer, a popular professor and Hope's successor as president, would hold forth. Hope and Archer were opposites. Dr. Hope, graduate of Brown University, classics scholar, a handsome, elegant, light-skinned man with silver gray hair, gave insightful, restrained homilies to the Morehouse men. Dr. Archer, a large, imposing man, a former football star at Colgate, shook the rafters with his big booming voice, his straight talk, and his hyperbole. "Both Hope and Archer were admired by the student body—John Hope for his depth of mind and Archer because he liked to, as they say today, 'tell it like it is.' " Despite the contrasts in their oratory, both men used the pulpit to preach about "character building," advice that combined intellectual, moral, and religious training. Their renditions were offered as "a very practical kind of advice."

Chapel also served as a forum for all the leading Negro figures who passed through Atlanta. The discourses of these central intellectual and political figures were generally expressed within a spiritual context, eroding the lines between religion and policy. Charles remembers Charles Houston, Leon Ramson, and later Thurgood Marshall voicing dual commitments to social justice and academic rigor. This parade of powerful black men was deeply inspiring for Charles.

In addition to attending daily chapel, Morehouse students were required to take one year of Bible. Bible was taught by Dr. Hubert, called "Big Boy Hubert" by his students because of his girth. Hubert, a graduate of Morehouse, had attended Colgate Rochester Seminary, where Raushenbusch had been his primary mentor. Raushenbusch, a central figure in the development of "the social gospel," influenced Hubert's views about the connections between theology and ideology. "The social gospel has to do with the here and now . . . with considering the relationships between labor and management . . . with the Christian socialist movement. . . . It was the tradition from which Martin Luther King, Jr., came." Hubert returned to Morehouse and enthusiastically transmitted these ideas to his students through his Bible teaching and through his sermons at the Providence Church, where he pastored as "a sideline." Charles "was ready to receive" Dr. Hubert's teachings. His professor's ideas spoke directly to his condition. "There was an emphasis on *not* being an old-fashioned fundamentalist. . . . For example, I began to see the Genesis story as a 'myth of creation.' . . . I began to perceive a difference between fact and truth . . . truth spoke to a deeper reality." Bible study in the first year was followed by a philosophy course in his sophomore year, which continued to shake and erode the fundamentalist foundations on which Charles had been raised. "In philosophy I experienced the usual confusions . . . I was wanting something that I could believe in."

During the summer following his sophomore year, Charles had an experience that fueled his transforming worldview. It was 1934, and, along with about ten other men from Morehouse, Charles went to work in the Civilian Conservation Corps (CCC). The CCC had been initiated in 1933, a federal program that extended through World War II. It was designed as a means of "taking care of unemployed youth" from urban and rural areas. College men were permitted to apply for a summer stint with the expectation that they would return to school in the fall. Operated by the army, the CCC had decided to "experiment" with taking in some "colored boys" for supervisory, white-collar positions. When Charles and his friends heard about this opportunity, they decided to apply for positions, and several of them were hired for work as company clerks and supply sergeants. The men were shipped off to an all-"colored" camp in western North Carolina between Asheville and Black Mountain. They wore military uniforms, adopted the army's nomenclature, and quickly adapted to the tough, male society. The pay seemed good, and the small measure of status was appealing. Most of them were paid thirty dollars per month, of which twelve dollars could be kept by them and the other eighteen dollars sent home to their parents. Because of Charles's slightly elevated rank in the CCC, he received forty-five dollars per month; thirty dollars went home to his folks and he was allowed to keep fifteen.

Even though Charles had learned how to survive macho toughness and teasing in the box factory in Utica, the CCC camp was a rugged experience. Isolated in a remote section of North Carolina, the men of the corps had no escape. Their frustrations and resentments built into rage. Violence erupted out of trivial differences. Charles watched on the periphery of this brooding, angry community. "These young men were quick to fight . . . they saw themselves as sex-starved. On Saturday night, they'd go off and visit prostitutes. Poor white families from the region would bring their daughters down to sell their services. . . . There was a fairly high rate of venereal infection . . . we got regular lectures from the white physician on the dangers of promiscuity and uses of the condom."

From the time of his arrival, the scene caused Charles distress— the frustrated young men directing their rage at one another; the physician issuing his platitudes and half-hearted warnings; and the white officers surveying the action from their lofty positions. He began to see them as all involved in a kind of maudlin theater, playing parts not of their own making but parts prescribed by the economic and cultural situation in which they were all embedded. Charles found himself playing a typical role as listener and interpreter—as the good, trustworthy boy who was different from the raging hordes. "The commanding officer would talk to me about all this [the promiscuity, venereal disease, and so on] . . . I got sort of singled out, as I so often do."

The story of CCC camp is told in typical understatement by my father. From his words, always spare and modest, it is hard to get a sense of the power of this experience and the meanings it held for him. It is only when you hear the CCC story juxtaposed with his emerging theological and political views that you begin to recognize how critical were those three months in western North Carolina. The CCC camp reflected, in bold caricature, the injustices and hypocrisies of the wider society. The hierarchies—of powerful, white commanding officers, on top; lowly, childish, "supersexed" "colored boys" at the bottom; and dutiful, civilized Negroes in the middle— were all-too-familiar echoes of the historical constructs of slavery. But this time, the colored boys were all dressed up in shiny uniforms. They were not doing the grueling, dirty field labor of their forebears. They were the recipients of a benign governmental policy; but the effects were anything but salutary.

Racial strife and economic caste were not the only disturbing echoes that Charles heard that summer. He seemed even more unsettled by the militarism, the mimicking of army ways that seemed to symbolize an even deeper primitivism.

When he returned to Morehouse in the fall, Charles threw himself into political activities that seemed directly related to his three months in North Carolina. He became an enthusiastic member of the Atlanta Interracial Forum, a left-wing activist group that pushed for interracial understanding and harmony. The ideology and rhetoric of the Forum were not terribly different from the "social gospel" preached by Hubert and his colleagues in the Religion Department. But there was an added ingredient. Claud Nelson, a southern white Methodist minister was an outspoken member. As the southern secretary of the

Fellowship of Reconciliation, Nelson's commitments to pacifism ran as deep as his determination to eradicate racism. Arthur Raper, a rural sociologist and professor at Emory University, was another member of the Forum. Author of *The Tragedy of Lynching*, Raper had been raised in Winston-Salem, North Carolina, in a Moravian community, a religious sect committed to pacifism and once active against slavery. He energetically combined the religious and political strains that were now woven into Charles's worldview, having found a way to cross the boundaries between his academic pursuits and his political commitments. Raper's study of lynching was an intellectual inquiry into something that he deeply loathed—the hatred and violence inflicted upon powerless blacks. As a sociologist, he sought to understand lynching as a social phenomenon; as an activist, he was determined to dismantle the system that rationalized it.

Raper's interweaving of morality, religion, and social and political action was not lost on Charles; nor was his synthesis of research and action. "Ready to receive" such lessons, Charles began to devour the writings of pacifist thinkers such as A. J. Mustie and Nevin Sayer. By the end of his junior year, he had joined the Fellowship of Reconciliation and "become known on campus as sort of a 'peacenik.'" By his senior year, Charles had taken on a part-time student job as a field worker with the Emergency Peace Campaign. On weekends he would travel around to other, primarily black, colleges in order to publicize the Peace Campaign and encourage the students to become politically active in opposing the war buildup. His proselytizing included trying to convince young people to take a "peace pledge" and "commit themselves to pacifism."

Charles was convincing, determined, and very serious. He was frightened, in a deeply personal way, by the impending war and understood the connections between the profound social injustices all around him and the war effort. There were only a few students at Morehouse who shared Charles's convictions. "There was a tiny group of us at Morehouse who agreed on the futility of war and the need to find ways for peace. . . . I was horrified at the approaching war. . . . It was clear we were headed toward disaster." Although Charles speaks about a "tiny group" of fellow devotees, I see him mostly struggling alone. Even he admits that when he sees his old college chums, they always remind him of the National Peace Strike when "all by myself, I picketed the main academic building the whole day long." Over the years, so many people have mentioned the picture of Charles walking the pavement, back and forth, carrying a placard, on his lone vigil for peace, that Charles almost admits that the story must have been true. He says, with typical modesty, "The story says I was out there all alone . . . but there must have been others walking with me."

Charles's feeling of not being alone came from the support he received from his peers. If he was called a peacenik, it was out of respect and loyalty, not out of hostility. Charles says, simply, "I received admiration from my black friends." They formed a circle of affectionate support even though they might not have shared his burning convictions. His political activities were also admired by some members of the faculty, particularly his professors in the Religion Department who had "some sympathy for what I was doing and supported the peace witness." After all, Charles was acting out the lessons from "the social gospel" that they had so clearly articulated and through his actions he was experiencing a "convergence" of his theological, moral, and political beliefs. "I found a rationale in my understanding of the Gospel."

Several years later, as part of an application for a graduate fellowship, Charles wrote about the connections between scholarship and activism, between religion and pacifism, and between domestic and international relations. Thirty-two years old when he put these words to paper, he still regarded his views as emerging:

The most important point of orientation for my philosophy of life, as I see it, is my religious faith. My ideal is the Christian way of life, a way of life that is constantly re-defining itself to me as I read, converse, meditate, and live. Despite these re-definitions, however, there are certain things which remain clear. Among these are (1) a faith in God (with no clear conception of what God is, save the source of life and goodness), (2) a belief in the sanctity of human personality, and (3) a conviction that followers of Jesus must work for the kind of society which will make for a realization of (2) under the grace of God. Right alongside my religious faith is a belief in the validity of the scientific method. Given the motivation for societal change that one receives through one's religion or other philosophy of life, one must seek to implement this through gaining knowledge of objective reality in the manner of the scientist—i.e., through conceptualization, observations of a systematic nature, and reconceptualizations. Finally, new knowledge gained through the application of the scientific method must be placed at the service of one's philosophy of life (religious or otherwise) so that it can lead to constructive social action.

I am a religious pacifist. I believe that this position follows logically from the demands of the Christian faith. I believe that my pacifism commits me to a spirit of good will and peacemaking as surely in my personal life as in international relations. . . . I need hardly add that this is an ideal almost, if not altogether, impossible to attain in this life. Even so, it is accepted as an imperative of my convictions as a Christian, constantly to be striven for though probably never more than fleetingly achieved. It is also fair to add that neither my religion nor my pacifist convictions which I believe to grow out of my religion are pragmatic in character. The test of their validity is not whether they will "work," in any manner which I can see and understand; it is rather whether or not they are ultimately right and in line with God's will for me.

. . . I believe peace to be indivisible. For our own country there cannot continue to be a neat compartmentalization of "domestic relations" and "international relations." As a religious man, I believe that peace is contingent upon a higher level of national morality among the great powers. For example, it seems that the beam of the white primary in South Carolina and Georgia and the poll tax in Tennessee somewhat beclouds America's ability clearly to see how to remove the mote of undemocratic election practices in Poland. As a member of an ethnic minority group, I believe that ethnic minorities in America have a responsibility to work for a greater extension of American democracy and American international morality, not for the sake of minority group people, but for the sake of a very sick world.

When Charles and Margaret, both nineteen years old, met in Vicksburg, the Morehouse man had a lot on his mind and found a willing and eager listener. On the porch swing, in the heat of the Delta summer, Charles told stories about his favorite professors: who challenged him to think critically; who worked on behalf of intellectual rigor and social change; who cared about him, had him over for dinner, talked with him for long hours into the night; who saw in these eyes the promises of the future. He talked about the camaraderie at college—his friends who loved him despite his burning commitments and seriousness, or maybe because of them. And Margaret listened, fascinated by this man's wide-angle vision on the world, intrigued by the way he took ideas and turned them on their heads. She loved his seriousness *and* his laughter, one following the other, leaping through their conversations. "He seemed so happy!" remembers Margaret. But more than anything, Margaret remembers his capacity to love and his insistence that she respond and initiate. "You see, this was the first affectionate relationship I had ever known. In my family, affection was assumed. You never hugged and kissed or stated your feelings about one another. . . . But Charles did all of these things and opened up a whole new world for me."

Even though in their long conversations Charles seemed to do most of the talking, the Cornell woman did not simply listen. Charles marveled at *how* she listened and at what questions she chose to ask. She pierced directly to "the core of the issue." He also was intrigued by her self-confidence (what Margaret would later call her "positive narcissism")—the way she could "be alone with herself." He found her "beautiful and brilliant." But mostly Charles admired and respected Margaret's single-minded pursuit of her dream. His visions felt fuzzy in contrast. "I never had a burning ambition like Margaret's determination to be a doctor. She was so certain, so sure."

VII

The Wedding at
St. Mary's

BRAINS AND MONEY

B Y 4:00 P.M. on June 5, 1938, St. Mary's Church was full. The
pews groaned under the weight of people dressed in their Sunday-
go-to-meeting best. The men wore neatly pressed summer suits with
crisp handkerchiefs in their breast pockets. The ladies wore wide-
brimmed hats decorated with fancy ribbons, and boned corsets to
give a firm foundation to their flowery cotton dresses. Many waved
church fans in front of their faces, to move the heavy, hot air. The
atmosphere was steamy both with anticipation and with summer
humidity. At the organ, Mrs. Ewing, Margaret's old piano teacher,
seemed to surrender to the heat, giving the notes a drawling pace.
Only the children seemed unaffected by the melting conditions. In
starched, immaculate outfits they squirmed close to the aisles, ready
to leap at the opening bars of "Here Comes the Bride."

Although the small church was bulging, the real crowds were
outside, lining the sidewalks each side of North Street and spilling
over the curbs. The spectators struggled to position themselves so as
to get a good view of the arriving guests. "This was a big deal in
the Negro community of Vicksburg.... The white community, of
course, just didn't matter. It was a great occasion! An upper-middle-
class wedding ... joining the Lawrences and the Morgans."

Not only did the two families have a special, revered status in
Vicksburg "colored society," but the young people about to be married
seemed to hold out special promise to everyone who watched them.

They were so good-looking, so bright and hardworking; and they just seemed to go together. When Vicksburg folks marveled at the pair, they would give "the biggest compliment anybody could give": "You look like sister and brother!" they would announce as satisfaction and pride swept over their faces. Even the young retarded man, known to everyone in the community as "slow-minded," didn't miss the special meaning attached to this union. He stood on the sidewalk across from the church, watching members of the wedding party arrive, and exclaimed for all to hear, "Brains and money. Ain't it grand. Brains and money." To which all around him nodded their heads in solemn agreement. The story told hundreds of times still causes Margaret to laugh with pleasure and incredulity. "When Charles and I heard that, we couldn't believe it. We both claimed to be the 'brains' of the couple because neither of us had any money.... Charles had borrowed money from his father to get the wedding license, and I think he had two dollars in his pocket, which was the change from the license."

After their first summer together in Vicksburg when they were both nineteen, Charles and Margaret had known that they would be married one day. All during the second half of their college careers in Ithaca and Atlanta, they had waited for each other's letters, plotted reunions ("Before our wedding, Charles and I had really spent very little time together"), and dreamed of the day when they would be married. Both of them knew that marriage was not possible until they had each established a career. Margaret, with her mind on medicine, thought it "wise" that they wait to be married until she finished Cornell and had safely survived the first couple of years of medical school. Charles, less certain of his goals, was nevertheless determined to do graduate study under "the giants in his field" at Atlanta University. He hoped that professors such as Ira Ried and W. E. B. DuBois would help him resolve the conflict he felt between scholarly pursuits and social action.

When Margaret and Charles set the wedding date, they knew that their studies, and their fragile financial status, would keep them apart for another year, and they did not relish the nearly one thousand miles' separation. But they were young and impatient. To them, marriage at a distance—however great—was better than waiting any longer. They yearned for each other's companionship, even if their embraces had to reach across half the country.

The wedding party was large, with Leah, Margaret's cousin from Richmond, as her matron of honor and six bridesmaids in long pastel dresses, like freshly cut flowers. "We needed eligible men," explains Margaret as we look at a picture of the entire wedding entourage and see the handsome, scrubbed faces of the ushers, all dressed in white. "Charles's father was his best man. Here is Henry Williams, a local friend of the Lawrences; here is Lucille Dillon's brother Bud . . . and Charles's good friend Ed, who is a physician . . . and, of course, Uncle Geoff. . . . Some of the main people came from a great distance." Mrs. Ewing had to play several refrains of "The Bridal Chorus" before the whole wedding party could make its way to the front of the church and form a neat U-shape at the altar.

Then everyone strained to see the bride, magnificent in flowing white lace, her face veiled. She paused for a moment at the church door, feeling the heat and energy from the congregation and trying to calm herself. The Reverend Morgan, also resplendent in his clerical vestments, waited at the front of the church, ready to officiate at the ceremony. With her father unavailable to accompany her down the aisle, Margaret was escorted by the treasurer of the vestry. As they marched slowly forward, Margaret saw a blur of faces and entered into a deep fog. She seemed to lose touch with everyone, going through the motions yet not registering the feelings. "The wedding *happened*," says Margaret in describing her semiconscious state. "I was in another world."

Fifty years later, she recognizes her spaced-out response as deep apprehension. She knew of no way to react to this extraordinary event. She didn't have the emotional repertoire. How could she show her joy and excitement, her anxiety? She had to retreat from it, not participate in it, and hope it would happen successfully around her. Margaret compares her young adult bewilderment to her middle-aged exuberance at my wedding. "At *your* wedding I enjoyed myself. I participated fully, was totally there." I listen to her and remember my mother's tears and laughter, her infectious spontaneity on my wedding day, and recognize the emotional distance she has traveled.

This anxiety of "not knowing how to respond" and escaping into another world felt familiar. A few months before, Jean Luke, her best friend at medical school, had given her a surprise engagement party. Jean, a spinster from a wealthy New York family, had entered medical school as a mature woman of almost fifty after returning to college in her early forties. Right from the start, Jean and Margaret had hit it off, enjoying each other's company and support, sharing each other's dreams. Perhaps they were attracted by the special kind of courage each saw in the other. Early in her life, Jean had been crippled by polio and later sent by her parents to a finishing school to learn the appropriate social graces. When she decided to do the unthinkable—become a doctor—she was going against the grain of deeply embedded family tradition. Women of her circle were to be ornamental, gracious, witty, and above all feminine. Medicine was a man's world. Margaret must have recognized, and identified with, Jean's determination and stamina.

When the young black woman from Vicksburg, Mississippi, became engaged, her middle-aged white friend greeted the news with great excitement and began scheming. For weeks she planned an elegant luncheon to which she secretly invited many of Margaret's friends and family members. On the day of the party, Margaret approached the suite in the medical school residence hall where she was anticipating an ordinary afternoon of student meetings. Instead she opened the door and heard a loud chorus of female voices. "Surprise!" they squealed with pleasure. All Margaret could feel was panic. Utter dread. The same deep anxiety that she was to feel on her wedding day rose in her throat. "My God, what will I do now?" Like the story of George Horse racing away from her mother, Mary, in Mound Bayou and the tale of her seven-year-old mischief cutting off her braid in Vicksburg, Margaret cannot remember what happened next. "Like painful dreams," she has buried the memory. "But Mom," I say, again feeling frustrated with the unfinished story, "what do you think *really* happened?" A long pause, then "I suspect I carried it off . . . that I managed to hide my panic."

Margaret's panic on her wedding day did not let her enjoy, or even register, the celebration. She, who loves music and ceremony, didn't hear the familiar refrains of the processional. She, who thought her husband-to-be was "unbelievably handsome," can't picture the sight of his face or the rush of excitement she must have felt when she saw him waiting at the other end of the aisle. All she remembers is the moment when her father spoke, his voice full and forceful. "Who gives this woman to be married to this man?" questioned Reverend Morgan. "I do" was how he responded to himself. "My father asked the question and he answered it," Margaret says now. But having heard and recorded her father speaking for two, she lapsed back into the fog. "I was in my own world through the whole thing. 'Where am I? What is going on? . . .' I was somewhere, but I don't know where I was."

While Margaret's dread on her wedding day was partly due to "not knowing how to respond emotionally," there was another, heavy anxiety that blocked her pleasure. She was feeling uneasy about getting married. She knew that she loved Charles very much and had never loved anyone as much as she did him. But she still worried over the extraordinary commitment of marriage. And she worried silently, always to herself, never sharing her ambivalence with anyone. " 'What am I getting myself in for? . . . What is this going to be like?' "

Not only did Margaret feel herself on a precipice, on an adventure that seemed both exciting and hazardous, she was also haunted by the echoes of her parents' marriage. Besides their constant bickering, there was the image of Mary kneeling at her bedside praying that her husband would not be unfaithful, the memory of going out in the streets of Vicksburg hand-in-hand with her mother in search of her father, the sound of her father walking down the hall and shouting: "You white bitch!" Margaret didn't want any of this. She wanted a union with Charles that was respectful and open and affectionate. She desperately wanted to break with a long family history of female dominance and male exclusion and form a more equal, loving partnership. She saw how the Smith women, "the Smithies," as her father called them, destroyed men. They developed riveting loyalties with one another that seemed designed to keep men out and make them impotent. The only way her father had survived the entangled Smith women was by staying far away from them. But even Sandy Morgan suffered. He always knew his wife's heart was with her mother and sisters. He knew he could never rescue Mary from the sadness that came over her when she was deprived of the other women's company. And he knew that his blackness was a source of both attraction and revulsion for Mary. In his suffering, all he could do, finally, was to lash out at her, and by extension, at all the Smithies. "Confound it, you white bitch!"

As she heard the organ pounding out "The Wedding March," Margaret must have tried to blot out these family echoes. Was she strong enough not to be drawn back into the family web? "I wanted my relationship to my husband to be different from my mother and father's. I wanted to be able to speak directly to my husband." While the family legacy was strong, Margaret felt very hopeful that her marriage with Charles would be a happy one. Already she could feel its special qualities: their friendship and respect, the way she was learning how to give and receive love. There is emotion in her voice as she remembers how she felt. "Charles was my first companion. I was fascinated by hearing somebody else's thoughts and feelings. It was my *first* experience of expressed affection. You are not related to a person unless you say something about it and let the other person know how you feel. I remember holding back at first and getting some requests from Charles that I respond."

These special qualities had been there from the beginning with Charles. Their relationship was so "natural," so nonadversarial, that it almost didn't feel like romantic love at first. To themselves and to the world, they had felt most comfortable calling it "friendship." In a letter to Mama Lettie a month and a half before their wedding, Margaret worried that her future mother-in-law might have felt some deception in the couple's claim that they were "only friends":

> *50 Haven Ave.*
> *New York*
> *4-22-38*

> *Dear Mrs. Lawrence,*
> *Just a note to confess that I love your son Charles and that I have promised to become his bride on June fifth at 4:30 P.M. There is also something else I felt the need of explaining since first I knew, long years ago in 1935. You and I had just met and you were sitting one day on the bank of Cherry Street School talking about the evils of*

the "younger generation"—when I said that being bored and weary
of the young men of my acquaintance, I was so happy to meet
Charles because at last I thought here was a young man that I could
be friends and pals with; play tennis, go on bikes and swimming and
play music and never feel that he would spoil all that by making love
to me in the usual "boy-girl" manner. And I remember quite well
that you said, "Do you know he said the same thing about you?"
And so what I've wanted to explain is that I said that in all good
faith and had no idea that this would happen at all. We have been
and still are such good pals and friends, and we find so many inter-
esting things and such good fun in life, that I cannot but see great
happiness in store for us. And besides I love Charles and think him
the most wonderful man ever . . . this I trust to you to keep a secret.

Margaret was not alone in her anxiety on her wedding day. The
groom expressed his differently, but he, too, felt butterflies. Instead
of "spacing out" during overwhelming moments, Charles would take
it all in, remember every detail, be fully, completely present . . . denying his uneasiness. In the long months before the wedding, Charles's excitement had threatened to overwhelm him. He
had counted the weeks, the days, the hours, and had written desperate,
endearing letters to Margaret:

Darling, do you miss me as much as I miss you and as much as I
think you do? Do my letters make you feel a nearness to me? I hope
they do for I want you to always feel that, in spite of our 900 miles
of separation, I am constantly with you, sharing your thoughts, reliv-
ing happy moments in the past and previewing happier days in the
future.—It is ever thus with me.

And humorous, teasing ones:

By the time you get this (letter) you will have less than two weeks of
maidenhood at your disposal. It has just dawned upon me that I have
only 15 days in which to sow my wild oats. It's really a heavy assign-
ment but I'll try to do my best. Meanwhile—in the midst of exami-
nations, et cetera—you must become a quiet, demure, innocent
looking bride . . . I can hardly wait to see you.

When Charles arrived in Vicksburg for the wedding, he was not
allowed to lay eyes on Margaret. They would not have dreamed of

not following tradition. "It was the old-fashioned business of not seeing the groom until the day of the wedding, and we hadn't seen each other for weeks!" So they each waited, apart. Margaret smiles at the evidence of Charles's premarital anxieties. "I learned later that Charles's mother had cooked a ham and there was much excitement on the hill at the Academy where the Lawrences lived. Charles said that he practically ate the whole ham single-handedly the morning of the wedding. He was really anxious!"

Although Margaret felt overwhelmed by the time her wedding day arrived, she had been pretty cool during the months of preparation. As her aunts went into frenzied activity in New York, Margaret threw herself more and more into her work at medical school. She was finishing her second year at Columbia and was determined to make it through her exams successfully. It seemed more important than ever to do well in her studies. After all, ever since she turned fourteen and announced that she was going to be a doctor, her aunts had doubted her. If she gave a boy even a sideways glance, "You'll never become a doctor," the aunts would protest. Now here she was, twenty-three years old, on the eve of her wedding. She certainly wasn't going to fail now. She wasn't going to give her aunts the pleasure of fulfilling their worst prophecies.

So when the aunts generously offered to give Margaret her wedding dress—custom-made from the bridal shop at Macy's—Margaret was cool. The more the aunts became involved in the dress, the more Margaret felt the need to keep her distance. It was a kind of punishment for all the years of doubt and suspicion. "I was in medical school, and I decided not to pay too much attention, but Aunt Hazel, in particular, and Aunt Ninnie were bound and determined that I have this bridal gown. . . . It cost them a magnificent sum, maybe over a hundred dollars! I was playing it cool and said, 'It's all right with me.' I doubt I showed the proper gratitude. If they wanted to do it, then okay. They had given me all sorts of mixed messages. I was paying them back. They wanted to make a lot over the wedding, so let them!"

Vicksburg, at least the colored folks in Vicksburg, had never seen such a beautiful wedding dress. It was so soft and flowing and seemed so beautifully to reflect Margaret's quiet grace. The translucent, filmy white material, embroidered with flowers, let her brown skin shine through. The bouquet of white roses completed the angelic picture. Five decades later, Margaret looks at her photograph, standing alone at the church altar. She shakes her head. "When Charles would look at this picture, he would say that it was just like my family that there was no picture of the bride *and* groom, only the bride." They both noticed the Smith family imprint—the powerful, elegant woman and the missing man. The next photograph, taken soon after the wedding, is a picture of Margaret *and* Charles. "Charles knew a good photographer in Atlanta, and I can remember he was very eager to have our picture taken together." Margaret gives it a satisfied look and exclaims, "Boy, are we good-looking!"

As she watched her aunts whip into action in New York, accompanying her to every one of the time-consuming fittings at Macy's, Margaret worried about the wedding preparations in Vicksburg. Would her mother be able to pull it off without her support and assistance? For as long as Margaret could remember, she had been the one in charge of pulling Morgan family gatherings together. If people appeared at the Morgans' house unannounced—as they often did, expecting bountiful hospitality from the clergyman's family— Mary would fall apart and Margaret would rush into the kitchen to prepare a meal for the guests. Mary's ineptitude and Margaret's competence became part of family legend and made Margaret apprehensive about wedding preparations. "I thought my mother wouldn't know what to do." To stave off worry and to make sure things would be done properly, Margaret was in constant contact with Marian Poe, one of the bridesmaids who was the niece of Mr. Bowman, the principal of Magnolia High, and whom Margaret regarded as thoroughly responsible. She asked Marian to take care of all the details of the flowers and the bridesmaids' dresses, and she felt certain that she could rely on her. But Margaret continued to worry about the rectory. Her mother was not a good housekeeper. She let "sally" (poorly fitting clothes, old books, dusty magazines and newspapers) build up everywhere in the house. Would her mother clean the place out in time for the reception, which was to be held at the house?

Margaret's concerns were heightened by the fact that she wanted things to be perfect for her aunts' visit. This was the aunts' first visit to the Deep South, and they were filled with dire images of this "godforsaken place." As daughters of Richmond's "colored high society," Hazel and Ninnie regarded Vicksburg, Mississippi, as uncivilized terrain, and they boarded the train for the long trip south with trepidation. "Mississippi was Hades to them . . . deep, dark South. Aunt Hazel told me that when they were riding along on the train, she decided to warn Aunt Ninnie . . . 'Now, Mary probably lives in a shack like that shack out there in the fields . . . so we musn't be upset by it.' " Part of the reason Margaret wanted her mother to have everything together, clean and organized, was so that the aunts might be fully disabused of their horrible caricatures of her home. She wanted them to see a shiny, civilized Vicksburg. She wanted to rid them of their insulting feelings of superiority. How delighted she was when she arrived home and found the "sally" gone and the house clean. How thrilled she was at the improvements her parents had managed without her help. "When I got there, my parents had bought new living room furniture and it looked very good!" I can still hear the relief in Margaret's voice.

While to her aunts Margaret boldly asserted her commitment to medical school, she felt uncertainty in her own heart about how she would arrange her life after marriage. One side of her might have wished to indulge herself in the blushing bride mode—to become the "demure and innocent *looking*" bride that Charles had urged her to be, perhaps only half-jokingly. In her letter to Mama Lettie proclaiming her love for Charles, Margaret presented herself as the negligent daughter, not able to attend fully to the important event and leaving the burdensome preparations to her mother:

> *Plans for the wedding are coming on fast. I only hope that I don't flunk medical school and that Momsy doesn't go into a coma from overwork. I suggested in a whisper that perhaps you'd help her a little in spite of the conventions, but it seems she thought of that first . . . Mother is a real wonder! She has not once said, 'you fiend, you devil, for asking me to work myself into a knot for June 5th.' But then both Charles and I have ever been conceited about our parents. It's going to be such fun having two more apiece. We were surely just born for good luck.*
>
> *. . . I will be very grateful to you for any help you can give Mom*

*in preparation for the happy day. It's annoying being in medical
school right now. I think I'll flunk just so that I can come home and
get ready like any other proper bride. Love to all family.*

Margaret

To her future mother-in-law, at least, Margaret was eager to be
seen as torn by the requirements of her career in the midst of wedding
preparations. Mrs. Lawrence surely knew better than to believe Margaret's playful threat that she might flunk out of medical school in
order to be a "proper bride." Anyone who knew Margaret, even
slightly, recognized her determination and her single-minded pursuit
of medicine. Her frivolous words to Mama Lettie seemed almost
scripted to match an image that neither of these strong women—
bride nor mother-in-law—subscribed to in their daily lives. Both
assumed that family and career would be important in their lives—
that they would give fully to each and struggle with the inevitable
tensions. These tensions would not come from Charles, who admired
her commitment. But on the eve of the wedding, somehow Margaret
felt more comfortable professing a convention she never expected to
follow. She knew it and Mama Lettie knew it.

As Margaret relives her wedding day, she occasionally glances down
at her hands, still slender and soft. She turns the wedding ring on
her left hand and is reminded of its origins. Before the wedding,
Charles had taken three rings to a jeweler he knew in Atlanta and
asked him to melt them down and make one thick band. After so
many years, the thick band has become a thin golden circle around
her finger, but the memories have not diminished. One of the gold
rings that became part of Margaret's wedding band was found up
at Quaker Lake, where Margaret and her friend Sarah Thomas had
worked as housekeepers. When Margaret saw the glint of gold under
some leaves along a wooded path, she thought it was a very good
omen. Maybe this meant that one day she would be married to
Charles. Maybe this was a sign that her love for him would grow
into a wonderful union. She put the ring in her pocket, believing in
its mysterious powers, and squirreled it away for safekeeping.

Before she found the ring at Quaker Lake, Margaret was already the owner of two gold bands given to her by Mrs. Kitty Lyle when she was ten years old. Kitty Lyle was an "aged white, blue-eyed colored lady" who lived in Vicksburg, in a two-room shack—the old servant quarters of a mansion several blocks away from the Morgans. Every Sunday, midafternoon, Margaret would take the dinner her mother had prepared over to Kitty Lyle. The old lady was bedridden and Margaret would sit beside her, making conversation or waiting in silence until Mrs. Lyle was finished, when she'd carry the dishes back home. It was a weekly visit that seemed to please both the old lady and the girl. "She was at the end of her life when she got these rings out, from her two weddings, and gave them to me. I kept them." The melting of three rings into one, the joining of North and South, Ithaca and Vicksburg, is one of Margaret's favorite memories of the wedding. She savors the symbolism.

The ceremony at St. Mary's was followed by a reception of ice cream and cake right next door at the Morgans' home. The bride and groom stayed until the last guests were gone and prepared for their journey to Jackson, the state capital of Mississippi. Due to report there the next morning for a teaching post that Charles had taken at Jackson College Summer School, they had to travel there on their wedding night. The accommodations at Jackson, in a boys' dormitory, were not the most hospitable setting for the newlyweds. "We had two rooms in the dormitory, and each room had two beds. If I was in the bathroom, Charles would go and stand guard at the door in order to warn the boys not to enter. (It was thought more seemly for us to live in the boys' dormitory than in the girls' because you wouldn't want a *man* to be in a girls' dormitory, even though he had just gotten married.)" So they spent their first night together crowded onto one narrow bed in a spare and unwelcoming dormitory room. The next morning they rose early because they had been invited to the president's house for breakfast. "We arrived there way before the scheduled time. I can remember sitting outside on the the front steps of the president's house waiting until it was appropriate to ring the bell."

Even though Margaret and Charles would have preferred a more leisurely time after the wedding, neither of them ever dreamt of taking a honeymoon. They felt fortunate to have found summer jobs and they needed the money desperately. Despite the proclamation of the wedding onlooker, their union was all "brains" and no "money." At Jackson College they could get free room and board and a small salary of which they hoped to save a portion.

While Charles taught sociology at the summer school, Margaret worked on a research project under the guidance of Dr. Haven Emerson, her professor of public health at Columbia Medical School. The project, a study of syphilis in the Negro population of Mississippi, would use data that had been gathered by the Department of Health, housed at the state capital. Knowing that Margaret had roots in Mississippi and knowing of her interest in public health and epidemiology, Dr. Emerson was delighted to sponsor her for the syphilis research. He wrote a letter of introduction to the director of the Department of Health in Jackson offering high praise for his student. The day after their arrival in Jackson, Margaret went down to the Department of Health to meet the director and begin examining the medical records. As she entered his office, his greeting made her feel like she had been hit in the stomach. "He immediately called me 'Margaret'... This was 1938 in Mississippi, and people were not in the habit of meeting and immediately calling each other by their first names." Her voice rises in anger as she relives the humiliation. "He made it clear that as a Negro, despite the fact that I was at this prestigious medical school, I had no title.... He knew who I was, 'Miss Margaret Morgan'... He had the letter from my Columbia professor saying how good my work was, how much he admired me.... But he needed to demean me. I was greatly offended."

Margaret left the office still shaking and hurried back to Jackson College to tell her brand new husband about the horrible encounter. She expected Charles to share her view of the incident and wanted to feel his support. She did not expect the explosion of rage. "Charles was infuriated.... There were very few times when Charles got violently mad. This was one.... He cried, he was so angry.... He was so angry, he was destroyed. He never forgot it." Margaret, too, weeps at the memory. "You see, Charles had lived a sort of protected life on the campus of Utica...a little safer from the assaults...but here he was in the South.... To have reached his manhood, to have married a wife, to have his wife not respected . . . he was destroyed. . . . In this place, he was rendered helpless as a man. . . . He could not protect his wife from indignity. . . . This was the most demeaning thing that could possibly be!" As she heard her husband's desperate words of pain and watched this normally restrained man shake in violent rage, the young bride felt their deep bonds. "For the first time, I knew what it was to be a wife and feel a kind of empathy with someone close to you. . . . You feel something he does."

Remembering this incident brings back other occasions for Margaret. In the first, the victim of racism is her mother, Mary. The other occasion is Margaret's triumphant return to Jackson, Mississippi, forty years after the Health Department experience. Margaret tells her mother's story first, perhaps in an effort to get it out of the way. Like the Jackson memory, this one still causes her some pain.

When Margaret was in her third year of medical school, her mother became seriously ill with a kidney disorder. Having been introduced to the best in medical treatment, Margaret decided to try and arrange for her mother to come to Columbia Medical School for the needed surgery. She spoke to the chiefs of medicine and surgery at the hospital and felt pleased at the support and influence she now had as a respected and admired medical student. "As a medical student, I had power to get my mother the best medical care." Margaret wrote her mother's doctor at the Vicksburg Infirmary who had been treating her for several years and knew of "her standing in the community." When the Vicksburg doctor wrote about his patient to his New York colleagues, he referred to her throughout the letter as "Mary." Suddenly the medical student, who had felt the "power" of being able to persuade her mentors to care for her mother, was rendered powerless. "He spoke so disrespectfully, calling her 'Mary,' as if this was someone who was working on his plantation! . . . I felt really ashamed to have made these contacts with all the people at Columbia responding to me respectfully . . . then have this man refer to my mother in this way."

The humiliation and anger Margaret felt at the insult are still visible on her face. Her response reflects the long shadow of black folks' tireless attempts to gain status as full-fledged human beings. When Margaret was a youngster in Vicksburg, the echoes of slavery were still resounding. In the first-name address, Negroes heard the old contempt, the brutal infantilization. When whites called grown-up blacks by their first names, they never expected to be addressed in the same terms. They expected a response of passive subservience— "Yes sir, Massah . . . Sho 'nuf, Mr. Charlie." In an effort to protect themselves from the daily assaults, blacks, in the generations close to slavery, and particularly in the Deep South, were ingenious in inventing ways to avoid being called by their first names.

In Copiah County, Mississippi, where Charles grew up, it was not out of the ordinary for Negro parents to name their children "President," "Deacon," "Mister," even "Secretary," so that whites would not be able to avoid calling them by a title. As a Negro priest in Vicksburg, Margaret's father only used his initials, the Reverend S. A. Morgan. Few knew his name was Sandy, and no one but the immediate family called him that. And the Reverend, in the intimacy of his own household, usually addressed his wife as "Mrs. Morgan."

Charles's mother, whose full name was Letitia Burnett Harris Lawrence, was even more circumspect. She refused to divulge the names attached to her initials "L. B.," which she wore with pride and dignity. When his parents owned the country store in Utica, Lawrence and Lawrence Merchandise, Charles can remember "the drummers" coming around to sell their wares. "The crackers were just aching to know my mother's name. . . . When someone discovered that her daughter's name was Lois, they began to assume that was my mother's name too. My mother never corrected them. She'd say that it was all right as long as they weren't calling her by her first name."

So when Margaret, who was in her third year of medical school at Columbia, heard her supervisor in Jackson, Mississippi, address her by her first name, and when her mother's Vicksburg physician referred to his patient as "Mary," her anger expressed generations of humiliation and oppression.

Leaving behind, for the moment, these painful echoes, Margaret hastens to tell me of her triumphant return to Jackson, Mississippi, years later. "It is 1979 in Jackson, a most amazing experience," Margaret says with fanfare. Forty years after being put down by the director of the Health Department, she is honored as "Dr. Lawrence," conquering heroine. She had been invited to give the keynote address at the annual meeting of the State Mental Health Association and accepted the invitation with a combination of anxiety and curiosity. She was eager to return home and savor the changes that would have allowed her to be the chosen speaker in this Mississippi city. But she also worried about the cultural inertia that would make things feel unchanged and bring back the hurtful memories. From the moment she got off the plane, however, Margaret felt "utter respect." "To find people knocking themselves out to honor me as a former Mississippian was incredible." She discovered that the executive director of the State Mental Health Association and the chair of their board were both black, a fact she had not discovered in their correspondence and telephone conversations. "The crowd I spoke to was thoroughly integrated. If I had closed my eyes in the room, I would have had no idea of who was black or white." After her speech, an elderly white man, the former state director of mental health, approached her with some half-formed recollections. Something about Margaret's poetic and passionate speech had seemed familiar to the old man. It turned out that he had lived around the corner from the Morgans in Vicksburg "and he remembered my father." Margaret's voice is incredulous and tearful. This encounter vividly expressed both the continuity and the change, all at once reminding her of her childhood in Vicksburg and the complicated feelings of privilege and powerlessness.

As Margaret describes these occasions, her explanations seem both to attack and protect her southern origins. Once again she struggles with the difficulty of giving her daughter "a flavor of growing up in the South ... the part of the world that everyone thought of as a benighted place." There was something about the crossing of race and class that had determined the quality of her life. Margaret's voice is tentative as she tries to figure it out. "I was in no way destroyed by racial separation. ... You were respected as belonging to your own class ... there were these class tiers on either side. When you met, you met as upper-middle-class Negroes with upper-middle-class whites ... you lived your life all the time in your own group ... you came together at the same class level." I listen, but I don't entirely understand. Is my mother saying that her class and station protected her from the ravages of racism? Did the upper-middle-class sector of the white population, "the tier" with whom she was related, possess a detached distance that allowed their Negro counterparts to maintain their dignity? But she has just told me tales of her victimization even when people knew who she was.

"Are you saying that you only related to upper-middle-class whites in Vicksburg?" I ask. Margaret's face shows mock amazement as she says dramatically, "Why should *I* have anything to do with poor white folks?" I pursue further. "But Mom, how about poor black folks?" Again her look is incredulous. "Yes, of course, poor black folks were a part of my life.... My mother was a teacher whose mission it was to teach *every* child ... and my father was a minister who made a point of going among the poor...." She smiles as she again sees the picture of Reverend Morgan in his dark suit with priest collar, often accompanied by his young daughter, carrying the word of God.

In the boys' dormitory at Jackson College, responsible for a large group of youngsters, Charles and Margaret still yearned to experience the full pleasures of solitude and intimacy. They took their noonday meals with their young charges, helped them with their studies, listened for hours to their late adolescent concerns, and responded to the occasional crises. There was precious little time to be alone and no chance to develop a sense of "household." But even in the midst of this communal dormitory scene, Margaret had begun to experience "what it was to be a wife."

In a letter to Lois, one of Charles's sisters who had missed their Vicksburg wedding, Margaret expressed her pride in being the "new Mrs. Lawrence." Her light and joking style reflected Margaret's first attempts to "act like the Lawrences." She was trying "very hard" to rid herself of the Morgan tightness and reticence and adapt to the Lawrences' lively exuberance. Today, she is amused by her self-conscious, twenty-three-year-old letter ("being much funnier than I felt"), and appreciates her determination "to survive" in the midst of the gaiety and openness of Charles's family.

Jackson College
Jackson, Mississippi
June 27, 1938

Dear little Sister:
It's Tuesday morning about eleven and Charles is still holding forth
over at the "schoolhouse." I've just finished my housewifely duties for
the morning and I thought I'd celebrate that and using Charles' type-
writer for the first time by writing you.——Needless to say we're no
end disappointed at your not coming home on the 16th—in fact
we're wading around in fishing boots up here—such is the abun-
dance of our tears. We won't give up tho—we're going to see you
anyhow. You can't work all summer you know—you just can't.
Them's orders!——We so enjoyed your lovely gift and wedding wish.
It kept us from feeling too sad about your not being there. Have you
heard all the details of the wedding? I hear it was right nice. But
then you'll have to listen to every little detail about the wedding
when we see you. We came right to Jackson College on June 5the
(am not getting proper—finger just slipped) and have been here ever
since except for two little sojourns in V'burg. Of course we went to
see Ann quituate (made up word for graduate)—the which she sol-
emnly did in cap and gown of grey. She looked very lovely. Then we
were at home week end before last.——It's lots of fun over here.
Charles, besides being the pride of my heart (if I can only manage to
keep him from reading this letter and at the same time get him to
sign his name—the report card stunt)—as I was saying—besides, he
is the pride of President Dansby's heart and the entire campus—and
his courses are tremendously popular—65 enrolled in one of them.
The courses are Rural Sociology, Urban Sociology, Rural Economics,
and Urban Economics. Meanwhile I go about and blush (??) nicely
when asked, "Aren't you the new Mrs. Lawrence?" There are quite a
number of Utica folk here—I'm sorry I can't remember names. Alas
and alack so many of them are Charles' old girls—e'en his first
love—that I sit at our window all the live long day biting my nails
and bemoaning my fate. We're living in Ayer Hall—the Boy's dorm,
you know, and we've two very nice rooms in which we do some light
housekeeping—featherweight. We have breakfast at home and supper,
but our noon meal we eat in the dining hall. I've had lots of fun
here and I'm enjoying myself no end. Both the students and faculty
are nice and congenial. We've made friends too.——I've liked my
new privilege of reading your letters home. I've read the last two and
have enjoyed following you thru your busy day. You certainly are a

smart girl. Don't let yourself get too tired tho. You've next winter to think of and you mustn't be too tired for that. We talk of you all the time and think of you oftener and wish you were with us even oftener than that. Write us—soon!

> *Love,*
> *Your sister and brother*

At the end of the summer school session, together with Charles's family, the couple took a four-week journey north—to Charles City, Virginia; New York; and Boston—which threatened to undo their newfound intimacy. Packed in the car with Mama Lettie, Papa Major, sister Ann, and Charles, Margaret felt overwhelmed. "I was closeted in with the whole family and that was difficult . . . I sort of retreated into my introspective self." The memories of Papa Major, who was "a quiet presence," and sister Ann, who "felt much younger," are not vivid. But Mama Lettie's image is still powerful. She was "in charge and in complete control" as she filled the front passenger seat next to her son who was driving. Margaret sat in the back, watching mother and son. Charles, with his wide shoulders, steered the car, but his mother called the shots, barking commands and directions. As the miles of road washed in front of them, Margaret felt more and more distant from her new husband—his eyes on the road, her eyes on the back of his strong neck.

The first stop was Charles City, Mama Lettie's old family homestead. The Lawrences arrived amidst the effusive welcomes of their relatives. Lots of hugs and kisses, exclamations of excitement and joy. "Everyone was so thrilled to be there!" recalls Margaret. "It was especially wonderful for Letitia." As the Lawrences got drawn into the extended family circle, Margaret felt more left out. Desperate for a contact of her own, she called her cousin Leah, her matron of honor, who lived in Richmond. They made arrangements for Margaret to travel into the city. "I escaped to cousin Leah's." The Richmond reunion brought a welcome quiet and woman-to-woman talk before having to return to the uncomfortable pilgrimage north.

After a stop in Elmsford, New York, to visit Uncle Charlie— Mama Lettie's brother—and his family, the Lawrences arrived in Boston, their final destination. Each place they stopped, they stayed with family, filling the houses, lining up to wash in the single bathroom, and gathering around tables full of food. Boston had a particular magic for the family. It was Charles's birthplace, and Mama Lettie had grown up in Cambridge. The family had returned to Boston several times during the children's growing-up years, usually for long summer visits. When he was eight, Charles had learned to ride the Boston subway system and negotiate the city all on his own. They all enjoyed returning to the city ways of Boston, which always seemed like a welcome contrast to their life in rural Mississippi. It was very important to have the Boston connection as a source of renewal and identity. Like the Morgan's every-other-summer journey to Harlem, Boston gave the Lawrences a wider angle on life. It was an escape from the provincialism of Utica, Mississippi, a connection to the wider world.

In Boston, the Lawrence family stayed with Aunt Julia—Letitia's sister—her husband, and their three children, Alex, Louis, and Catherine, who "were somewhat older than we were." Again the house teemed with people; the laughter was loud, the conversations boisterous, and the food bountiful. "This house was hopping! . . . Aunt Julia was a great cook. . . . On Sunday morning she would fix fresh rolls, fried fish, oyster stew, and beans." Margaret felt as if she were watching a three-ring circus, looking at a family scene that was both attractive and frightening. "I felt so unrelated."

Margaret did manage to make a quiet connection with Alex, the oldest cousin, who was a studious and gentle man. They would have long conversations together on the front steps or go off on leisurely walks. Alex expressed an interest in Margaret's life. He was intrigued by her combination of driving ambition and inner peacefulness, and softly questioned her about her medical studies and plans for the future. He, too, thought the Lawrences were a "noisy lot," sometimes difficult for quiet, reticent souls to be with. "I found him very comfortable," says Margaret appreciatively. "What a relief!"

One afternoon, toward the end of their Boston visit, Margaret and Alex went off together. The household was busy, as everyone prepared to go on a big clambake at the beach. The two of them sought some peace and quiet from the family bustle. As they walked and talked, Alex and Margaret lost track of the time. When they strolled back to the house, they were horrified to see the waiting relatives. Margaret felt a riveting panic when she saw Mama Lettie's fury. "I can't remember Charles, but Mama Lettie was really pissed off!" There was a deafening silence as Margaret slipped quickly into the back seat of the car that Charles was driving. Mama Lettie assumed her usual position beside him and unleashed her anger through rapid-fire commands. "Don't go this way . . . go that way . . . turn here." Charles was silent. He seemed very far away. Then suddenly the sound of brakes squealing and crushing metal. Their bodies lurched forward. An accident. Charles, since boyhood the safe and confident driver, had had an accident! Although, as far as Margaret can remember, no one was hurt, the festive clambake that everyone had been looking forward to all day had been ruined by this awful chain of events. First their lateness, then the silence, then Mama Lettie's yelling, then the accident. But most awful was Margaret's sense of having lost her husband. "I was feeling very young, like a child . . . I wasn't relating to Charles as if he were my husband. . . . It was as if I were with strangers under the supervision of Lettie. I thought, 'Oh my God, is this what marriage is about?' This was my real sadness. . . . Thankfully, this was the last time I had to tangle so thoroughly with the family."

VIII

My People's Wound

T H E Lawrence family entanglement, the overwhelming power of Mama Lettie, her new husband distant and withdrawn, the loud crash of car fenders, all caused fear and trepidation in the young bride. At twenty-three, Margaret could only shudder in silence, hoping that the ominous cloud that was hovering over their beginning marriage would drift slowly away and there would be open sky. She had no words to express her grief. Fifty years later, however, Margaret, the psychoanalyst, welcomes the opportunity to revisit the tortured moments of her life. It is she who asks that we spend some time talking about "trauma."

When I interpret this suggestion as a wish to focus on the "traumas of her professional training," Margaret reminds me that "I had my share of childhood trauma as well." By now I know that images are likely to flash into Margaret's mind, and they are usually worth pursuing. The connections often weave a free-floating narrative, "like what happens in analysis."

In the childhood picture that comes to her now, she and her mother are on the train traveling from Vicksburg to New York. At a station close to the end of their journey, a large group of people crowd onto the train and look for seats. They are a raucous bunch returning from a big picnic, white people with foreign accents. Margaret is sitting with her head in Mary's lap. A man swoops in and sees the brown child taking up a seat next to the "white woman" and says, "Make her move that child." When Mary does not move, "Knock *it* in the head," the man bellows. The pain that Margaret still experiences is not so much related to the crude man or his rude ways as it is to her mother's hysterical response, for Mary explodes when she hears the man's threat. She rises up out of her seat and begins to make an impassioned speech about her life in Mississippi—a life where she has been deprived of the company of her mother and sisters; a life of service as the wife of a missionary; a life of deprivation; a life of always giving to others. "My mother was making a spectacle out of herself and doing it on my behalf. . . . I was ashamed of my mother who was exposing herself hysterically . . . on this crowded train. . . . I was embarrassed by her speech." Margaret's words seem to reverberate with the child's pain and humiliation.

A kindly, polite black gentleman calms the hysterical woman, urges her to sit down, and talks her gently into silence. When they reach New York, he helps mother and daughter off the train, hails a cab, and accompanies them all the way to the front door of the aunts' and grandmother's apartment. It is an unusual gesture of kindness, but Margaret remembers the embarrassment of this stranger's attention to her mother; that, too, is part of the lingering trauma. "I was always embarrassed if a man, other than my father, attended to her."

On the heels of this memory of excruciating childhood embarrassment is another one of Margaret as a young woman, again on a train "going somewhere . . . I don't know where." The image that flashes through her mind is no longer of a helpless child but of an adolescent feeling the new sensations of womanhood. "I am wearing a brown and white knit suit. I am alone and I am looking good . . . I am aware of my body . . . and aware of men admiring me. . . . I'm coming into womanhood. I can take care of myself . . . and it feels good." As Margaret describes the brown knit suit, the glorious sensation of independence and sensuality, I am struck by how much she values her independence. The worst traumas of her professional training are perhaps those that made Margaret feel forced into a childlike dependence. When Margaret's dream is threatened by capricious, malicious decisions over which she has no control, she again feels the helplessness of when the brutal man on the train said, "Kick *it* in the head."

The next such moment came in Margaret's senior year at Cornell.

She had concluded her career there with a flourish. As she moved closer to medical school, the momentum and energy of her academic pursuits increased, her grades soared, and she knew with increasing certainty that her dream would be realized. In the beginning of her senior year, she took the medical aptitude exams required of prospective medical students. Margaret remembers that "it didn't so much depend on past knowledge, but on aptitude, on figuring things out." For the first time since she had come north, the girl from Vicksburg managed to do very well on a standardized test. When the dean of the medical school told her she had done "very well" on the examination, she was overjoyed and newly confident. This was another sign that "medicine was right for me."

When the same dean called Margaret into his office toward the end of her senior year, she assumed that this would be the ritualized visit offered to all incoming medical students. She expected that he would offer acknowledgment of her fine work in college and congratulations for her successful admission to medical school. "I took it that everyone was having these conversations with the dean." As she sat in the chair facing the dean, Margaret's mind savored all the anticipated events. "I recall happily considering medical school, looking forward to my graduation, planning for my parents' arrival, working on renting an apartment for them to stay in . . ." Her pleasant reveries were interrupted by the dean's voice, which seemed to be cautious and apologetic even before Margaret could hear the words. Then the message—with all its horror—began to penetrate, and Margaret grew blank and silent. "The dean said there had been a number of meetings of the Admissions Committee about me, that my application had been carefully considered, that I was a very good student and a promising physician, but that I would *not* be admitted. He said he was sorry."

This was impossible. Margaret couldn't believe what she heard. Still stunned, she heard his explanation for the rejection. "You know," he said, without a hint of emotion in his voice, "twenty-five years ago there was a Negro man admitted to Cornell Medical School and it didn't work out. . . . He got tuberculosis." Each of the dean's words was like a knife. There was nothing to say. "I cannot remember my response . . . I *must* have said something. . . ." She left the office in a daze, devastated by the death of a dream she had pursued with all her energy since she was a young girl. "You go along, you make your plans ... you do your work, then suddenly someone has passed a sentence on you. This had been my plan since before I was four- teen ... my parents expected this ... they had taken me seri- ously ... there were my aunts and the ladies in Harlem. Charles was already involved. We already had the plan for the health clinic and social service center in Vicksburg. All these expectations, and I couldn't fulfill them."

She saw the long parade of loyal supporters who believed in her and who had attached their hopes to her dream. She heard their advice and guidance and remembered the gifts of love and confidence that they had so generously bestowed upon her. Now she would have to disappoint them. Margaret sensed that they would feel more than frustration. They would feel the despair of people who have been robbed of their own dream.

Margaret's pain cut right to her soul. "My experience was one of depersonalization. ... It was as if I was lost in a strange world ... I walked around like this for days and days ... I remember one brief conversation with my comparative anatomy professor ... but there was nobody who could really be with me where I was." The reliving of this tale nearly fifty years later brings back the pain and tears as Margaret speaks of a "lost identity." "Who am I?" she wondered.

Somehow out of the depths of despair, Margaret was able to reach out. After days of aimless wondering, she managed to make a tele- phone call to Madeline Ramée, an administrator with the National Council of the Episcopal Church, a group that had awarded Margaret a scholarship for her undergraduate education. With the Regents Scholarship she had at Cornell that paid for her full tuition, her domestic work for room and board, and her money from the National Council, Margaret had managed to sustain herself economically. Miss Ramée was more than an administrator dispensing funds, however. She had developed a great fondness and admiration for Margaret, and they were in constant touch. It was a connection that had special meaning because it had been initiated by Margaret's father. "My father had put me in touch with them, and they very proudly took me on and gave me money."

As she remembers Miss Ramée, Margaret explains how unusual this New York lady was, for she came from a set of sophisticated, affluent society ladies whose benevolence was usually accompanied by a heavy dose of condescension, and sometimes unbelievable ignorance. One evening Miss Ramée had invited Margaret down to the city for an evening of Shakespeare. Dressed in one of her favorite tailored suits, Margaret looked forward to the elegance of the occasion. Miss Ramée had also invited one of her woman friends to go along, eager for her to meet this lovely, intelligent Negro undergraduate from Cornell. At intermission, the friend turned to Margaret, her voice registering both amazement and innocence: "You know, Margaret, I don't see how anyone could object to being related socially to you. . . . You are so *normal*." Margaret says with mischief in her eyes, "I had felt pleased to be going to the theater with these ladies . . . but they must have gotten some kicks out of this as well!"

This mixture of racism, benevolence, and innocence, veiled in polite talk, reminds Margaret of still another such experience. This one took place her first year at Cornell. As the only black undergraduate, "if I walked across the campus, people would stop talking, turn their heads, and ask, 'Who is that?' " One Sunday a white woman from one of the local churches invited Margaret to come and speak about her experiences in Mississippi. The Vicksburg girl responded with style and grace as she told the Ithaca folks about her life in the Deep South. We can only imagine it was not the exotic tale or the rags-to-riches story that they had anticipated. Perhaps disappointed by the girl's sophistication, or perhaps unknowingly resenting it, the woman who had invited Margaret approached her after her talk. Her smile was sugary sweet as she took Margaret's hand. "I am so pleased you came," she gushed thankfully. Then, without skipping a beat: "You remind me so much of a maid I had. The only problem she had was that she would steal." Margaret tells the story with lightness and humor, as if these white "ladies" had done her no injury. They made fools of themselves. "How did you react?" I ask with shock and anger at the humiliation that my mother does not seem to be feeling. "Obviously I remember it. . . . You would think that I would have felt like I had been hit with a ton of bricks . . . but I didn't experience that . . . I felt the way I felt in Vicksburg when a white child yelled

'Nigger' at me ... well, that was *her* problem ... I was not overwhelmed by these things. Living with my parents in Vicksburg, I got a firm feeling about myself.... When this white lady spoke to me in this way, it was *her* responsibility, it wasn't me ... but I checked it in my head and it stayed there."

The stories of the theater and church events are told lightly in contrast to the heaviness and sadness that still clung to the Cornell rejection. While the white women's social patter remained "checked in her head," the dean's words penetrated her soul.

Miss Ramée received Margaret's painful news with a welcome equanimity. She did not share Margaret's panic but moved quickly to think about alternatives. "She wrote back and said, 'Hold on! ... We have contacts at Columbia Medical School. Make your application.'" By now, it was very late in the spring, well past the usual application deadlines, but Margaret moved quickly and Miss Ramée pursued her contacts. Before she knew it, Margaret was on her way to New York to be interviewed by Columbia's Admissions Committee. The stone-faced, gray men sat in a line before her and asked lots of questions, one of which Margaret remembers: "Suppose in your clinical years you go on the ward and a white patient refuses to have you as a doctor. What would you do?" Margaret's response was straightforward and seemed to satisfy the concerns of the committee. "I would come back to my clinical supervisor and I'd ask for another patient." She was admitted. "So that was that," says Margaret of the smooth conclusion to her terrifying experience. "I had fallen apart ... but I came back." When Margaret Morgan was admitted to Columbia Medical School in the fall of 1936, she was the third black medical student and the second black woman to attend, although she was the only black there during her four years of school. She was also one of ten woman students out of a class of one hundred and four.

The only other time in her life that Margaret experienced the same sense of "acute depersonalization"—"floating through space somewhere"—was at the end of her psychoanalytic training sixteen years later. When she had arrived at the Columbia Psychoanalytic Center in 1946, she was the first and only black trainee. The center was dominated by Dr. Sandor Rado, its founder and director. Rado had been a close associate of Freud's and was a major figure in the interpretation of Freudian theory and practice in this country. A short Jewish man of Hungarian background, he was opinionated, outspoken, and uncompromising in his power. The trainees both revered and feared him, treasuring every pearl of wisdom that came out of his mouth. Margaret, although questioning of some of his assertions, had great respect for Rado and admired his single-minded commitment to the field. Margaret remembers one of his favorite homilies to students about the antagonism between religious belief and productive psychoanalysis. Rado's words were unforgettable to Margaret who, of course, was the daughter of an Episcopal priest and a believer. "If anyone applies to you to go into analysis and they say they are religious," Rado warned, "refuse them because they are too dependent." As Margaret listened, her skepticism and resistance did not appear on her attentive face. She did not accept Rado's view but kept her feelings to herself. After Rado's speech, one of Margaret's peers approached her and asked with great concern, "You know how Rado feels about people who are religious. Do you have any worries you'll have trouble?" Her friend was "amazed" by Margaret's response. "I don't intend to tell him," she said without hesitation.

At the conclusion of her training, now thirty-seven and the mother of three children, ages six, seven, and eight, Margaret took the oral examinations required for the final certificate of graduation and was eager to push on with her life. This had been a costly and consuming process, in terms of both time and psychic energy, and she could almost taste the feeling of relief and liberation she would feel when it was all over. On the eve of her departure, having successfully passed the oral examination, Margaret was called into Dr. Rado's office. Just as in the conference with the dean of the Cornell Medical School, she arrived with the expectation of a ritualized, appreciative encounter. After all, she had thrived in her training analysis, successfully completed the required course work, learned a great deal in supervision, and passed the final examination. But, as she was now more sophisticated and skeptical, it occurred to her that the Rado meeting might not be merely ritual or congratulations. She was not, however, prepared for what she heard: "The committee has decided that before awarding you a certificate, you should have a consultation with Dr. Abram Kardiner to see if you need further analysis." This time the blow did not leave Margaret speechless. She was fighting angry and "by now I was free enough to say my piece." "Why?" she inquired. "I won't tell you," Rado shot back. "You'll have to go to Kardiner. That was the committee's decision." "Why can't you tell me?" said Margaret, her voice steady but her insides ravaged. Dr. Rado, unaccustomed to any questioning of his authority, rose from his chair, his body rigid with anger. Margaret looked into his red and contorted face as their confrontation escalated. "You will have to go," he finally threatened, to which she replied, "I refuse to have this consultation." Then there was silence as the two adversaries tried to figure out how to extract themselves from the deadlock. Margaret, her mind racing furiously, offered a compromise. "David Levy has been my supervisor, and Gene Milch, my analyst; I would be willing to talk to one of them but not to Kardiner." But after she offered this suggestion, she asked once again, "Why can't you tell me?" And Rado kept turning away, refusing to answer, as if he were harboring some terrible, unspeakable truth. Finally he spoke the words that ended the session, words that felt unsatisfactory to both of them. Both of their faces showed defeat. "You see Levy, but if that is not satisfactory, you will have to see Kardiner."

"This was on Friday afternoon," recalls Margaret as if it were yesterday. "I made an appointment to see David Levy on the following Monday morning . . . that was a weekend of *suffering*." Once again, the pain was so deep that Margaret "lost her identity." Again the question from the depths of her soul: "Who am I?" This time the loss seemed more severe because she would be taking her family down with her. Charles and the children had been part of this quest. They, too, had made sacrifices and now they, too, would have to endure this blow. Margaret passed through the long weekend in a daze, wandering and detached. "Charles was *there*. He couldn't tell me why this had happened, but he was there. . . . This long investment, all this energy, all these plans . . . had just gone down the drain. Having Charles there with the children meant that I could afford to be out of reach."

Margaret had made plans to see Eugene Milch, her analyst, that very weekend. Weeks before, she had invited Dr. and Mrs. Milch to dinner at their home in Corona, Queens. Her analysis concluded, this was to be a Saturday evening of good food and conversation. "We had grown very fond of one another," says Margaret about a relationship that had a lovely tenderness and mutual respect. With Margaret feeling so crushed, Charles managed the children, cooked the dinner, and made conversation. When she told Milch about the meeting with Rado, "he was furious"; he promised to call David Levy to express his outrage and try to undo the shocking decision.

"This was the longest weekend I have ever lived." Margaret felt like a puppet in the hands of these powerful men. Her fate hung on their impulses, their needs, their fears and apprehensions. The drama was further complicated by the nature of the man whom Rado had wanted to pull into the act, Abram Kardiner. Kardiner, an analyst and professor at the institute, was also the author of *Mark of Oppression*, a popular and controversial book about the Negro psyche. A few years before, when he had been gathering data for the book, he had asked Margaret to be a research assistant. He had wanted her to go into the field and spend several months interviewing Negroes in the Deep South. Margaret had declined his offer. "I said I couldn't do it because I had three children and a husband, and I was in the midst of psychiatric and psychoanalytic training." She was also suspicious of his perspective and his methods, and worried that in his research Negroes might be portrayed as powerless and inarticulate. But she did not mention these apprehensions. It was enough to offer him the facts of her already overcrowded life. Kardiner was furious that this black trainee—the only one he had available to him—would dare to refuse his offer. He needed her to make his work legitimate, and she had the nerve to decline the chance to work with him. From that moment on, he stopped talking to her. "He exploited people like mad," says Margaret, referring to his relationship to his research assistants, who were often forced into the fairly typical but unfortunate position of doing the professor's work and receiving little credit. Margaret knew better than to get caught in that thankless role.

After *Mark of Oppression* was written and published, Kardiner broke the silence. He called Margaret into his office and asked her opinion of the book. "He wanted a pat on the back from me. He had gotten a lot of criticism from Negroes about this book. He, of course, thought he had written *the* definitive book about Negroes . . . and he wanted my assurance." Margaret's voice reveals the distaste she felt for this man who refused to speak to her for years because she didn't permit herself to be used by him and then who broke the silence because he wanted her support and reassurance. When he pressed Margaret for her opinion, she was glad she had not read the book and could simply tell the truth. "All I could do was say I hadn't read it."

How could she possibly go to Kardiner for a consultation about her analytic training? Here was a man who had written a book that many critics claimed misrepresented the psychological life of Negroes—a book that argued in part that ambitious and productive blacks experience so much guilt when they are successful that they eventually become paralyzed and immobile; consumed by ambivalence. How would he see Margaret's ambitions? How would he interpret her motivations? How would he diagnose her state of mental health? She dared not disturb this hornet's nest. "Thank God I refused to see him!"

But the story was even more complicated than Margaret had suspected. The characters were more entangled than she dared believe. The final complication Margaret discovered only years later on a pleasant weekend at the Milches' summer house on Fire Island. With all the children tucked in bed, the adults were savoring the quiet and the chance to talk. The conversation, as it often did, drifted to shop talk and the goings-on at the institute, and Margaret heard herself exclaim, "I can always tell the people who have been analyzed by Kardiner; they are all a bunch of *cold* fish." Her assertion brought side-splitting laughter from Milch and his wife. When she managed to stop laughing, Mildred Milch explained their howling. Kardiner had been Milch's analyst. "Kardiner was my analyst's analyst!" says Margaret, her face still registering disbelief.

When Dr. Rado insisted that Margaret pass through Kardiner's gate before being permitted to exit from the institute, he was exposing her to a web of complicated, incestuous relationships in which no one could be trusted to have a clear and unencumbered view.

On the Monday following the agonizing, long weekend, Margaret arrived at David Levy's office. This was a friendly place and she trusted him. Levy had been her supervisor and they had developed a satisfying, caring relationship. "He was an easygoing quiet man . . . serious, but you knew he was warm." Margaret mostly appreciated his respect, the way he used their sessions to teach *and* learn. She recalls a session when she felt his admiration, and it brings tears to her eyes. "I was telling Levy about using finger paints to help children create changing scenes, scenes that offer them the chance for alternative interpretations about feelings." Levy listened attentively to Margaret's detailed rendition of how she helped the child unravel his feelings and was awed by her sensitivity and wisdom. Even before Margaret finished describing her work, David Levy reached for his phone, dialed a number, and exclaimed to his close colleague, "Henriette [Klein], let me tell you something that Margaret Lawrence did. Isn't that amazing!" Having delivered the good news, Levy hung up and returned to the session with Margaret, urging her to "write this up." This appreciation was deeply satisfying to Margaret. In this highly patriarchal, opinionated, and competitive environment—in this place where so many of her teachers seemed so committed to dogmatic, unyielding views—David Levy acknowledged her special talents as a psychotherapist and admired the way she used her own feelings in her work.

Her appointment that Monday was made slightly easier because she believed he would never want to hurt her. She repeated her conversation with Sandor Rado, trying to remain distant and cool, and trying to pull herself out of her weekend daze. Levy had already heard a short version of the confrontation from Milch, who had called him with the news the night before. He then revealed the terrible, hidden secret that Rado had refused to let Margaret hear. His voice sought clarification but had no edge of condemnation. "Someone told Rado that you had said that you didn't want to work with Negro patients. . . . Is that true?" Margaret couldn't believe her ears. Nothing could be further from the truth. She shot back, "Absolutely not!" Levy's reply was both relieving and deeply troubling. Almost casually, he said, "Well, just forget it then. I'll take care of it."

So easily remedied. Just a phone call from this powerful person would remove the nightmare. "What extraordinary power. . . . In the meantime, I had been devastated for two days, thinking my life was in ruins. The whole thing seemed so unreal. Where did this idea come from? Where did Rado get this accusation which he couldn't tell me? How could they accuse me of rejecting my identification as a Negro? *That* was a lie. That I had never done! Those people who were supposed to be experts on motivation telling me I didn't want to be a Negro." Margaret is raging as she speaks.

How could this rumor have gotten started? Why wasn't it stopped by those mentors who knew her well? Was there anything she had done—some slight slip of the tongue, some almost imperceptible gesture, some challenging question she asked—that might have given them the impression that she was forsaking her people? Were they trying to put a barrier in her path, forcing her to jump extra hoops in order to test her mettle? When she declined Kardiner's offer to work on his research, did he misinterpret her response as a decision not to work with Negro patients? But she had not wanted to work for *him*! Even today, for Margaret it remains a murky mystery. The whole scene still seems "unreal," impossible to comprehend, and she shakes with the memory. Then her voice grows calm as she puts it back in the past where it won't hurt so much. "David Levy was powerful enough to say, 'Let's drop it'... then life went on after that... with just enough scar to remember."

The third experience with racism during Margaret's professional training was not as deeply traumatic as her rejection by Cornell Medical School or the crisis at the end of her psychoanalytic training. At the end of medical school, Margaret applied to several residency programs in pediatrics. Her first choice was Babies' Hospital. She knew it was an excellent program and she was familiar with the place and staff because of its connection to Columbia Medical School. She also wrote applications to hospitals as far away as Chicago and New Orleans, and applied to several that primarily served Negro patients and had large Negro staffs. Although her preference was for Babies' Hospital, Margaret did not have her heart set on it. "I don't remember whether I expected to get in or not."

She did have her heart set on becoming a pediatrician. Ever since she began making plans to become a doctor, Margaret always imagined herself working with children. Even after recognizing that Candy

Man had a congenital illness that she could not have corrected as a physician, Margaret hung onto her original goal. Her impulse to save children remained strong, and she never considered any other medical specialty as she applied for internships.

When the list of those who had been accepted for internships at Babies' Hospital was posted, Margaret's name did not appear. "This was in no way the same feeling as not getting into medical school." However, when Dr. Rustin McIntosh, chief of pediatrics there, called her into his office, his explanation reminded Margaret of the pervasiveness of discrimination, "of what it meant to be the token Negro." "He said he was pleased I had applied . . . that I was well qualified and they had hoped to accept me for internship." By now Margaret knew that such preliminary proclamations were likely to precede bad news. She waited to hear the "but," and one followed rapidly. "*But* since there were no quarters for women interns at the doctors' residences, women interns had to stay in the nurses' residence . . . and the superintendent of nursing had said that they could not possibly accept Negroes in the nurses' residence."

Margaret received the news sadly and quietly. Her sadness came less from the feeling of personal rejection than from her frustration with the discriminatory attitudes and behaviors that were constant reminders of her special vulnerability. This time, instead of being crushed, she was reminded of the unyielding institutional and interpersonal racism. McIntosh's words offered her another painful reason to ruminate about "what it meant to be a Negro." "As I went along, I continued to assess my relationship as a Negro to the world around me, to people and institutions." This "rejection" did not feel like a shocking assault. It felt like the slow erosion of her spirit.

By the time the letter came from Ruth Campbell, the superintendent of nursing at Babies' Hospital, addressed to "Miss Lawrence" (not Dr. Lawrence or Mrs. Lawrence), Margaret gave it only a cool, cynical appraisal. (The letter came from Miss Campbell, rather than from Dr. McIntosh, because the tiny group of women interns had to be housed in the nurses' quarters, and Campbell, as the superintendent of nursing, was the gatekeeper.) Naturally, the letter omitted any mention of the discriminatory policy that had led to her rejection:

May 19, 1940

My Dear Miss Lawrence,
I am sorry to have to tell you that the positions on the intern staff of
Babies' Hospital have been filled for the period January 1, 1941 to
July 1, 1942. It is unfortunate that we are not able to accommodate
all the promising candidates who apply."

Very truly yours,
Ruth Campbell
Superintendent

Miss Campbell's letter came on the heels of another letter from the clinical director at Grasslands Hospital, in Westchester, New York, not far from Babies' Hospital, where Margaret had also applied for a pediatric internship. This time the greeting was partly correct— "Dear Mrs. Lawrence" (still not Dr. Lawrence)—and the rejection had a different discriminatory basis:

We have received your application for internship. According to hospi-
tal rules, we do not accept married internes [sic]. You will note a
statement to that effect in the information booklet which we sent to
you. However, if you wish to leave your application on file, we shall
place it before the Interne Committee, but I doubt it will receive
favorable consideration because you are married.

In an immediate response, Margaret asked that her case be reviewed by the Interne Committee. She did not hold out any hope for a reversal of their earlier decision, but she knew that she would never forgive herself if she did not pursue this matter fully. Within two weeks, the committee returned with the answer she expected:

Yesterday, our Interne Committee met and gave serious consideration
to the various questions of policy pertaining to the selection of in-
ternes for the coming year. Among questions considered was that of
married internes. It was decided that we will not deviate from our
past policy of not accepting married candidates.

The rejection from Grasslands Hospital felt distant and impersonal. It hurt even less than the letter from Babies' Hospital because Margaret had had no prior association with the institution, and because at least Grasslands was willing to honestly convey its criteria of exclusion. The committee's letter felt clearer, unencumbered by personal association or hidden meanings. The Grasslands decision, however, did revive for her the haunting warnings of her aunts and the Harlem ladies. As Margaret quickly put the letter aside, she could picture the Harlem ladies, so defiantly single and so unambivalently single-minded in forging their career paths. Once again she heard the shrill voices of her aunts: "You'll never become a doctor. You'll get married and have a houseful of children." Here was a case where marriage did, in fact, seem to limit her career choices, where the institution forbade the joining of work and family that Margaret had envisioned.

New York

ALONE AND TOGETHER

AFTER getting turned down by Babies' Hospital, Margaret decided to pursue her application for a pediatric internship at Harlem Hospital. Not only was it considered a fine training ground, but it served the community in which Margaret had spent her adolescence. She could remember the sound of ambulance sirens racing through the night to Harlem Hospital; she heard of babies born there, and lives saved there. It was a proud and vital institution. In 1940, most of the interns at Harlem were Italians and Jews, "who had themselves suffered discrimination," although there was a handful of Negro interns and residents. Most of these young doctors were excellently trained, and if it were not for their ethnic and religious backgrounds they would certainly have had their choice of any number of prestigious internships. In addition to the required transcripts from medical school and personal interviews, Harlem Hospital required that prospective interns take a written examination. When Margaret passed the examination and was accepted, she was "very pleased." Not only did she look forward to returning home to Harlem and working with good attendant physicians, she also looked forward to working with colleagues who had a reputation for being politically active. "They were a very smart group that tended to be 'left' . . . some were open Communists . . . others were oriented toward public service and social change . . . very interested in fighting for good medical care for patients."

Life at Harlem Hospital made medical school seem sedate and

sheltered in retrospect. Not only were the patients of different colors and social class from most of the patients Margaret had worked with in her undergraduate clinical training at Columbia, but now she felt more responsibility for them. She was a doctor, still in training, but relied upon as a member of the hospital staff. In Harlem, her eyes opened to the connections between physical illness and community health. She saw how history, culture, and economics shaped patterns of disease in Harlem. She saw the corrosive effects of poverty and racism, and recognized that to be a doctor in Harlem meant fighting against the oppressive conditions of her patients' lives.

Margaret saw a Harlem that she hadn't known as a protected adolescent living with her aunts and grandmother in the Dunbar Apartments. Although her aunts' ever-present fear that Margaret would get pregnant while in their care, combined with their constant warnings about staying away from the city dangers—hucksters, rackets, the numbers, pimps—made Margaret aware that there was another life out there, her own life had been innocent and secure.

As a young doctor, she was introduced to the other faces of Harlem. Margaret took in the scene, sometimes feeling herself a stranger to the grim realities. On the days when she felt overwhelmed, she would sift through her responses in a journal. Her notes to herself recorded the theater of the ambulance rides:

Beautiful Blasphemy

Female age 34 to Male age 40 who had beaten his wife age 35— thrown her out. She had been rescued by female. Male said in presence of cops and doctor "What she had to take her in for. Must be somed'n between 'em

(With hammer à la main) "Take dat back you dirty nigger. Nobody can sinuate dat 'bout me. What I want with her when she got what I got. I'se a man's woman and my paw was mean" Say that again and I'll piss on you till you're green as a lizard. You fucking bastard. Now get out fo' I kill you."

The Law Will Git You If You Don't Watch Out

Female age 35 being transferred to Riverside. Diagnosis. Adv. Bilateral PID. (Pelvic Inflammatory Disorder)
Well I'm glad I'se going. Now maybe he can't find me. . . . The

*man I was livin wit for 4 years. You know I just couldn't git away
from that man. His wife was in the hospital & he went right in there
& beat her up. Dat's what I was afraid of. He would come up here
from Chattanooga. It don't take much—just 10 dollars. And he could
get 10 dollars if he worked hard & come right there & climb thru
the windows. Being nothin but wimmen dere he could do anything
he want to. You say this hospital is cross the water. [The hospital was
on Wards Island.] Dat's good. Maybe he won' fin' me.*

*Liscen—is that the law drivin this. No. Well if it is—I ain't wor-
rin none. Cause if de law get you there ain't nothin you can do
about it. Corse I ain't done nothin as I knows of—but there ain't
nothin you kin do about it anyway. You say dat ain't the law. Down
in Chattanooga cap & badge like that means de law. Corse I ain't
worrin. I gotta get well.*

*You say we on the river—right in dis car. Ain't that wonnerful.
Das right. I wanta ask you. Has you seen one of them thins—like
they had in the hospital—call it radio? radiator? I ain't never heard
of one in Chattanooga—but I heard one on de ward. They say it
look like a can. It play music and talk & can tell what you doin
wherever you is. [She thinks the radio can hear her and knows everything she is doing.] . . . Never had nothin like dat in Chattanoog. [We
arrive.]*

*Well ain't it pretty here. I'se so glad to come. He kin never find
me here.*

At Harlem Hospital, physicians newly minted from medical school
entered into a rotating internship for eighteen months, with three
months of training in a variety of medical services—surgery, medicine, obstetrics/gynecology, pathology, and so on. The rotating internship was followed by six months of a "houseship" (referred to
as a residency in most training hospitals) in which the new physician,
by then having experienced a wide range of clinical services, selected
one for specialization.

The first assignment of Margaret's rotating internship was the
ambulance service, offering her the chance to become quickly acquainted with the underbelly of Harlem life. "People would call the
ambulance for everything." If neighbors heard a domestic battle next
door . . . if someone was threatening a child with a knife . . . if an old
lady woke out of a dream with terrifying hallucinations . . . they'd

pick up the phone and call the ambulance. The interns assigned to the ambulance service worked "twenty-four hours on and twenty-four hours off." At the hospital, "there was a small admitting room next to a tiny, closet-sized space for the ambulance dispatcher . . . and behind this dispatcher's office, there was a spare room with a naked bulb hanging in the middle and four cots where you could flop between calls." When a call came in, the dispatcher would come to the door yelling out the location of the emergency. Margaret, who never had trouble falling into a deep sleep in just a few minutes, would hear the voice penetrating her dreams, wipe the fog from her eyes, and sit up on the edge of the cot. "Even if I was reluctant to go, I somehow never had trouble functioning."

Dressed in her white uniform—jacket, skirt, and blouse—sporting woolen red, yellow, and blue kneesocks, wearing a blue hat with a visor, and carrying her doctor's bag, Margaret was off and ready for action. In the early days, when Margaret rode the ambulance, she and the driver were the only ones to go out on a call. "It was up to the driver, and the kindness of his heart, whether he would choose to leave the ambulance and come in or whether he'd just sit there and wait for my return." Later on, because the young doctors sometimes met with hostility and violence or just needed help parting the crowds, they began having policemen ride on the ambulance as well. With the sirens blaring, they would race to their destination—a knifing in a dark alley, a bloody traffic accident, a desperate woman threatening to jump from the top of an elevated train, or a child lying on the kitchen floor writhing with convulsions. Onlookers would spot Margaret's white uniform and announce the arrival: "Here comes the doctor!" Some would express amazement at the sight of this attractive young woman rushing to the emergency. One man said to the "sweet young thing" he saw tending the patient, "You may be a doctor, but you look like a chippy to me."

Margaret would make her way past the curious crowds with a combination of fear, dread, and excitement—her blood pulsing, her heart quickening, and her head calm and clear. It was almost as if her mind became more sober and precise as the action around her grew more frightening and chaotic. It was intoxicating, this mixing of clarity and chaos, fear and fearlessness. But even more than the excitement, Margaret loved her mission, the chance to make a difference.

Margaret remembers one painful time when she thought a life might have been saved if she had arrived earlier. "I went out on a DOA (dead on arrival)." As he lay there motionless, Margaret felt for the young man's pulse. Nothing. Then she pressed her stethoscope to his heart. Nothing. The silence was especially shattering because this man—strong, slender, and muscular, in the prime of his life— had just returned from the emergency room where they had "found nothing and sent him home." Margaret shakes her head, still feeling the loss. "There was *nobody*. He lived alone. I was shocked and frustrated."

At other times, medical intervention seemed almost miraculous. A woman suffering from asthma seemed on the verge of death—gasping helplessly for breath, the color of ash. Margaret knew immediately what was wrong but not what to do. Thinking quickly, she grabbed the syringe and she pumped a dose of epinephrine directly into her vein. (The epinephrine should have gone into her muscle!) Margaret watched the woman's body shake, shiver, and shudder out of control for a few seconds. "My God, I thought she would die!" Then suddenly the frightening movements stopped and the woman lay there peaceful and bright-eyed. She grabbed Margaret's hand tightly, and said, "Doctor, ain't nobody made me feel well so fast before." Her face broke into a big appreciative grin as the doctor sighed with relief. Margaret enjoys this tale, its drama and its lessons. "In medical school, they taught me how to diagnose *periarteritis nodosa* (nodules along the arteries). . . . They acquainted us with all kinds of strange, exotic diseases that you rarely see. . . . But they didn't tell me how to treat asthma!"

It was not only the fancy curriculum of medical school that sometimes made Margaret feel unprepared to face the ordinary diseases of Harlem, it was also the contrasts in life experiences between the mostly middle-class interns and the people in the community they served. The ambulance ride took her so swiftly from a world she knew and felt competent in to a place where her skills and expectations seemed useless or inappropriate. When Margaret thinks of the contrasting worlds, and the discomfort it sometimes caused her, she recalls an evening when one of her fellow interns—an upper-middle-class, well-trained Jewish woman—decided to ride along in the ambulance with Margaret. Her colleague was eager to see Margaret at work in Harlem, "with her own people." The ambulance call took them to a dilapidated, two-room apartment inhabited by eight people. "There was no privacy . . . no privacy for the sick person to go to the pot." The room felt hot, tense, crowded with people. The black and white doctors surveyed the situation, and as Margaret moved toward the sick patient, she could hear her colleague's shrill voice—a voice that at once expressed innocence, accusation, and alarm. "Do *all* of you live here?" she asked. Her question drew dark, sullen stares. Finally, a cynical voice interrupted the silence—"What kind of people do you think we is, doctor?"—and the room erupted in angry laughter. Margaret remembers feeling the clash of worlds and sensing the treacherous tightrope she walked between them. "I felt embarrassed for her . . . and very uncomfortable . . . I could feel what the folks in the room must have been feeling."

On the way home from ambulance runs, Margaret would often feel ravenously hungry. She could hardly wait to go to the hospital's kitchen, which was a friendly place, open each night until midnight. She would ask one of the cooks ("I always made friends with the folks in the kitchen") to fix her an egg sandwich, and then make a "critical" inquiry: "Do you know how to cook a hard egg?" Sometimes the new staff did not know Dr. Lawrence's special brand of hard fried eggs ("with the yolk broken and the whites very crisp"), so Margaret would heat up the skillet, take the spatula and demonstrate. The details of the egg fry are vivid. Margaret can still feel the satisfaction a good egg sandwich brought to her weary body. When the ambulances rolled in after midnight and the kitchen was already closed, Margaret would find a fellow intern who was also working the night shift. They would walk over to Lenox Avenue to one of the soul food joints and fill up on ribs, sweet potatoes, corn bread, and greens. "Or the Jewish boys [fellow interns] would come up from downtown with big packages of chopped liver and rye, lox, bagels. . . . They'd rap on our doors, we'd all pile out of our rooms, and go eat together."

Margaret's introduction to the other faces of Harlem brought new commitments. She joined other interns and residents who saw the need to link medicine with social and political action. Many of them became active members of the Interns Council of America, a group that pressed for better medical care for poor patients. Margaret remembers the gung-ho spirit of this group, energetic, outspoken, and militant, and also the feeling of camaraderie as they pursued these broader responsibilities. "We would go down to the Board of Estimate [of the city Public Health Services] dressed in our white intern uniforms. . . . We would demonstrate and try to petition for more funds for patient care. . . . I remember one time going down for a hearing and meeting with the commissioner of health who used to be director of the School of Public Health at Columbia. He had known me there. When he saw me with this protesting bunch of interns from Harlem, he said, 'Margaret Morgan, what are *you* doing here?' . . . He couldn't believe that I was part of this rabble!" The commissioner remembered the quiet, studious medical student at Columbia, and her transformation into an outspoken activist surprised and disturbed him.

Much to her amazement, Margaret occasionally found herself speaking for the group. She could feel the anger and passion rise as she stood up on behalf of patients' rights or better working conditions for the hospital staff. She always felt great anxiety as she voiced her concerns publicly, but she never fell apart. The activism felt good and brought her a new kind of self-assurance. The night before the presentation she would jot down an outline of the major points she wanted to make. In front of the audience, the dry outline seemed to come alive.

1. Harlem Hospital ambulance serves the majority of the population in the place of private physicians.
2. The H.H. ambulance makes an average of 125 calls in 24 hours. On bleak winter days 250 calls, on dull summer days 95.
3. The types of cases vary from mild headaches and measles to cases for which hospitalization is necessary.
4. In 1940, 4000 of the 40,000 ambulance calls made ended in hospital admission. 10% of the calls were hospital cases.
5. The home relief [visiting nurses] set-up is inadequate to care for even home relief patients and the patients prefer the ambulance to the clinic. Urgent calls are delayed.

6. This method of medical care for the Harlem population is inadequate as far as medical service is concerned and wasteful financially to the city.
7. Private physicians who actually are not in excess if Harlem patients could use them are deprived of the opportunity to serve this population.
8. This condition exists to a lesser degree in other hospitals in the city.
9. There are several plans offered to alleviate this condition
   a. Enlarge the Home Relief set-up.
   b. Distribute patients to neighborhood physicians—who would be city-paid.
   c. Establish a home medical service set-up with physicians who from a central office would serve the poor of Harlem.
10. The magistrate's committee to study Harlem should be made interested in the problems of medical service to Harlem.

The first year of Margaret's internship at Harlem Hospital was active and exciting. She felt comfortable in Harlem and glad that the fates had brought her back home. She found new friends and comrades who shared her commitments to first-rate medicine and social change. And finally she was doing what she wanted to do: being a doctor, working with her hands, healing. She knew she had found her calling.

Even in a landscape that often felt strange and ominous, the sense of familiarity, of being "home," ran deeper. As Margaret fought for Harlem Hospital, for the Negro community, for the survival of black babies, for Candy Man's memory, she saw images of her own childhood. She wrote about these later in her career:

Throughout my life I have felt that I never wholly left Harlem after the age of three. I was born in New York, but not in Harlem. Negroes in 1914 lived, among other places, in the West 60's and my mother had come there to have her baby. Grandma had arrived in the West 60's not long before, from Richmond, Virginia. I was not born in Harlem Hospital, where my first child was born, but in Sloane's Hospital for women, which later moved to Columbia-Presbyterian Medical Center. I went to medical school there in 1936.

Some years later, my Aunt took a picture of me on 137th Street between Lenox and Fifth Avenues. She shot the photograph from the apartment window, and one could hardly tell that there were two people, one very large and one rather small. Harlem Hospital loomed up behind us. It looked very big. Grandma moved to 137th Street because it was a good neighborhood, and not too expensive. Two years later, when my mother and I made our bi-annual trip to Grandmother's . . . Grandma had moved to a swankier neighborhood on Seventh Avenue and 141st Street. There was a park with nice green plantings in the middle between the uptown and downtown sides of the street. Parades passed nearly every Sunday. In those days, nearly all of Grandma's friends went to Harlem Hospital when they were sick, and called the ambulance freely.

(*Young Inner City Families*, 1975)

Yes, Harlem Hospital was home. Margaret could hear echoes of her own adolescence as she rode the ambulance through the dark, throbbing city streets as a young intern.

Columbia Medical School, thirty blocks to the north, had been a vastly different experience. Here Margaret had found the pleasures of disciplined retreat, not the excitement of adventure and commitment that she felt later during her internship. In medical school, she kept her eye on the clear connections between the curriculum and her dream. Unlike many of her classes at Cornell, there was no wasted motion. Her days were filled with study, in lectures, laboratories, and libraries, and she went from one to the other, hardly looking up from her work. With persistent and focused study, Margaret was successful, winning good grades ("not extraordinary but very respectable") and the distant respect of her professors and classmates. Never once did she doubt her purpose or wish to turn back.

Not only did Margaret feel that she could finally see a clear path to her goal, she also loved the nature of her work at Columbia. Her particular strengths seemed to match the requirements of the curriculum. She discovered her incredible ability to commit pictures to memory after studying them carefully. Anatomy, with its detailed drawings of skeletal structures, became an engaging exercise once she put her mind to it. Biochemistry also appealed to Margaret. "Preclinical medicine came easily to me. You had to learn it, so you learned it . . . much of it by rote. I was very methodical about it." Most of the basic science courses she took demanded exactly what

Margaret seemed to possess: stamina for study and concentration, a good memory, and a penchant for detail.

Margaret lived on the second floor of Bard Hall, the residence hall for medical students, where the women occupied the first two floors. Her simple dormitory room was distinguished by its view of the Hudson River, the beautiful Palisades, and—if you stretched your neck—the sight of the George Washington Bridge. This scene provided hours of quiet, ruminative pleasure. As Margaret composed her daily letters to Charles, she would sit at her desk, gazing out at the view—so stark and angular in the winter, so soft and lush in the spring—and feel comfort in her connection to the river. Every evening she would turn on her radio to the same station that Charles was listening to in Atlanta and they would "share the experience together," almost a thousand miles apart. Except for very occasional dining out, Margaret ate all her meals in the cafeteria, usually with other women students, trying to ignore the flat taste of the mediocre food. To pay for her meals, Margaret worked in the kitchen drying silverware, a mindlessly repetitive job that seemed almost attractive to the medical student whose mind felt constantly overwhelmed by new material.

In the third and fourth years, when her studies became more clinically based, the appeal of medical school remained just as strong, but the attractions were different. Now Margaret was working with patients, and her work required much more than the memory of facts or the understanding of empirical relationships. The practice of medicine was relational; it depended on developing trust with patients, learning how to listen to their stories, and piecing together the diagnostic puzzle. In the practice of medicine, Margaret felt even more at home. She was competent, even skilled, at digesting the sciences in which medicine was rooted. But there was heart and soul in clinical medicine, and as soon as she was allowed to taste it, Margaret knew it was right for her.

Margaret remembers the formality and ritual of the hospital rounds, when the medical hierarchies were expressed visually in the way "people fanned out . . . students at the very back." Often they would have to stand for hours, barely able to see from their place on the fringe and hardly able to hear the whispered diagnoses. Margaret never knew when the attending physician would cut through the crowd with his sharp voice demanding a response from her, so she strained to catch snippets of talk. Margaret's friend Claire, who suffered from hypotension, had trouble standing for too long. At any moment, she would fall over in a dead faint and "I would catch her."

Claire's passing out reminds Margaret of a strange experience she had during her first observation of surgery. She was standing alone in the small, glass-enclosed balcony overlooking the operating room. She looked down, saw the body opened up, and then saw black. Nothing but black. "I had lost my vision." She opened and shut her eyelids trying to bring back the image, moved her head about, talked to herself, hoping to discover she was dreaming. But she saw only black. With her hands out in front of her, she felt her way along the glass windows, out of the balcony, then down the steep stairs. Once in the hall, she moved slowly with her back pressed along the wall, feeling her way to the elevator. She backed into the elevator, guessed at the correct button, and finally landed where she wanted to. Margaret can't remember when the blackness gave way and her sight returned. But she can still feel the panic of this episode of "hysterical blindness": the darkness that enveloped her, which she feared might surround her forever. Her account feels cool compared to the moments of terror. "It didn't last long and it never came again . . . this [the surgery] must have been something I didn't want to see . . . so I became temporarily blind."

Throughout her clinical years, Margaret was also haunted by another, less terrifying but uncomfortable apprehension. As she began seeing patients on the wards, Margaret could hear the stone-faced man on the Admissions Committee who had asked her: "What will you do if a patient refuses to see you because you are a Negro?" Margaret had answered calmly, but now that she was facing the real situation, she did not want to have to test the cool resolve she had expressed in the admissions interview. "Always in the back of my mind was a worry about the possibility of patients rejecting me because I was a Negro." Happily, she never had to face an explicit rejection. No patient ever refused her. In this hospital, where it was rare to see a black patient, most reached out and pulled her toward them. "Sick people are waiting to be taken care of . . . they are hungry for company. They also hoped I might know something more about what the doctor was thinking. They would try to use me to interpret information."

Margaret had never worked so hard at, nor been so rewarded by, her schooling as she was at Columbia. The work rarely felt grinding or distasteful. Most of the time, it felt challenging and productive. "I was a willing part of the structure . . . I didn't object to anything." When she was not in the library, in class, or on the hospital wards, Margaret found welcome companionship. Among the ten women in the class, several became Margaret's devoted friends. With ten, they could avoid the meanest distortions of tokenism and buffer each other from whatever discriminatory assaults came their way. Margaret and her friends relished the company of women in a sea of men—sharing dreams and fears, inhibitions and temptations; sorting out the responses of the institution to their presence. They were unusual women, pioneers, and Margaret felt identified with their ambition and drive. She has warm memories of sitting with women friends in their rooms in Bard Hall, telling stories, laughing, singing, knitting . . . charting career plans. All these women were aware of the doubts of male peers and professors who felt they were "wasting" seats in the class—who believed the women would get married, have babies, and never practice medicine. But you could tell from the determination in these women's eyes that they did not plan to waste their training.

All ten women graduated from Columbia University Medical School. All ten had distinguished careers, as clinicians, academics, and researchers. Each year, for the next thirty-five years, the women met annually for an elegant lunch at Jean Luke's house. As an adolescent, I remember fetching my mother from one of these lunches and finding the women sitting around the table finishing off their lemon soufflé and fancy cookies. Some were dipping their hands in dainty, antique finger bowls. This was light-years away from how our hustle-bustle family lived, and I could sense the contrasts between my mother and her best friend from medical school days. But more impressive to me than the finger bowls was the sense of history and kinship among these women—the support and mutual respect that seemed to warm the reunions.

Margaret was not a token women. She was a token black. Two

blacks had preceded her through Columbia University, a man and a woman, so she was not the first. But in the four years she was at Columbia, Margaret was the only black student. The sting of her isolation was somewhat diminished by her women friends, but not completely. Her professors and peers slowly got used to her demure, black presence and would occasionally offer her the kindest compliment they could think of: "Margaret, you don't even seem like a Negro . . . you fit in so well." She knew they meant well. She even knew they spoke out of some combination of ignorance and innocence. But their "compliments" still caused her discomfort, a knot in the pit of her stomach.

A picture of Margaret, with her two white male laboratory partners, reminds her of how she was perceived by her peers in medical school and brings back the small pleasures she derived from her exotic status. In the photograph, the three of them, dressed in lab coats, are in their anatomy class hovering over a female cadaver. Margaret struggles to remember the name of the cadaver whom the students revisited every time they were introduced to another organ. She cannot retrieve her name, but she easily recalls the names of her laboratory partners— Hank Standwick and Chuck Russell. She speaks their names with affection and talks about the easy way she reminded them of her origins. "They were very comfortable to be with. They would enjoy my jokes; they liked to hear stories of my life. I would sometimes sing spirituals." As Margaret would croon the melancholy notes of "Nobody Knows the Trouble I've Seen" or shout the hopeful beat of "Walk Together Children, Don't You Get Weary," Hank and Chuck would listen intently, as though hearing sounds from a distant land, relishing the strange and seductive strains. In turn, Margaret relished the attention and enjoyed being the stranger. As we examine the photo, she points to Chuck Russell who has his eyes fixed on Margaret. "You can see how he was looking at me, a little surprised and sort of admiring. Mostly, these people had never seen a Negro or had any contact with one, so I was amazing to them and somehow I didn't mind that."

Listening to herself express pleasure in her peers' awe at her dark and luminous presence, Margaret is momentarily pensive. She struggles with describing her mix of feelings—the difference between

1937, when she enjoyed the special attention of her tokenism, and 1987, when she is understanding, but critical of, her responses. "I can remember being self-preoccupied, with what you'd probably call 'narcissistic' tendencies . . . Now I distinguish between 'positive' and 'negative' narcissism. With 'positive narcissism' you have a sense of your own self-worth. If you don't know your own self-worth, then you have to pretend . . . in 'negative narcissism' you have to keep checking yourself out with others. . . . I remember praying about being preoccupied with myself. It's hard to say when I began to recognize that I needed to be thinking more of other people." In her mind, Margaret's sense of self-preoccupation is joined with her response to the benign racism that crept into her relationship with her laboratory partners. Singing spirituals, sharing stories, making jokes, were all ways that she found to lighten the heavy role of stranger. Even as she relished the attention, she knew it was not the stuff on which to build a strong self-image.

For the most part, the issue of race did not loom large inside medical school. Margaret was always aware of "what it felt like to be a token Negro," but she experienced very few malignant racial encounters. As soon as Margaret hit the streets of Washington Heights, however, she felt diminished by her Negro status. In her book *Young Inner City Families*, Margaret traced these continuities of racism in her own life:

> History, in fact and in symbol, contains the germ of the future. In my own life, I walked across the street from my childhood Mississippi home again and again to hear the story of a doctor-husband tarred and feathered and run out of town because he dared to treat white patients. Years later, in Washington Heights, while a medical student at Columbia Medical Center, intending to vote for the first time for a president of the United States, I had to take a "literacy test." I framed the certificate of literacy. On the same streets I had several offers of "day work."
>
> (*Young Inner City Families*, 1975)

The oblique racism encountered during her medical school years contrasted with the unambiguous quality of racism in Vicksburg, Mississippi. Despite the prejudice in this "benighted place," she was made to feel strong and confident. "To be able to say over the telephone as a child, when someone called and asked 'Is Morgan there?' . . . to say 'you mean my father, the Reverend Mr. Morgan?'" showed ten-year-old Margaret's ability not to let the white world undermine her sense of self-worth. The great separation between the two worlds is evident in Margaret's memory of having "crashed" a special centennial celebration service at Christ Church, the white Episcopal church in Vicksburg. It was a "state occasion," and Margaret was intrigued and decided on her own to attend. The young brown girl arrived at the door of the church filled with white people. She felt adventurous, not scared. "I was greeted by the usher and led up to the front pew to sit down." "But how did the parishioners react?" I ask. Margaret seems not to have paid very much attention to the sea of white faces. "Well, you know, it was usual that when white folks visited black churches they would always be ushered up to the front . . . I guess they thought, here was a little squirt who had dared to come in . . . who certainly didn't belong with the white folks . . ." Her voice trails off. The service proceeded smoothly and without incident, and Margaret left, having now successfully crossed the rigid color line, feeling no sense of victory, only interest and amusement. "You handled most of life living completely separately." The separateness, so deeply ingrained in people's psyche, had a protective and clarifying dimension.

This clean-cut separation of races was very different from the Northeast. Margaret had anticipated the relief of integration and instead found discrimination in more veiled and ambiguous forms. "When I moved to the 'integrated' Northeast, I felt discrimination as more of an attack." She never knew when racism would appear and in what form. She would begin to get comfortable in a setting, begin to trust the people surrounding her, and a subtle remark or gesture would make her feel vaguely uneasy. Then the dull pain would come and Margaret would try to discover its source. In the Northeast, so much energy had to be put into fathoming the scene, discerning the nuance, and waiting for the surprise attack.

Several years later, when Margaret was at Columbia's Psychiatric Institute, the first and only Negro resident, racism subtly insinuated itself into the clinical work with patients. Her white colleagues, sophisticated and worldly, welcoming of Margaret's presence, would offer their Negro patients patronizing and limiting care. Margaret would listen as they explained to her, "We can only give this [Negro] family *supportive* therapy because they can't use anything deeper." Her colleagues, of course, felt fully justified in these clinical assessments. But Margaret tasted the bitter discrimination, for herself and for the black patients who came through the institute. Two decades later, she wrote about the distance between occasions in her southern childhood filled with honor and sustenance and others at this northern psychiatric institute where Negro patients were often treated as second-class citizens:

> The distance does not seem far between the rural Thanksgiving table, groaning with food, provided by a "grass widow" member of my father's church and made elegant by her admonition to one of her sons, "Brother, take your elbows off the table," to the conference room in a psychiatric institute devoted to research. When I heard there that a ten year old black boy and his mother were not suitable for psychodynamic psychotherapy, and that recourse had to be taken, in our despair, to "supportive measures," my mind began to drift to one of these older rooms in my own history.
>
> (*Young Inner City Families*, 1975)

Sometimes these contrasts made her want to correct the arrogant perceptions of northeasterners toward the "unenlightened South." "In my analysis, I remember arguing with my analyst (who was *not* arguing with me), 'Don't think I grew up thinking I was nobody. This was not the case. In Vicksburg, I felt like someone special." And Margaret's last declaration from the couch, just before concluding her analysis, spoke of her commitments to the full development of her "self" and the liberation of her people. "At the end of my analysis I remember saying 'The thing of first importance to me is knowing myself as a person . . . the second thing was making my contribution as a Negro. My concern as a person was for myself and others. My concern as a Negro had to do with the welfare of the Negro people."

Even with the strong finale that concluded her analysis—powerful words of self-affirmation—Margaret admits to "layers of response" in relation to her training in the Northeast. As a medical student at Columbia, she did very well, "felt very comfortable," "had good friends," "felt productive and rewarded." That was the top layer of response to her medical training, smooth and successful. But there was another, deeper layer of response that Margaret feels viscerally. Almost fifty years later, when she goes back to visit Columbia Presbyterian Hospital, a feeling of "self-consciousness" comes over her when she gets on the elevator. "Something about getting on the elevator ... I think it's the closed space ... I feel especially self-conscious about my hands ... I think, if only I had on my white coat, I could put them in my pockets."

As Margaret tells the story, she holds out both her hands in front of her, and they tremble slightly. "Here I am, black as you see me." Her voice is full and tearful. "Here are my hands, *exposed*.... I am in the elevator, confronted with the difference." Margaret's laugh cuts through her emotion as she describes her response. "An infant will put something over his head and think that you can't see him ... maybe if I put my black hands in my pockets, they won't notice the difference!" The ravages of racism run deep, penetrating the subterranean layers of the soul. Even when you emerge victorious and sing songs of sweet success, there are wounds that are not thoroughly healed. For Margaret, the feeling of being in the elevator at Columbia Presbyterian Hospital opens up the old wound of self-consciousness. "You can recognize the difference between the level at which I lived happily ever after and the deeper level. When you dig more deeply, the difference makes a difference."

It was after Margaret's second year of medical school that she and Charles were married. Although they had been "promised to each other" for at least four years, they both finished college and moved onto two years of postgraduate work before they dared get married. Even then, they knew that their studies and career plans would force them to live apart. After the June wedding and their summer together in Jackson, Mississippi, Margaret had returned to medical school at Columbia and Charles had continued his graduate training in sociology at Atlanta University. He supported his studies by working full-time as an English teacher in one of Atlanta's junior high schools and serving as a dormitory counselor at his alma mater, Morehouse College.

While Margaret memorized formulas with single-minded purpose, Charles struggled with finding the connections between scholarship and activism. As they pursued these separate paths, Margaret and Charles hung onto their plan to open up a center for social and health services in Vicksburg. In the fall of 1936, when Margaret had just started medical school, Charles had written to the Episcopal bishop of Mississippi seeking support for this plan:

October 6, 1936

The Rt. Rev. T. D. Bratton,
Chapel Hill
Jackson, Mississippi

My Dear Bishop Bratton:
A few weeks ago, Miss Margaret Morgan of Vicksburg was granted an interview by you for the purpose of discussing the establishment of a social settlement house and clinic at the present site of the Vicksburg Industrial School. She had talked the possibilities of such a venture over with me before her interview with you. Immediately I voiced my interest in the social settlement side of the project. She tells me that you seemed to be favorably disposed toward the idea, and asked that I write and tell you of my interest in the venture.

Margaret has told me that I might write you and speak very frankly concerning the matter. This I shall do. One thing that she neglected to tell you I think is the fact that we are engaged to be married at some future date which is as yet unsettled. I think that I should tell you this in order that you might see the possible advantages or disadvantages in having us work together in this venture.

I have been interested in the field of social welfare for longer than I can remember. For fifteen years my father was a teacher in the Utica Normal and Industrial Institute at Utica Institute, Mississippi. My mother was very active there in community improvement and social welfare. Since 1931 my father has been employed as Boys' Work Secretary at the Vicksburg Colored Y.M.C.A. By this you can see that I have a background of social work. Last June I was graduated from Morehouse College of this city with the degree of Bachelor of Arts. While in college my fields of major interest were economics and soci-

ology. During this time I was very active in extra-curricular activities especially the Orchestra, Band, Dramatics, Debating, and Y.M.C.A. I was president of the Y.M.C.A. during my last year in college and am at the present time a member of the Kings Mountain Field Council of the Student Y.M.C.A.

At the present time I am employed as a teacher in the Atlanta Public School System. This offers a good field of service and a fairly good salary as teachers' salaries go. On the other hand, I have always wanted to return to Mississippi to render whatever service that I can. For a long time I have seen the need of a real community center in Vicksburg where anyone would feel free to come and enjoy the facilities for recreation, study, and fellowship. The difficulty that I have always run up against in my mind is in finding some one to back the project. I truly believe that Margaret and I can do a good piece of work on a much needed task.

Along with my regular teaching work, I am availing myself of the opportunity to advance myself by taking work in Atlanta University leading to the Master of Arts degree. I take this work in the evenings after I am out of school. I am doing my work in the field of Sociology. When I shall have finished my work at Atlanta University, and have secured means wherewith to pursue further studies, I plan to take some special work in community organization.

Margaret and I are collaborating on the plans for the center. I am hoping to see her at Christmas. At this time we hope to finish them and prepare them for presentation to the proper persons.

We greatly appreciate the great interest that you have shown. I am very grateful to you for having read so long a letter. I trust and pray that our plans—now in the embryo state—shall burst forth to be a real source of service to my people for the glory of Him whom we all love and serve.

Respectfully yours,
Charles R. Lawrence, Jr.

Charles's letter followed one from Reverend Morgan to the bishop:

April 17, 1936
Vicksburg, Mississippi

Rt. Rev. and Hon. Sir,
Please permit me to sincerely thank you for your very inspirational visit to us, which indeed meant more to us than can be expressed on

Margaret Morgan Lawrence, St. Mary's Episcopal Church, Vicksburg, Mississippi, 1938

Charles and Margaret Lawrence,
1938

Charles Radford Lawrence II,
1941

Margaret Morgan Lawrence, 1941

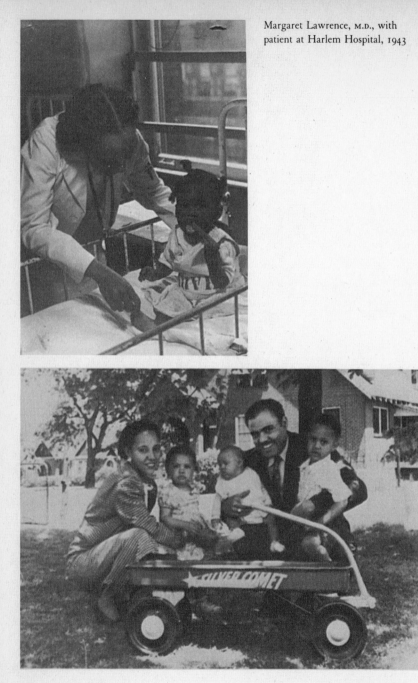

Margaret Lawrence, M.D., with
patient at Harlem Hospital, 1943

The Lawrence family
FROM LEFT: Margaret, Sara, Paula, Charles, and Chuck, Nashville, Tennessee, 1946

Margaret and her children,
Easter Sunday, New York, 1949

Paula, Sara, and Chuck Lawrence, 1949

Margaret Morgan Lawrence, 1983

paper. I am also writing you as you suggested in the interest of Mar-
garet C. Morgan, our daughter, the one of whom I told you . . . You
said, if she desires to be a Missionary Doctor, you would help her. In
answer to this, she said she wants to formally make Vicksburg her
life's work. Starting the Clinic, finally to become an Infirmary. We
have sufficient buildings for a beginning. If need be I will have her
write you and tell you of her plans and will be glad to write you
further myself.

Thank you again for our visit which has meant so much to us.
I am faithfully and humbly,

The Rev. S. A. Morgan

The bishop's response to Charles's letter was immediate and positive. His connections to both the Lawrences and the Morgans made
Charles and Margaret feel a burning optimism. One day the clinic
would be a reality; the plan would be more than a vision!

Oct. 29, 1936

Dear Mr. Lawrence:

I was very glad to find your letter on my return home. Margaret
had already introduced you to me as a kindred spirit with her in the
desire to do social service work for our Negro people, particularly in
the South, for which she is preparing herself. I am hoping to live
long enough to help her initiate the plans which will be maturing
during her medical course.

She interested me in you and I hope that you will continue to col-
laborate with her in her cherished wish. I find I have also another
connection with you through your father whom I have met I think
both at Utica and Vicksburg. I am very glad to hear of your success-
ful college course and of your connection with the Atlanta schools. It
will be a pleasure to hear from you from time to time as your plans
mature and you have time to write me.

With very warm regards, I am,

Respectfully yours,
Theodore D. Bratton

The plan was a major source of bonding during their first year of
marriage when they were forced to live hundreds of miles apart. It

promised a togetherness of purpose and vision and offered a connection to their southern black roots that seemed strained by the tug of professional training in the north. Their plan represented the future. The present was held together by daily, sometimes twice-daily, letters. For Margaret, the letters were deeply sustaining. They were another way of learning to communicate feelings and experiences, and of defining one's self in marriage. There was a need to say things explicitly in writing that might have been assumed in the daily routine of living together. Charles's letters reminded Margaret of her good fortune in marrying someone so skilled and uninhibited in expressing his affection. As though continuing their long talks on the porch swing in Vicksburg, Margaret was challenged to respond, and she could feel herself, long distance, learning the art of building a relationship.

Charles's letters were declarations of love, celebrations of the heart, extravagant expressions of longing and loneliness:

9/13/38
Friday Night 11:15 P.M.

My Own Little Wife,
Despite the fact that this is the frayed end of Friday the thirteenth, I remain the luckiest man alive. I can sit down and write a letter to the loveliest, sweetest and best wife extant and call her my own. It is such a happy thought to know that when this letter arrives Sunday, you will rush to read its contents with as much enthusiasm as I always have in reading yours—though lately I've taken to putting yours in my pocket until I get to my room. It does several things for me. It makes me rush to my room when otherwise I might loiter, it gives me a much-needed lesson in self-restraint, and allows me to enjoy your letter in the proper leisurely environment, surrounded by all the equipment of my room that reminds me so much of you.

9/25/38
Sunday Morning

My Lovely One,
... This is our first Sunday apart since we were married. I miss you even more than usual, however, inasmuch as I have more time to do

so. Yet I am extremely thankful on this day of worship for the great happiness that many future Sundays portend. It is a very beautiful day; and as I sit at my table looking at the Western hills of Georgia, I see the hills that are a symbol of the strength that comes from Him who makes our happiness possible. It is on this strength that I depend to make your absence bearable—a strength which He has thus far given in a measure that I certainly don't deserve....

10/29/38
Saturday Evening 6:00

My Darling Wife,
... I haven't written you for several days because I have been in a state of near-melancholia, so much has been the extent to which I have missed you and longed for you. I didn't wish to convey to you any of that feeling so I refrained from writing. I feel much better now—I guess that these attacks are my form of the "curse." The only difference is that where my presence helps you, your presence entirely obliviates my malady.... I think I shall go over to Spellman tonight to a Halloween Party as a sort of mushroom. I may decide not to go at the last minute ...

Charles's letters also conveyed the everyday rhythms of life in Atlanta:

9 25/38

... Yesterday I did quite an extensive piece of laundry. It included a dozen handkerchiefs one of which I am enclosing since it doesn't fit me, eight suits of underwear, two large bath towels, one small one, five pairs of socks, and three pairs of pajamas. All of these have been pressed. Am I not smart?

10/4/38

... I have moved! The room is going to be very comfortable, and eventually, attractive. As soon as I started moving in a student suggested that I exchange the privilege of cleaning my room for the privilege of paying his way to the show twice per week. An angel must have sent him!

10/14/38

... I came directly from school today past the post office where I received your lovely letter. From there I went up to band rehearsal in the Chapel where I remained until six, and went directly from there to supper. After supper there was a pre-game parade, and I lugged that sousaphone from the A.U. [Atlanta University] Dorm to Graves Hall via the Library. I have helped one frosh with his English, heard Hollywood Hotel, and President Roosevelt, and an interview of the coaches of Morehouse and West Virginia State. By the way, W.S.V. is playing Morehouse here tomorrow, and everyone is enthused. (And there is such a word. I just looked it up.) ...

11/20/38

... At nine o'clock this morning I was at Morehouse Chapel as usual where I heard a good sermon. At eleven o'clock, I was at the Congregational Church where I acted as a guest soloist with the choir— vocal soloist. At four o'clock this afternoon I found myself at Big Bethel Church where our Annual Thanksgiving Teachers' Vespers was being held—our Teachers Choral Group sang and Rev. Mr. Kelsey (Remember?) delivered an excellent sermon. Seven-thirty saw me at the Providence Baptist Church—my church—for a literary program at which I played a trumpet solo. Is this sufficient service for a recalcitrant husband stranded from the finest, sweetest, loveliest, bravest, most considerate wife in the world?

Margaret found her husband's daily record overwhelming. The way he reached out and embraced the world, his energy and commitments, seemed astounding to her. The texture of Charles's days was so dramatically different from her own. As Margaret went through the predetermined routines of medical school, Charles put together the various pieces of his life—weaving together his work as a junior-high-school teacher, dormitory counselor, and graduate student, and finding the connections between his political agendas and his academic pursuits. There were so many people in Charles's life—people who depended on him to offer guidance and support. Margaret felt fortunate in her primary responsibility to herself. Charles carried his responsibilities with a seriousness that resembled the fatherly role he had always assumed in relation to his siblings. Sometimes these obligations tugged at his loyalties and emotions, and he would use his letters to talk to himself as much as to his wife:

11/4/38
Thursday evening 7:40

My darling Margaret,
... I think I mentioned slightly the fact that I remained up until four Wednesday morning. The trouble was this: Some boys had complained to Mr. Williams and me that there had been some peculiar action in the adjoining room. We went up and talked to the man who had complained and his roommate. They suspected their neighbors of homosexuality. We did not enter the room in question inasmuch as we thought to do so would only run whatever existed—or might exist—"underground." About two o'clock I was awakened by a knock on my door. When I opened it I found a boy there—the boy who had complained—crying, "Mr. Lawrence, we've caught them in the act!" I pulled on my bathrobe and found that the boy was telling the truth. Several boys had actually found the two boys in bed together with all of their clothes off. Since then we have been trying to work out a satisfactory solution to the sordid mess. We don't wish to punish the boys, but to help them to reconstruct their lives. Between this and the last paragraph one of the boys involved came in. We talked over his future plans. He has suffered a great deal; has been close to suicide, he reports. Everyone has tried to help him. He thinks all of us have been, not only kind, but helpful. Both boys will have to leave the institution as part of their attempt to reconstruct themselves. Yet I think each of them will know that those of us who have to do with working with them have tried to do our best to act as friends rather than censors or police....

When Charles wrote about his intellectual work and his career commitments, he showed his greatest ambivalence, an uncertainty that was both attractive and baffling to his young bride who had no such stirrings in her heart. How could she support him through these struggles and where would they lead?

9/27/38

... I was by to see Ira Reid last evening. He suggested several problems on which I might work. The one I liked most was on Negro

Homicide in Atlanta. He thinks that if I work hard on this one I should be able to get a Rosenwald, and if I do well, get it renewed after a year. Wouldn't that be wonderful?

11/3/38

... The problem on which I am to work is one which will cause me to take a major in population problems and theory and a minor in anthropology. This means that I will have access to the best men at Columbia in the Department of Sociology, namely Chaddock, Mac-Iver, and Klineberg. I think that it will be a problem in the social history of special groups. It sounds challenging and will take a great deal of time. Pray that I may have the perseverance to work hard and get something decent ready to go to the Rosenwald people.

Even as Charles searched for an intellectual "problem" that would galvanize his energy and intellect, he admired Margaret's steady focus, which seemed to make his indecision seem less threatening. In fact, he was warmed by the "reflected glory" that Margaret's accomplishments allowed him. Charles's declarations of love were often accompanied by pride in his wife's career, a double message that was reassuring to Margaret and made her feel optimistic about combining family and work:

9/27/38

I am as proud of you as I have every right to be. I have exhibited the Times *clipping until it's frayed and torn, yet I've protected it with all my heart. Don't I have every right to be proud of you? ... you are a woman of whom any man might well be proud. Your accomplishments only add to my joy. ...*

9/29/38

... At this point (two hours ago) the Courier *newsboy came in and said, "Mr. Lawrence, I know you are going to buy a paper this morning, your wife's picture's in it." I almost tore it out of his hands. If I didn't know they were underestimating you I would have expected a bill for publicity. It's wonderful, Lil' Precious! Yet, you de-*

*serve every word of it—and more . . . By the way are you wearing
lipstick all the time or only for pictures? Or does the camera just give
that illusion? . . . Of course, I ran straight for Miss Usher and the
other faculty members to show you off. Pride was fairly oozing out of
my pores and my eyes and I was smiling my broadest grin. I am
easily the world's proudest husband.*

10/1/38

. . . The article in the Courier *has really boosted our collective stock.
You have no idea how much better I am looked upon by my friends
and associates. I am justly proud.*

10/29/38

*. . . Congratulations on the fact that you have completed "Fractures!"
The way you have worked with this particular phase of your course
causes me to agree—as I have always agreed—with the sentiments of
the janitor who says that you will "get somewhere in the world." . . .*

Both Margaret and Charles counted the days until Christmas, when
they would be reunited. They marked off the days on their calendars
and indulged their fantasies about the reunion. With their meager
resources, they often found it hard to scrape together even the money
for stamps. Telephone calls were a rare extravagance. Once, between
September and Christmas, they permitted themselves the pleasure of
hearing each other's voices. It was bittersweet.

11/3/38
Thursday evening 7:40

My darling Margaret,
  *Less than an hour ago I was talking to you, listening to your voice
as we talked for two and one-half minutes: the most precious minutes
I have ever known. As I said to you, it was wonderful to hear your
voice. When I walked in to that booth, I was a lonely man. Since
Sunday, I had been contemplating that call, and had planned to
make it Saturday night in celebration of our fifth luniversary. But
somehow I could not wait. I had to talk to you tonight; just hear*

your voice. When I left the booth, I was a happier man; I was exhil-
arated, joyful—yet saddened, ever so slightly by the fact that I could
only talk to you for less than three minutes. I started over to the
Library to do some reading—actually went into the building—but
realized that I was too disturbed—by my own happiness—to do con-
centrated work. I love you almost too much, my Darling Wife. I
hope we never have to spend another year so far apart....

For both of them the Christmas reunion in New York loomed bigger than life, and Margaret worried privately about these great expectations. Was it not inevitable that they would feel disappointed if they anticipated too much? For months she followed the enter-tainment sections of the newspapers and consulted Charles about which theater and concerts they would splurge on. She carefully arranged her academic commitments so that she would feel freer about taking time off when Charles arrived. "I wanted to experience fully our short time together!" While Margaret schemed to create the perfect conditions for their ten-day reunion, Charles measured his contentment by the distance until Christmas:

11/20/38

... This is a beautiful night. It is one of the many nights when I
have an acute longing for the joy of having you with me. The fact
that it is slightly cool reminds me that it is just a little more than a
month until I shall have the joy of holding you in my arms. The
only fear that I have is that I shall not be able to let you go....

Although Charles's letters were uninhibited in their joyous expec-tations, he, too, showed some signs of apprehension:

11/8/38

... I ruefully admit that in the last three months I have developed a
bald spot and added three inches to my waistline. I tell you this in
order that you might be prepared for the worst....

Beyond Charles's minor worries about his wife's response to his slightly changed physical appearance (and his typical self-deprecatory humor), he was harboring a deeper concern. As he anticipated the trip north, he began to feel uneasy about being pulled into the Smith women's web. Mom Margaret had died, but Aunt Hazel and Aunt Ninnie were still living in one of the posh sections of Harlem, the Dunbar Apartments, and Margaret had arranged for the newlyweds to be housed at their apartment. But Charles was traveling to New York to be with his wife, alone. He knew that if they accepted the aunts' hospitality, the visit would be diminished. He knew that unless he resisted their intrusions, the aunts would dominate their days, demand Margaret's allegiance, and move him to the periphery. In addition, he felt that he couldn't count on his wife to be fully aware of the dangers. After all, she had had years to learn to handle the aunts' controlling ways. She was deft in the skills of avoidance, silence, and adaptation. Besides, she was a woman. How could she ever know how men felt in the presence of these powerful and unforgiving sisters?

It wasn't that the aunts were ever rude to Charles. They were far too civilized to be less than polite to "a stranger." As much as they could like any man, they liked Charles. They particularly liked his fair skin ("They were glad he wasn't black; I had redeemed myself finally, I think"), and were also proud of his fine upbringing and superior education. But even though he had their distant respect, Charles noticed the way their noisy gossip and easy rapport would cease whenever he entered the room. Suddenly the aunts would freeze into haughty stone statues, silent and inscrutable. He also noticed that when he was around, the aunts seemed to pick on Margaret more, as if she were taking the resentment that they did not dare inflict upon him. Margaret remembers the heightened assaults. "If they had anything mean to say, they managed to say it to me or about me." The thought of sharing the apartment with the aunts, even for a short time, seemed intolerable to Charles:

11/4/38

... With the Aunts in their present state of interference do you think it wise for us to impose on their hospitality? Of course, other than there and Uncle Charles', there is no place for us that we can afford

in New York. However, there is Atlanta and train fare is the same both ways....

11/22/38

...I am disturbed at the rather officious attitude of your Aunts...I must agree that they are getting into our domestic affairs. First they send a wedding present to a couple with whom neither of us is intimately acquainted. Then they are kind enough to buy cards and have them inscribed altogether without any knowledge nor apparent concern about our own ideas of the cards that we are to send out. It's bad to waste two dozen Christmas cards, but my male ego would hardly allow me to sanction a card inscribed "Margaret and Charles Lawrence Jr." It sounds much more like two unrelated people than would "Charles and Margaret Lawrence" (without the Jr.). Though we believe in complete sex equality, it is still customary to sign the husband's name first when something goes out from a happily married couple. Plus, I don't like not being able to pick my own Christmas cards or have you pick them—Now that's off my chest...

12/12/38

...Margaret, I am convinced that in light of present circumstances we shall be imposing unduly on your Aunts...I am afraid we shall take all of the privacy away from the apartment and be generally a nuisance. For this reason I am again doubting the wisdom of my coming to New York this Christmas. I have even considered postponement of seeing you until either your or my Spring holiday. If I do come now, I think I shall wait until Christmas eve.... You speak of rest and going in the same breath. Somehow I had hoped for the slightest bit of the "home life" out of which we are cheating ourselves. I don't care if I don't see New York and its wonders. I had hoped to spend whole days with you....

Never had Charles been so stubbornly angry. Margaret knew that he wasn't the least bit worried about the *aunts'* privacy. His professed concern about intruding upon them and his threats that he might not even come were his way of making clear the entrapment he feared. At first, Margaret had neither anticipated nor fully understood her new husband's reactions to her plan to stay with the aunts. But when she finally let herself hear Charles's point of view, she began to feel empathy for his position. After all, it *was* a household where men were devalued; it was a place of female power where men sat on the edges. Charles knew the patterns of this household and wanted to start their married life by breaking the pattern, by experiencing "the slightest bit of home life." Finally, she understood.

So Margaret searched for a place in New York where they could spend Christmas all alone. "I found a sleazy apartment hotel with a room, a bath, a kitchenette," remembers Margaret. The dirty, crumbling surroundings didn't dampen the wonderful magic of their romantic interlude. Margaret smiles with the memory of her first Christmas present from her husband. "Charles had bought me a little radio for Christmas. When he arrived at this place, he hid the radio very carefully and then brought it out as a big surprise on Christmas morning." Margaret's eyes fill with tears as she recalls his exuberance and the festivity that they managed to create in this seedy place. "There he was on Christmas morning with practically nothing on, presenting me with this radio. He was so proud of himself!"

The moments of celebration were followed by tender, peaceful hours and serious conversation as Margaret and Charles searched out what it meant to be a couple. "I remember a discussion of how my name would appear on the medical degree ... Charles did not have his doctorate yet, and he said he never wanted to be in the position of having people call him 'Mr. Morgan,' which they might if I graduated as 'Dr. Morgan' ... This was at a time when women rarely used their married names in their professional lives ... in fact, this was a time when most women physicians never got married. ... Charles asked me if I would have 'Margaret Morgan Lawrence' written on my degree." Charles's request had a gravity about it that reflected weeks of worry and indecision. Was he asking too much of this strong woman with her single-minded dream? Margaret understood. "I could see it was important to Charles." But to her, the request did not feel weighty. She was touched by his concern, but did not feel as if he was asking her to give anything up. "I was charmed to be Mrs. Lawrence ... I was Mrs. Lawrence before I was Dr. Lawrence ... so I said yes with ease."

For the most part, Margaret and Charles kept to themselves during this holiday, ignoring the shabby surroundings as they focused on one another. The tiny apartment became a nesting place to which they returned for the intimacy and warmth that they hoped would sustain them until the following summer. They shared Christmas dinner with Ninnie and Hazel and calculated how many visits would make the aunts feel content. (Margaret barely remembers Uncle Jimmie's benign presence, cooking in the kitchen and forming a quiet bond with Charles.) They enjoyed the New York theater but had neither the money nor the inclination to sample more than a couple of plays. They delighted in walking arm in arm through the cold city streets, peering into ornately decorated stores, savoring the sensation of being a couple—handsome, young, hopeful about the future. They went to Margaret's church, St. Martin's in Harlem, listened to the Reverend Johnson give a rousing sermon, and felt themselves joined in spiritual commitment. And they searched out all the free holiday concerts they could find in churches, schools, and symphony halls, feeling their hearts raised by the Hallelujah Chorus. As long as they could stave off Charles's inevitable departure, they felt wrapped in a safe and luxurious cocoon.

There were echoes of their early days in Vicksburg. As he had in Vicksburg, Charles tended to do most of the talking, wrapping his imposing intellect around his current preoccupations and thinking out loud about social problems and political strategy. On this Christmas visit in 1938, he spent long hours worrying about the threat of a second world war, waking early to hear the radio news, the reports of attacks and counterattacks in Europe, and feeling the mounting danger in a deeply personal way. Margaret listened, again enraptured by Charles's worldliness, his grasp of issues, and his comfort with abstract language and thought. But now she also listened to her own role in their conversation. To her surprise, she discovered that her role was far from passive. She found that her questions could be focused and penetrating, and that sometimes she persisted boldly in her pursuit of the truth. Nor was her talk limited to inquiry. She had lots to say to Charles and he valued her spare, perceptive remarks. But most important, Margaret began to recognize one of her major contributions to their relationship: she was helping Charles live fully in the present, to enter into the moment, to experience "the I-Thou that Buber speaks of." If Charles was good at drawing the broad map and sketching the contours, she was good at illuminating a segment and delving deeper. There was relief and pleasure in the discovery of her own powers and she was overjoyed when Charles expressed admiration of these:

1/2/39

> *Dear Lil' Doe:*
> ... *My visit with my wife during the holidays has worked wonders with me. I am a much better and happier man since I returned than I was when I left Atlanta. I am so happy over having seen you, Margaret, that my work is easier. This is an addition to the inspiration that I have as a result of having seen how hard and how well you are working and having seen how cheerfully you have gone and do go about your tasks. To see how you chose to enjoy fully our few days together rather than to worry about their inevitable termination was an object lesson in the art of living—One of the myriad lessons that you have taught me and the boundless reasons for my being grateful to so good a wife.*

By the fall of 1939, Margaret's last year in medical school, Margaret and Charles were reunited. Charles had been admitted to the Ph.D. program in sociology at Columbia and been awarded a prestigious Rosenwald Fellowship. They took an apartment on Manhattan Avenue across from Morningside Park. It was a modest little place that the young couple furnished with second-hand things from Goodwill. "We had a food budget of nineteen dollars per month," remembers Margaret, "and it seems to me that everything was nineteen cents.... Butter was nineteen cents a pound ... oh, fish was ten cents a pound." They watched their budget very carefully but felt no deprivation. There was such happiness in being together, experiencing the regular, everyday quality of life. "We did our wash and hung it in the tiny bathroom. We had friends over. We took long bike rides on the weekends ... we savored the simplicity of it all." Margaret pored through magazines, searching for inexpensive recipes that could liven their diet. For dinner on Tuesdays, she fixed Sweet and Sour Frankfurters from *Woman's Day Kitchen*:

Sweet and Sour Frankfurters

Costs 46 cents

Serves 4   Woman's Day Kitchen

3 cups cooked carrots	3 tablespoons dark corn syrup
1½ cups sliced tart apples	Juice 1 lemon
Salt and pepper	4 frankfurters

Arrange several layers of sliced carrots and apples in 1½-quart casserole, sprinkling each layer lightly with salt and pepper. Pour syrup and lemon juice over all. Cover and bake in moderate oven 350 F., about 20 minutes; top with scored frankfurters, and bake covered about 25 minutes longer until apples are well-done.

Mrs. Elizabeth Daniel, Birmingham, Ala.

Note: Thick slices of bologna or sliced ham may be used instead of frankfurters.

On Wednesday evenings, they devoured the Rice and Cheese Skillet Dinner, featured in the same magazine.

Rice and Cheese Skillet Dinner

Costs 40 cents

Serves 4   Woman's Day Kitchen

1 cup rice	⅓ cup chopped green pepper
2 tablespoons margarine	2 cups tomato juice
1 large onion chopped	Salt and pepper
a clove garlic minced	½ pound processed American cheese, shredded

Cook rice in boiling salted water, about 18 minutes or until barely tender. Drain . . . etc.

Although their life together had a light newness about it, Margaret recalls one concern that hung over them. Charles's father had lost his job in Vicksburg as boys' secretary for the YMCA and was out of work for several months. His father's unemployment hit Charles very hard. A great sadness came over him that weighed heavily on their life together. "It took a long time before Papa Major landed a job, and it was very painful for Charles to have his father out of work." When he finally managed to secure a position as secretary of the colored YMCA in Memphis, Tennessee, his son was greatly relieved and the cloud lifted from Morningside Heights.

In the third year of marriage, Charles and Margaret were again forced to live apart. They simply did not have the resources to afford full-time training for both of them, and Charles was feeling ambivalent about his purely academic diet at Columbia. He was growing restless and preoccupied by the grim international events and by the connections he saw between the impending warfare and the oppression of blacks in the United States. The lure of activism, the desire to voice his commitments more directly, and the need to make a living finally forced his departure from New York. He returned to Atlanta to work for the Southern Field Council of the National YMCA, and Margaret moved on to her internship at Harlem Hospital. Another year apart. Another year of daily letters, long distance declarations of love, and promises that they would never permit anything to force a long separation again. But this time the experience did not feel as raw and as treacherous. They had spent a year living together and had built up a short history that seemed to cushion the pain and anxiety of living apart. And they were freed of the illusion of a perfect, harmonious togetherness, an illusion that had made their first year apart seem almost unbearable.

By September 1942, Charles had returned to New York and Columbia, and they had found an attic apartment in Brooklyn. Margaret was now in her "houseship" in pediatrics at Harlem Hospital. She remembers how she would finish work at the hospital, travel on the subway from Harlem to Brooklyn, and walk slowly home, her body drooping from weariness. She remembers climbing the five flights of stairs to their tiny apartment: one small room, a bath, and a kitchenette at one end of the room. She can hear the constant crying of the year-old baby who lived with his mother on the floor below. The mother used to sit the baby on the toilet for hours at a time. If one peered down the stairwell, through the open door, one could see his little body uncomfortably perched on the throne. The baby hated sitting on the potty and would scream at the top of his lungs, begging to get up; his mother would yell back at a matched volume. Their painful duet would rise up into Charles and Margaret's place.

While Charles studied and went to classes, Margaret had the rigorous schedule of a resident. "I was on every other night at the hospital and every other weekend." The work load felt steady and unrelenting, and rarely left time for scrutiny, reflection, or complaint. However, the pace often energized her. "We were able to be together several times a week, and on my weekends off we lived it up. . . . We had a great time!" remembers Margaret of the year that felt adventurous, intimate, and unencumbered. It was the year that Charles learned to cook. When Margaret returned home from the hospital, their little apartment would be filled with wonderful smells. "He made a great stuffed cabbage. . . . It wasn't your usual stuffed cabbage. He would scoop the whole insides out of the cabbage and then fill it with meat and rice. . . . *Delicious*!" says Margaret, smacking her lips and relishing the simple pleasures that made their life good.

Harlem to Meharry

GETTING STARTED

During Margaret's pediatric houseship, the final six months of her tour of duty at Harlem Hospital, she wrote to Charles, referring to her medical specialty as "my beloved pediatrics." The ward was small, clean, and shabby, with antique equipment. But the feeling was warm, almost familylike. The nurses seemed to like working with children, and they immediately rallied to assist Margaret in any way they could. This was the most hopeful part of the hospital. Young children would arrive very sick, looking frighteningly close to death, and leave a few days later, after treatment and care, smiling and robust. Even when their tiny systems seemed to shut down completely, the children could often be brought back to life.

One day Margaret was preparing to draw blood from a seven-year-old boy's arm. The boy stood stiffly in front of her, holding out his arm like a sacrificial offering, his brown face looking gray with fright. Before taking out the needle, Margaret described to him exactly what she was about to do. "I had begun to get a notion of how important it is to help children anticipate what will happen." The boy kept his eyes glued to Margaret's face and listened intently to every word. As soon as she uttered the word *shot*, the boy dropped to the floor in a faint. Margaret put her stethoscope on his chest and felt a surge of panic. "His heart had stopped." Within seconds, Margaret injected Coramine into his arm and watched the limp, lifeless body begin to move. The child's eyes fluttered open and he looked at her directly. With a foggy voice, he said, "I'm okay, ma'am." The young resident could only hug him. "He came to! . . . But he scared me half to death."

There were days when beneath children's vulnerability Margaret would find a deep, resilient strength. There were other days when their bodies withered right before the doctors' eyes, despite their best efforts. Margaret particularly remembers the seriously undernourished babies who would be rushed over from the emergency room. One scrawny, weak ten-month-old was brought to the ward weighing eight pounds. The baby's mother, ravaged by a hard life of drugs and alcohol, barely staggered behind the stretcher carrying her child. The medical staff leapt into frenzied action over the frail little body. "We worked on that baby for hours." Margaret, who was considered "the master of the 'cut-down'" (an emergency procedure used to give fluids to infants intravenously), moved rapidly to get nutriment flowing into the veins. "I would look at the baby's wrist, find a little vein, make a sharp cut—a quick surgical procedure to expose the vein, then pump in the infusion." Even with the all-out effort, the baby died, and silence fell over the ward. "You could never, ever get used to it." Margaret went to find the baby's mother, who was nodding off in the lounge. She gently awakened her and told her the news. The mother's eyes looked distant and lost as she refused to see her child. "I just want to remember her like she was," she muttered sadly.

At Harlem Hospital, Margaret could feel her world expanding. She learned to balance sensitivity and toughness. The routines of delivering babies and saving lives struck her as both ordinary and miraculous. But Margaret could not deliver babies and ignore the unforgiving world into which she was bringing them. Watching the new black babies arrive—so vulnerable, so dependent—the new doctor's eyes saw the lives that lay ahead of them and felt compelled to respond. Right in the hospital, she saw the inadequate resources and impoverished conditions, and joined her politically active colleagues who pressed for better patient care and more modern facilities. In the community, she felt the deadening force of racism mixed with deeply rooted poverty and felt compelled to participate in civil rights activities. She feared the rising war efforts and began to explore, and finally accept, the values and "spiritual commitments" of pacifism.

Margaret could feel the inevitable joining of her professional training and her social responsibilities. How could she be a doctor in Harlem without being an activist?

Margaret's activism had been building for some time, especially since she met Charles. In many ways, he had been her mentor, her guiding light, on matters of politics. He introduced ideas to her that she had simply never considered—troubling realities and provocative theories that she had not yet made her peace with. Much of their courtship had been centered on their developing understandings of the society and world they inhabited and on coming to terms with their obligations to it. But these conversations were almost always initiated and guided by Charles. In 1941, alone at Harlem Hospital, Margaret had been forced to consider realities in her patients' lives. It was an extraordinary opportunity, and her letters to Charles recorded her fears and excitement. Her letters spoke of the daily struggles of a young doctor in a big city hospital and traced her emerging commitments to broader social issues.

Thursday night
12/9/41

. . . Today I arose at 9:30 having bedded myself about 2:00. After a shower and dressing I went over to 1C and there saw all my kiddies—there and on 4A. This afternoon all of us gathered in my room (all the pediatric staff) for an informal discussion of infant feeding. Shortly after we got two new admissions—one being a suspected diphtheria. We had worked on the little fellow all evening when it dawned upon the superintendent that the child should have been sent to Willard Parker from Accident. We managed that and now we're quarantined till some report comes back on the diagnosis.

Monday 6:30 P.M.
1/5/42
43rd Luniversary!

. . . Last night we resuscitated a 1 lb 4 oz baby in a most heroic manner. Unfortunately, he had the nerve to up and die today. Today also I've done 4 circumcisions. I feel like a rabbi.

Thursday 4:00 P.M.
1/29/42

... *Last evening in preparation for my job as night senior I had a troubled sleep in which people played handball in the attic of Dad's church, breaking the rafters and making the roof soft. (I could dent it with my fingers.) I was almost glad for midnight. Things were slow the first of the morning but soon as I returned to my bed about 3 A.M.—so soon I had three cases. I did three deliveries on my time, the last at 9:00 this morning—a forceps....*

Saturday P.M.
2/2/42

I've just been in my room where I reclined for a moment and read.... The reclining was an antidote for a very strenuous morning—mostly mental. We had a 21 year old woman whose baby for some reason went bad and when he was delivered by forceps lived to but a few minutes. Then the placenta refused to be delivered and had to be taken out manually under ether and she lost a lot of blood. Everyone ran in circles and was a little upset. 'Tisn't often that we lose a perfectly healthy looking baby....

12/9/41

... *I've just finished the outline of a talk for the Manhattan Medical Society tomorrow night. Dr. Aubrey Maynard demanded a pre-talk outline. The talk of course is about the ambulance—none of which will concern anybody at all at the moment I'm quite sure. I shall go thru with it though as prearranged....*

Hysteria has descended upon the environs since Sunday. For two days we've heard the air raid warnings (screeching sirens) and the evening Post *carried—besides the red, white and blue flag on its front page—foot high words saying "Bombers sighted off New York." While we had our little infant feeding chat, two mamas called their intern sons present telling the news of the bombing planes over New York and communicating their fright. I wonder how hysterical are the powers calculating to get the populace?*

2/16/42

... *Yesterday was more or less completely devoted to the "Cause." I
needed it because during the course of last week I had allowed myself
to become depressed—something that hadn't happened in a long time.
I was supposed to work until twelve but I managed to rush off in
time for church and the first lesson. The worship was inspiring. Rev.
Johnson's sermon on "Blind as Bartineus" was in the main not inspiring. His discussion of what the attitude of the people of Harlem
should be to crime and the criminals, and his idea concerning the
belief of some millions of Japanese in a masterful destiny left a lot to
be desired. After Church Mrs. Seabrook and I came uptown on the
bus and at Harlem there was a better chicken dinner than usual. In
my room I had a 45 minute piano concert all on my own....*

*It was snowing gently most of the day, so in kerchief and rubbers I
went down to Labor Temple in time for the worship service preceding the lecture. I was happy to play the piano for the hymns. Thelma
Burge gave an excellent talk. Her topic was "Strength Through Suffering." She is a librarian and apparently she has read widely. She
got her material from autobiographies and biographies. Some of the
people were: George Fox, St. Francis of Assisi, Sidney Lanier, Marie
Curie, John Bunyan. She told these stories so well that she made you
want to read the books suggested. A point of information: I didn't
know that Thomas Jefferson in his original draft of the Declaration
of Independence wrote in a clause calling for the abolition of slavery.
Did you?...*

*One of the Ashram girls—Ruth and Jay's eleven year old Kath-
leen, who styles herself a "junior pacifist," and I came back to the
Ashram together. Jay was there. On the basis of a deep conviction
that pacifism must be an all-consuming way of life rather than just
an extra-curricular activity to pacifists as well as others, that people
in general are more disillusioned about war than ever before, and
that pacifism can and must offer an alternative (to war) of real active
non-violent direct action in such fields of present importance as race
discrimination—he suggests the formation of groups of people thruout
the country who will devote themselves actively to this active pacifism. He would call them non-violent volunteers....*

3/2/42

... *Last night I went to hear James Farmer, Race Relations Secretary
of the F.O.R. (Fellowship of Reconciliation). He believes that now is*

the time for a movement to get to the bottom of race discrimination. This movement, he suggests, should be a national movement with three types of people entering into it. One group would be those who believe in racial equality but who do not agree on methods, 2) Those who would produce (on farms) cooperatively and market their products, 3) The action group who would protest non-violently.

As Margaret became increasingly active in the "Cause" (the movement for peace and social justice), it grew to feel like her own personal struggle. The problems of race discrimination, the war effort, the impoverished lives of black babies, appeared to her to have common roots. In her letters to her husband there was evidence of this developing synthesis of professional, political, and personal responsibility, an integration made possible, she maintained, because of the "beautiful harmony" she found with Charles and because of God's grace. In the following long letter, written without paragraphs, words and feelings followed on one another as she connected various spheres of experience:

12/12/41

My Own Husband,
  More than ever I long for the day that brings you here, for more than ever I feel the need of nearness to the one of whom I am a part—to gain comfort and strength by that nearness and thru his understanding to better see the light. Since it is necessary that we live in this world at the present time and rightly share in its guilt, it is good that between us this beautiful harmony, this spark of life exists. Kept alive, it may be God's instrument to help—somewhere. Tonight being off I was assailed by various opportunities to spend my time various ways. First of all Scheinblum and I went to P & S (College of Physicians & Surgeons, Columbia University) and deposited some blood for Coburn's lab to test for rheumatic fever. Coburn was there and our conversation included a promise by Coburn to be available to help me in any way in getting further jobs. I stopped at the bookstore for a light bulb and an ear spectrum (for babies). I came back for hotdogs at Harlem. A friend dressmaker of Freddie Phillips is repairing my maroon dress that Moms sent last year, so I was obliged to visit her on 110th Street to try it on. From there on—was a little mental conflict—because I had said that I would go to the emer-

*gency ILA meeting downtown if possible. I couldn't persuade myself
to make it possible so I walked uptown and on my way stopped in to
talk to Rev. Johnson—on the matter of the protest to the YMCA/
New York against discrimination. He wasn't in so I looked in the
store windows along 125th Street and visited every 10 cent store. I
went into Xmas card stores too but apparently the* Peace On Earth
*message is somewhat hard to put across this year. I didn't like what I
saw. . . . Back in my room I chatted with Freddie a while. We went
down to eat when Rev. Johnson called, made his regrets, asked my
mission and said if I could come to the rectory then he'd drive me
back. I caught a ride down with Rodino and discussed with the Vicar
whether he should or should not write a letter to the Board of Direc-
tors of the YMCA. He was not very favorably disposed to it since he
says that he doesn't think that that type of protest does any good. He
believes the Board knows it is discriminating and we would do little
but antagonize it. We differed widely on various points including the
question of whether New York is the Negro mecca and whether we
saw hope for any improvement in the South. Somehow I got the
impression that he was fairly envious of the optimism and hope of
youth.*

Margaret was beginning to be critical of Reverend Johnson's cautious views on race relations. When she had arrived in Harlem at
the age of fourteen, Johnson had been a very important force in her
life, a larger-than-life-sized figure. He was the "heavy uncle," the
one to whom Margaret's father entrusted his precious daughter, the
one to whom she turned for guidance and support. Not only did he
watch over her and gather her into his orbit with avuncular pride,
he also introduced Margaret to the powerful and supportive circle
of Harlem ladies.

When Margaret returned to Harlem as a young doctor, Reverend
Johnson continued to be the person to whom she often turned for
consultation and advice. She valued his political savvy, his connections
to the community, and his unwavering belief in her dreams. But at
twenty-six, Margaret was beginning to see a different Harlem—
meaner, grittier, more threatening. She was beginning to see Harlem's
plight as inextricably joined to the deteriorating world conditions.
And she was beginning to feel a shift in how she defined herself in
relation to the struggle. Now Reverend Johnson's views no longer
went unquestioned. In his refusal to protest the YMCA's discrimi-

natory policy, Margaret could hear a cautious tone that was a source of disquiet for her. She could feel herself growing away from him, and the new distance felt both uncomfortable and invigorating.

Actually, the fact that she and Reverend Johnson were even engaged in this dialogue meant that a new equality was being established between them. Two adults were challenging each other's views. The new symmetry of their discourse was disquieting in another way, which Margaret described to Charles:

> ... Later on in the conversation he [Reverend Johnson] thought it wonderful that we had a married life so calm and free of turmoil in contradiction to his own. These things my intuition bade me not to develop further—for though I have known the vicar for a long time it has been rather from a distance—and didn't feel myself a close enough friend to share confidences or hear of his personal life. Then too one feels sort of queer when one has had a child-adult relationship with a person to attain a full adult-adult relationship in a few conversations. Somehow I felt a bit uneasy and was not unwilling to arrive back at the hospital. . . .

Reverend Johnson represented the old Harlem of Margaret's adolescence—the cautious, middle-class, protective Harlem that had guided Margaret safely through her high-school years. His church had been an asylum, a retreat from the overbearing instrusions of her aunts. She had relished the activity at St. Martin's: Sunday school, drama club, choir rehearsals. Now, a decade later, as she listened to Reverend Johnson's sermons, he sometimes seemed hundreds of miles away from her life in Harlem. She felt a growing identification with the larger, poorer Harlem and Johnson's soliloquies seemed too comfortable. Her work at Harlem Hospital had forced Margaret to see that "all Negroes faced the same fates," that all blacks experienced victimization and "guilt," that there was an indissoluble bond that they all shared.

In her emerging view of the larger Harlem, Margaret could hear the echoes of the lessons she had learned as a young girl in Vicksburg from her mother's "fierce" teaching, her determination that every black child—no matter how poor—would learn in her classroom. And she could experience again the feeling of holding her father's hand, walking the red light district of Vicksburg, bringing God's message to the prostitutes and pimps. "My father would go *anywhere* to spread God's word." So, while Margaret's life in Harlem, her activism in the hospital and the community, was new, the motivations and obligations she felt were deeply familiar:

> It is not difficult to find myself, a black, identified with poor, black, needy people. I share history, culture, communities with them. I live, however, on a social class and economic level somewhat different from that of many of the families with whom I work, although oft times their relatives or families down South share my relative affluence. Nevertheless, I share the conviction that regardless of social and economic class, they and I have identical goals and dreams for our children.
>
> (*Young Inner City Families*, 1975)

By the end of her residency at Harlem, Margaret had learned a great deal about pediatrics and about the practice of medicine under fire. She had fully incorporated the quick pace, the grinding routines, the triumphs and casualties of work in a big city hospital. There was some feeling of victory in battling the odds and learning the craft. But her experience at Harlem also left her with an overwhelming sense of all that she did not know. In order to be a good doctor, she knew she needed to understand more about the connections among history, culture, and disease; between public policy and medical practice; between physical disorders and psychosocial forces; and between poverty and vulnerability to illness. As she neared the conclusion of her residency, it felt more like a beginning than an ending. There was so much she yearned to know in order to be ready to pursue "the plan" and return south.

Margaret's decision to spend a year at Columbia's School of Public Health seemed almost inevitable, a natural extension of her training. It also fit nicely with Charles's decision to continue his studies at Columbia. They had been separated for two years and had promised each other that they would never again live apart. They had tested their independence and had survived the test, but now had no more energy for lonely, autonomous pursuits. From now on, they would unite forces and daily reaffirm their partnership in work and love.

This time they both applied for Rosenwald scholarships. Charles's application proposed work with Professor Robert Merton on the "Racialistic-Radical Social Movements in the Harlem Negro Community," and Margaret applied for a year of study in "public health— emphasizing child health—in preparation for pediatric service in a southern community." Her proposal to the Rosenwald Fund outlined the pieces of her training that Margaret hoped would finally prepare her to be, as her father called her, a "missionary doctor":

> ... Following a two year general internship which ends July 1, 1942, I would like to take a one year course in public health paying particular attention to child health. With this increase in armamentarium I hope to become associated with a Southern university-hospital system which will allow me to do pediatric hospital work, to work in or institute well-baby and other pediatric clinics, and to cooperate with health authorities in matters of child health. In the meantime, I would wish to continue with the study of pediatrics under the staff of this hospital. Authorities in both pediatrics and public health advise me of the wisdom of securing public health training in preparation for child health work—especially in view of the present trends in medical care.
>
> The DeLemar Institute of Public Health offers a one year course leading to the degree of Master of Science in Public Health. This course of study has as its required subjects, 1) the elements of vital statistics, 2) a study of methods and laboratory exercises in epidemiology in which methods of collection, tabulation, and analysis of epidemiological data are studied and these methods applied to the study of recent epidemics ... 3) public health engineering—a study of its principles and laboratory practice in various routine procedures, 4) a single course in industrial hygiene—a study of industrial and home environments as they affect the health of the worker, and 5) two courses in public health administration.
>
> The elective courses offered in the third and fourth quarters of the year are chosen to suit individual needs. There are electives which would serve my interests. The clinical instruction in child hygiene is such a course. In this course the modern practice of preventive pediatrics is studied and various agencies are observed in regard to their methods of child care. I would also elect instruction in dealing with the diagnostic procedures used and the treatment available in the care of the clinic patient ill from tuberculosis or syphilis. Other studies of nutrition and deficiency, growth and de-

velopment—from a clinical standpoint—would surely be chosen.

... This well rounded public health training—emphasizing child health—would, I believe, prepare me to serve in the Southern community which I have previously described. In addition, my husband, Charles R. Lawrence Jr., a 1939–40 Rosenwald fellow in Sociology, and I dare to hope to work in the same university-hospital system, and further, to collaborate at some point—most probably on a problem concerning the family. My entire preparation so far has been made with the service of southern children in mind. My ambition is to continue to that end.

Both Margaret and Charles received the Rosenwald Fellowships and felt doubly launched in their joint venture. The *New York Times* announced the winners: "Rosenwald Fund Gives 72 Awards, 56 Fellowships Worth $90,000 in all to 35 Negroes and 21 White Persons." Congratulatory notes came from far and near, adding fuel to the young couple's already keen "sense of responsibility."

From Ira Ried, Charles's southern mentor:

> *Atlanta University*
> *May 11, 1942*

> *Dear Lawrence,*
> *A few hours after I asked about the Rosenwald Fellowships I heard that both of you—Margaret too—had received them. I was pleased to no end. My full congratulations to both of you. I do believe that your individual and collective possibilities are limitless.... Plan to spend some time with us here on that thesis. I want to help.*

> *Cordially,*
> *Ira D. A. Ried*

From Robert Merton, Charles's northern professor:

> *Columbia University*
> *May 7, 1942*

> *Dear Lawrence,*
> *I am of course delighted but not surprised to hear that Mrs. Lawrence and you have both been awarded the Rosenwald Fellowship. It is one more reason for my devotion to Sears Roebuck even at this late*

date. I shall promptly order another catalogue.... Mrs. Merton and I
hope that you will come out to see us shortly after your arrival in
New York.

> Best regards,
> R. K. Merton

Margaret smiles softly, thinking of the relationships Charles achieved with his teachers—a combination of intimacy and distance that allowed both professor and student to feel rewarded. Charles found a kind of intellectual companionship and avuncular caring in his teachers that Margaret had never known in her professional training. His professors looked into his eyes and saw their careers projected forward. In Charles, Merton and Ried could see their intellectual imprint. The attractions were mutual. Charles studied his teachers' minds, scrutinized their ideals, and made what he admired his own.

During her year at Columbia's School of Public Health, Margaret finally had an experience with a teacher that had the powerful, transforming qualities Charles had enjoyed with his mentors. For several months she participated in a seminar led by Dr. Benjamin Spock at the Kips Bay–Yorkville Child Health Station. Spock was then a young pediatrician with a gentle manner and an inquiring style. He was the first physician Margaret had ever met who talked about the connection between physical health and psychological well-being, between social and cultural forces and family life. When Margaret had plunged into her studies in public health, she had been yearning to hear the message Spock preached, but this was the first time she had heard it so clearly and forcefully articulated. Her own inner murmurings, her inchoate but strong feelings, found their voice in Spock's classes. He seemed to be speaking directly to her. "His exciting and well-integrated vision of the child, the family, the community, and society never left me."

But there was an even more powerful lesson in Dr. Spock's teachings. The message was conveyed less by what he said than in how he interacted with mothers and their children. There was in his manner a wonderful, simple respect—a reverence for the ordinary intuition and common sense of mothers. And there was an abiding belief in the strength and resilience of babies. "I can still quote him," says Margaret as she relishes the potent memory. "If a baby has a feeding problem you must first look to the parents, to the mother, for clues about why the infant is having the problem. . . . One of the first things you have to make sure is that the mother knows this child is not going to starve . . . and what's more, that the child is likely to find a way of eating a well-balanced diet so you don't have to push food on him. The cure is to help this mother to relax, and the child will be all right and he won't starve."

Margaret carefully watched the way this rare doctor gathered information, offered assurance, and listened to mothers' stories. She carefully observed the connections between Spock's words and his actions, and she promised herself that she would pattern her practice after him. "It was Spock who gave me my first firm feeling of being a pediatrician and a child psychiatrist." The rest of her training at the School of Public Health paled in contrast to the transforming experience with Spock. The regular courses were gray and formless against the flame that Spock had lit within her, a flame that would continue throughout her career.

Margaret felt a new sense of direction and a validation for her own emerging views on the practice of medicine. She could see how she might translate Spock's approach to the child-health center she hoped one day to open in the Deep South. As she watched Spock examine and treat babies, she could feel her attention shifting over to the mothers. She noticed the special qualities of maternal compassion, their fears of ineptitude and failure, the ways they looked to the doctor for advice and then tried to incorporate what was useful for them. She felt their passion, the deep rapport between mother and child, the barely muted anger and frustration, the mother's glowing happiness in the child's expression of pleasure. Part of Margaret's pleasure in observing Spock was in witnessing his support for the mother's strength and intelligence and his way of understanding the raw and powerful feelings of motherhood.

By the time Margaret finished the Spock seminar, she had learned that she was pregnant. In her growing identification with the mothers, she found herself hoping that she was about to become one. She had never doubted that she would one day have children of her own. From the moment Charles and Margaret knew they were promised to each other, they had planned on becoming parents. In fact, part of Margaret's attraction to Charles grew out of her admiration of his fatherly qualities. From a very young age he had been a parent figure to his siblings. "There go Charles and the children," people in Utica would say as they watched the parade of four young Lawrences walking off to town. Margaret loved the way Charles took care of people. She called him "my strong oak tree," encompassing and protective. So Margaret had chosen a husband whom she expected to be a good parent.

Margaret, too, had plans of becoming a good parent, although being an only child, she had not had much practice. In some ways, however, she felt as if she had done her share of mothering. When Mary "couldn't cope" and fell apart—usually just before guests would arrive—Margaret would take over, tidying the house, cooking, and welcoming visitors. Her mother could count on Margaret rising to the occasion. "If people would drop by, as they always did, I was the one who would say to my father, 'I'll make some biscuits.' My mother would panic and get upset . . . 'What will I do?' I never knew whether she would make it or not. Naturally, part of that was in my own head. Often I felt I was more capable than she, and my parents sort of felt that way too."

In her role as "the capable one," Margaret also "felt some anger" at having to take on these responsibilities before she was grown. There were so many ways that Mary's mothering made her want to raise her children differently. Margaret wanted to "be there" for her children, available, open, listening—not depressed and withdrawn. She wanted to feel vitality for both family and work, not reserve her best energy for work and then close down and draw the shades when she came home. How could she forgive Mary's lying there in bed "like dead" all weekend long, unresponsive to her husband and daughter . . . only to rise on Monday morning dressed and ready to teach? She wanted to have a relationship with her husband that would allow her children to feel safe in their love. She didn't want her children to suffer as she had, in the shadows of parental conflict, feeling the constant strain of divided loyalties. She wanted to be happier as a mother, to enjoy her children—not like Mary, consumed by sadness, wanting to be close to the mother and sisters that she had left behind, facing backward, not forward.

Even though Margaret wanted to be a very different kind of mother from Mary, she realized that her mother had helped her to become the capable, confident person she was. While Mary had been sad and withdrawn, she had always believed in her daughter. Mary had great admiration for Margaret, a respect and deference that sometimes made Margaret feel like a third adult in the Morgan family. Both her mother and father took Margaret "seriously," never doubted her career decisions, and responded fully when she made requests. Margaret still marvels over her parents' unquestioning approval of her decision, at fourteen, to move from Mississippi to New York "to get a first class education." "This came from me. I announced it to my folks . . . and that was that." When Margaret graduated from Cornell, she asked her parents for a bicycle. "I got a beautiful blue bicycle . . . I had never ridden one, but I always wanted to learn . . . I said I wanted one and so my parents bought it for my graduation. *They always did what I wanted if they could.*" This deep loyalty, this unwavering belief, gave Margaret a solid and sure foundation. Even as she yearned for signs of love from Mary and felt her mother's passionate bond to "the Smithies," Margaret was always secure in her mother's glowing respect.

When Mary Morgan heard the news of Margaret's pregnancy, she expressed her joy in a long, affectionate letter that underscored her belief in Margaret's future as mother and doctor:

> *St. Mary's Episcopal Mission*
> *and Vicksburg Industrial School*
> *Monday, 10:45 P.M.*

> *My dear Honey Bunches,*
>   *I don't think this epistle will be very long, as I am so late starting it. I have such little time in the evening, as I get out late, and I feel I must get in my walk. On Mondays I get up clothes and tonight I was determined to write this note or letter.*
>   *Well, first thing I want to tell you is that Mrs. Oliver came to church Sunday after an absence of a month or so, and put ten ($10) dollars on the alms basin and after service greeted me and the next*

thing she said was "Uh huh! You didn't tell me," and I said "What?" and she said "that you are going to be a grandmother." I told her I had not known it long myself. She wouldn't tell me where she got it from, or from whence it came, but told your Dad she heard it at the club meeting. So I'm assuring you it is on the go, since Mrs. O. has it. I am wondering whether it came from Atlanta, although she said she heard it at the club. So they are all looking for the little Morgan Lawrence.

Mrs. Edwards has been coming every Sunday since she started and is very friendly at church with all. Mrs. Ewing sings out louder than ever trying to hold up the choir. We asked Mrs. Edwards why she didn't use her alto voice in the choir and she says she will as soon as her eyes get better and she can see to sing the words. . . .

Oh! I forget to say that everyone seems happy that you are going to increase your family, so there is happiness on all sides.

School is going fine as to numbers. I have now about 45 pupils in my room and your Dad has about 33 in his room, and some have registered who are out picking cotton and will be in soon, so you see we have our hands full. . . .

I hope you come out okay in your exams. I am sure you did as I am certain you put in some hard work. I know you will be glad to get to your journey's end when you have finished as all of us are when we have a task ahead. You both have much to think of now and more plans to make, and to perfect. I am glad you are seeing that Honey Bunch (No. 1) is taking good care of herself and that you are doing your part to take care of him or her. Since you all say you are not concentrating on boy or girl, I have stopped concentrating, too.

Well, I must stop and get some shut-eye. Safe airplanes of love, hugs, and kisses to all three.

Your loving Momsy

As Margaret awaited the arrival of her first child, she thought a lot about the challenges of mothering and the difficulties of inventing different family forms. She worried over how she would balance mothering with working, a feat that had been imperfectly accomplished by Mary, Mom Margaret, and almost every maternal figure in her family. Marriage and professional life had been comfortable companions because she and Charles cared so deeply about both pursuits, and because her husband felt enhanced, not diminished, by her ambitions. But the prospect of a child felt different. A mother could not expect her baby to appreciate her other endeavors. Margaret also wondered how she would feel about leaving her baby in another's care. That was something you could never fathom until the baby actually arrived.

Despite these worries, Margaret never considered not working. It was too important to her to "make a contribution"; she had worked too hard to become a doctor, and she knew that given the discriminatory practices, both subtle and explicit, if she abandoned her precarious position in the field she might never regain it. Her struggles with herself, therefore, were not related to choosing between work and family; rather, they were related to balancing them. She had no illusions that this would be easy. She knew, at its best, her life was always going to be too full, that she would always experience moments of guilt and feel torn in many directions.

Margaret's concerns about this balancing act were heightened by Charles's plans. It was 1943, and Charles, a committed pacifist, had decided that he could not participate in the war effort and would have to declare himself a conscientious objector. This decision meant that he would have to leave his family and devote two years to "alternative service." Most likely, he would be sent to CPS (Civilian Public Service) Camp, where he would do hard physical labor: clearing land, chopping down trees, building dams. Although the thought of abandoning his family was excruciatingly painful, he felt "he had no choice." He could not be part of the inhuman, barbaric violence. His decision cut to his very core, reflecting a deeply felt moral and spiritual stance. So as they anticipated their first child, Margaret and Charles both knew that Charles would probably be gone soon after the baby arrived. "The question of whether Charles would have to go to CPS Camp" hung over the young couple like a heavy shadow. "We knew he'd have to go somewhere and I would have to be responsible for supporting the family."

The pregnancy was "uneventful" except for this haunting worry. But Margaret was beginning to expect her husband's absences. She remembers the moment when her obstetrician announced to her that she was pregnant, and she sighs, a long, weary sigh. "We discovered I was pregnant while Charles was on a march to Washington. . . . The A. Philip Randolph Civil Rights March. . . . He joined them late somewhere along the way in Baltimore. . . . But he was gone, un-reachable . . . no one to tell the big news." The sigh turns into a gentle smile, as if Margaret still experiences the dual feelings, of pride in this man who lived by his convictions and of concern for the new family who awaited his return.

She wrote Charles right away:

Saturday 2:30 P.M.
9/5/42

Darling,
I could fly to you with the news. THE RABBIT SAID "YES". It was a nice young black and white rabbit and it was almost a shame to see her die for the cause. But her ovaries were large and had nice big hemorrhargic spots over both of them—just as they should have been. And Kornolen—nice old hen that he is—was so pleased to be in on the secret, he nearly burst. Of course yours truly was so calm she nearly choked and could hardly taste the junk they fed her at the hospital noon meal. It all happened at noon today. I had to talk to somebody at the moment and the safest person was Geraldine on ac-count of she's a doctor and a married woman and she has hopes her-self. She says she's just plain jealous and wants me to tell you not to fly home immediately but to continue your walk to Washington. I don't agree with her. . . .

As her belly swelled, Margaret pounded the pavement looking for a job, urged on by the worry that she was about to be the sole breadwinner of the family. She remembers endless interviews and skeptical looks as people saw the pregnant young doctor and felt they couldn't trust her commitment to medical practice. She also remem-bers the racism. "I recall an interview at Planned Parenthood when I was very pregnant with Chuck. The lady gave me a long stare and said sweetly, 'Well, you look like a healthy one. . . . You'll just drop that baby and keep right on moving.'" Margaret shakes her head. "Like I was some 'darky' working in the fields . . . I would just leave my cotton chopping, crouch on my haunches, and drop the baby."

Just before Margaret completed her studies at the School of Public Health, in early May of 1943, the baby arrived. Born in Harlem Hospital, Charles Radford Lawrence III, always called Chuck, came two days after his father's twenty-eighth birthday. He was a brown, robust, beautiful baby. As Margaret held him close, she felt a wonderful coming together of the strands of her life. She had great ambitions for their firstborn child, "good health and strong ego" being near the top of the list. But another of her hopes for him was that he would always feel related to the community into which he was born—that his roots would be in Harlem, even though his life would stretch out in distant directions.

By the time Chuck was six weeks old, the three Lawrences were on their way to Nashville, Tennessee. Charles and Margaret had not planned to head south at this point in their lives, although they expected that would be their final destination. Since Margaret had trained in New York and had begun to build a network of professional connections there, they had expected she would find work in the Northeast. But the prospects in New York were not promising. Either Margaret felt discouraged by jobs that did not begin to approximate her interest in the integration of pediatrics and public health, or her potential employers shied away from this very pregnant woman doctor, or subtle exclusionary tactics might have been at work. Margaret felt discouraged and frustrated in her attempts to ferret out what the problem might be. Did they express no interest because she was black, because she was a woman, because she was pregnant, because of her unorthodox blend of interests? She would never know. Both Margaret and Charles felt anxious living with this uncertainty. Their anxiety sometimes threatened to eclipse the joy of anticipating their new baby.

In the middle of the winter, their prospects changed with the arrival in New York of Dr. Charles Johnson, the president of Fisk University in Nashville. Dr. Johnson, a renowned sociologist, whose book *Growing Up in the Black Belt* was a carefully wrought study of Negro youth in the rural South, had come north on a fund-raising trip. He also hoped to do some faculty recruiting, and at the top of his list was Charles Lawrence, whose career he had followed with eagerness. From his colleagues Ira Ried and W. E. B. DuBois, Johnson had heard about this promising scholar, and like Ried and DuBois he felt drawn to the young man's social and political commitments as well as to his scholarship. He already knew that the chances were great that Charles would be forced to abandon his work at the university because of the alternative service. But he was willing to risk the almost-certainty of Charles's quick departure in exchange for the energy and intellectual vitality he might bring to Fisk.

As Charles listened to Dr. Johnson's offer to teach sociology at Fisk and initiate research on Negro community organizations for the Race Relations Institute there, his mind raced in many directions. Johnson's proposal felt like an invitation to return home to the familiarity of his black roots, to the action of the civil rights movement, to the heart of the Negro intellectual community, to colleagues who understood and appreciated his deep commitments. Charles's mind also leapt to the promising possibility that Nashville could be a fertile place to start Margaret's career. Perhaps she could teach at Meharry Medical College right across the street from Fisk. Meharry had for years been one of the primary training grounds for black physicians. Along with Howard University in Washington, D.C., Meharry had produced more than 98 percent of the country's black doctors. A very few black trainees, like Margaret, had managed to break through the discriminatory gates of prestigious white medical schools, but everyone regarded them as the exceptions, and most blacks recognized the distortions and suffering that accompanied their token status.

Beyond the possibility of a medical school position for Margaret, Nashville had another appeal. It seemed like a good way to test out the viability of their plan without the risks of creating and sustaining their own institution. In Nashville, Charles could explore the integration of social theory and political action in his work at Fisk's Race Relations Institute and Margaret could pursue her interest in child and public health as a faculty member at Meharry. They could test out their skills and commitments in these already established black institutions. Dr. Johnson responded enthusiastically to Charles's query about the possibilities of a position for Margaret at Meharry. He promised to contact Dr. Edward Turner, the president of Meharry, as soon as he returned to Nashville, and he urged Margaret to write Dr. Turner directly.

Margaret wrote to Turner in late March, introducing herself, describing her training and interests, and inquiring about faculty positions. By May, Margaret had signed a contract for a yearlong appointment as instructor in preventive medicine and pediatrics at an annual salary of $2,400. She was to begin on July first. The original offer was for $1,800 annually, but Margaret had firmly insisted on a higher salary and Turner wanted very much for her to come. The president saw in Margaret a bright, energetic, well-trained physician, one who might bring new insights and high standards to Meharry. He also was eager to have a woman on his all-male faculty of medicine, and each of his letters spoke to this point: "I am deeply interested in a thoroughly well trained young woman physician being added to the staff." And in another piece of correspondence: "We are especially interested in having a woman physician in the department to handle some of the problems of the young women at Fisk University as they present themselves in the Student Health Clinic." As she read Turner's letters, Margaret understood the twin attraction she represented. She was a northern-trained physician, a rare black graduate of an elite white medical school, and she was a woman. To the white president of a Negro institution, she seemed like a precious, exotic bird. Although he did not want to go overboard in his enthusiasm for her—his letters showed the typical bureaucratic restraint—he very much wanted Margaret to come.

Turner's enthusiasm was not without ambivalence. Although he wanted Margaret's fancy training and elevated northern status on his faculty, he harbored worries about the modern ideas she might want to import to Nashville. Would she be one of those radical, irreverent types who might want to change the comfortable institutional patterns that had worked so smoothly for so long? And while Turner was most eager to have a token woman on his faculty, he felt a little wary of a professional woman who was also a mother. Could he trust her commitment and sense of obligation to Meharry, or would she be a person of divided loyalties, torn by the demands of family and career? Ideally, he would have wished for a single woman—like most female doctors were—so he could count on her undivided devotion to medicine. In his second letter to Margaret, after he had been informed of her pregnancy, Turner revealed his concerns about hiring a mother: "I am wondering what your own plans and program will be once the baby arrives. I should be very glad to hear from you again within the next month. If after the arrival of the baby you still feel that you might be interested in work down here I will be glad to correspond with you further."

This letter sounded to Margaret as if Turner were about to back out. With her baby due in less than two weeks, and with the probability that Charles would soon be called away, Margaret felt great urgency in landing this job. She focused her energies on composing a letter to President Turner designed to allay his fears. The letter assured him that he needn't worry about the child-care issue because she had that under control (which she certainly didn't) and presented herself as a serious, professionally committed young physician eager to join the faculty community (which she certainly was). Her well-phrased letter apparently calmed Turner's anxieties. Four days after Chuck's birth, Margaret received a letter offering her the job.

By mid-June, Charles and Margaret had dismantled their simple apartment in New York and decided which of their possessions were worth transporting south. A mahogany chest from China, their most beautiful treasure, which had been given to them by one of Margaret's medical school classmates, made the long trip to Nashville. Most of their other well-used "Goodwill" furniture was given away to appreciative friends who were glad for the modest inheritance. The new parents and their six-week-old son arrived in Nashville with few things but with a great deal of hope. They had no place to stay, so the three of them lived for the first month at the home of President Johnson. When a small house on the Fisk campus was vacated by a departing faculty member, the Lawrences moved in.

Almost immediately, before feeling the least bit settled in Nashville, Charles and Margaret began working. In the few weeks following their arrival, Margaret had arranged for a young teenager from Vicksburg to come and live with them to take care of Chuck. Although this seemed like a reasonable plan, it quickly became apparent that the arrangement would not work out. No amount of attention, training, or reinforcement could turn this grim, moping adolescent into an adequate caretaker. She lugged herself around the house all day, resenting any requests from the baby for attention, resenting the very modest housework that was required, and resenting the enthusiasm and interest of the young parents. Her presence hung over the household like a dead weight, and Margaret hated to go off to work and leave Chuck in her care.

The Vicksburg girl was sent packing. She seemed as relieved to go as Margaret was glad to see her leave. Luckily, she left before her lethargic, resentful presence became a hazard for the cheerful baby or caused great guilt on the part of his parents. She was replaced by a Mrs. Catherine Sellers, a widow with five children of her own who loved babies and felt completely comfortable taking on another one. Margaret's face brightens as she remembers her. "Mrs. Sellers was a fine lady." She came every day and eased herself smoothly into the household, doing some cooking, caring for Chuck in a relaxed but loving manner, and mostly neglecting the housework. Mrs. Sellers was fat and slow-moving. She would plant her large body on the couch and then welcome the small baby into her arms, content to sit there for as long as the child could tolerate the peace. Her style, her way with Chuck, contrasted sharply with the high-energy, talkative style of the baby's parents. But like most infants, Chuck adapted easily, calming way down in Mrs. Sellers's comfortable arms and brightening up and bouncing in her lap at the sound of his parents coming home. Because their little house was right on the Fisk campus and near Meharry, Margaret and Charles would often come home to have lunch with Chuck or to play with him for half an hour. Both parents became very adept at sandwiching in short visits home into their strenuous schedules. Chuck looked forward to the lively interludes; Mrs. Sellers marveled at the strange and wonderful people she worked for who seemed to want to "do it all." Margaret and Charles felt resolute in their determination to combine work and love. Occasionally, Margaret would carry Chuck over to the pediatric clinic and let him sleep or play in one of the cribs while she supervised residents or attended to sick children.

Most afternoons, Mrs. Sellers would put Chuck down for a long nap from which he would wake in time for his parents' return from work. When Margaret or Charles arrived, weary from the workday, their son would be wide awake, ready for any action his parents could invent. Margaret smiles at the memory of the bright-eyed, expectant infant. "We would come home and the day would begin!"

The nap schedule had been worked out with Mrs. Sellers (who welcomed the rest herself) in order to give Charles and Margaret more "awake time" with Chuck. With several hours of sleep in the afternoon, Chuck could easily manage to stay lively until midnight, when his Dad often fell asleep before his son, rocking the baby and drifting off in the middle of a goodnight song.

Teaching was a brand new experience for Margaret, who had never been responsible for preparing a course curriculum, developing a lecture style, or responding to the needs of students. At Meharry, she had to learn all of this very quickly and the first weeks felt awkward and stressful. "I can remember being fairly self-conscious about the idea of teaching." She had formidable models, whose practiced images contrasted with her hesitant first attempts. Margaret thought of her mother, Mary, the "fierce" teacher, who was at her best in front of a classroom full of children. Teaching brought out her strongest qualities—her energy, her determination, her sharp mind. Against such a powerful image, Margaret felt inadequate. And Charles, too, was a forceful model. By the time he reached Fisk, he had already taught at Jackson College Summer School and at a junior high school in Atlanta, and had lots of experience counseling and tutoring undergraduates at Morehouse. He had also carefully watched his own professors in undergraduate and graduate schools with an eye toward emulating them. Although young, Charles was already an inspired and confident teacher.

Margaret also knew that Charles's comfort in teaching, his sheer joy in fashioning an intellectual argument out loud in front of students, did not derive merely from practice. She knew that he was temperamentally suited to this work. His mind came alive when he taught. Margaret loved to listen to Charles think through an idea. She loved his natural inclination toward abstraction and theory, but she also recognized the sharp differences between them and often felt diminished by them.

These differences often come up in our conversations as we work on this book. Trying to impose some order on her wandering recollections, I ask from time to time, "Mom, when did that happen? What year?" This quite ordinary request always stops Margaret in her tracks. She fumbles around trying to happen on a date or to reason it out based on a date she knows. "Let's see," she starts, "Charles and I were married in the summer of 1938 and so that must have been 1941 ... or was it '42 ... I don't know, but Charles will. He's very good at dates." Charles remembers dates, not just years but months as well. He places himself in time, in relation to the world's events (World War II, the Depression, the Harlem renaissance, the union movement) and also personal events (their marriage, Margaret's second year of residency, the family's move from Nashville). The dates spill off his lips with ease and precision.

These contrasts, which went far past an ability to remember dates, troubled Margaret in their early years together. The recognition of her own strong intelligence came slowly and was always measured against Charles's. Early in their marriage, Charles became a Fellow of the Society for Religion and Higher Education, and together they attended the annual gathering. The discussions among the Fellows were heavily theoretical and abstract, and Margaret felt herself on the periphery. She remembers a conversation with a psychologist she met there, a senior member of the group: "I remember talking to him and saying I felt I needed to have someone give me a list of books ... I needed to be more widely read ... needed to know more about the world. ... I talked to him about my rather intuitive approach to things." The psychologist's response was clear and reassuring: "You put things together in a different way. People have different kinds of intellectuality; the intuitive approach has great value. If this is the way you see things, you should write about it." Margaret must have been ready to hear his words because the simple advice of this stranger felt like a significant moment. "This helped a great deal."

Several years later Margaret recalls a similar experience. She and Charles had formed a reading group with another couple who were good friends and aggressive intellectuals. They would assign themselves readings and then get together to discuss the work. In this group, Margaret always felt like the odd-woman-out. "The other three always seemed well read, sophisticated, and worldly." Then one week they read Martin Buber's *I and Thou*. She remembers listening to the others struggle with the text. They talked in a language that was contrary to Buber—far away from the author's intent, she thought. Finally, in exasperation, one of them exclaimed, "What does he [Buber] mean?" Margaret was disbelieving: "What do they mean, 'What does he mean?' ... Had these intellectuals not understood what Buber was saying?" Yes, she knew what he was saying, and her knowing was almost effortless.

Slowly Margaret learned to appreciate her way of seeing the world. Once she did, she began to use her gifts to great advantage. Her particular, intuitive approach proved to be "very useful in the way I function as an analyst and psychotherapist ... I can pull dreams back over the years and hand them to the person ... I have the capacity to integrate matters of feeling and understand the development of intergenerational things ... and I know how to push to get this material." Her voice rings with victory, and I smile at the poignancy of her long journey. I smile also because I know how my father admires his wife's "brilliance" and cherishes their opposite tendencies. "It took me time to make my peace with this," says Margaret.

Nashville

CAREER AND FAMILY

MARGARET's anxieties over her first teaching experiences melted away when she was actually engaged in clinical work with children and their families or when she was closely supervising medical students on the wards. In this concrete work she felt at home; her intuitive mind seemed to flourish. "I particularly loved being in charge of the outpatient pediatric clinic and going to the child-health stations. I also loved supervisory-type teaching, where I worked closely with students and dealt with them one-on-one."

In a letter written to her department chairman, Margaret described her work at the city Well Baby Clinic in East Nashville, a project she initiated soon after her arrival at Meharry:

> This has been a worthwhile and rewarding project for we have seen in a very needy neighborhood twenty to thirty babies each week (except in bad weather) and have seen at least a dozen tiny two and three month olds, on adequate feeding schedules, grow to be sturdy, plump toddlers. And their new siblings follow them to the clinic— which to me is the proof of the pudding—despite the opposition of a few griping old-line neighborhood doctors. Since the inception of this program of feeding, immunization, routine examination and doctor patient conferences we have each week supervised two senior students as they actually carried out their work. The response, even in the most lackadaisical, has usually been enthusiastic. . . .

Leaving home early in the morning, Margaret would fill a couple of thermoses full of hot coffee and fetch her students at school. They would pile into her small blue car and ride together out to one of the child-health stations. The grinding competitiveness that generally dominated the medical classroom would momentarily be replaced by a camaraderie among the students. The usual chasm between the dominant teacher and the reticient, submissive students seemed, for the period they were together, to be bridged by feelings of colleague-ship. And the typical cynicism toward patients that usually marked medical student conversations would be eclipsed for a few hours by sincere attention to diagnosis and cure.

Away from the authoritarian structure of the classroom, away from the cramming of formulas and facts, Margaret could see different qualities in her students—of concern, of generosity, of insight. Some-times, as she watched them examine a patient and piece together the child's history, she would see how well they communicated with patients, how they integrated what they learned or picked up by intuition—qualities rarely called for or rewarded in other parts of their training. These pilgrimages to the child-health stations, then, were rewarding to Margaret on a number of levels. They allowed her to use her own strongest qualities; they seemed to make her students more human; they allowed for a different kind of teaching and learning; and they captured the "missionary spirit" that was always at the center of Margaret's interest in medicine.

The contrasts in how students behaved in different settings fas-cinated and worried Margaret. Why was there so much comfort, camaraderie, and caring for students in the real, challenging world of the child-health stations and so much awkwardness, competition, and panic in their classrooms? The dissonance, she knew, reflected to some extent her own love of the clinical, supervisory work. She was at her best in those environments and students mirrored her enthusiasm. But as time went on, she knew that the contrast reflected more than her personal predisposition. She began to see a broader picture: how the educational structures, practices, and philosophies of the medical school did not inspire the best in students.

After several months of quiet observation at Meharry, Margaret felt compelled to write them up for the faculty Curriculum Com-mittee at the college. She knew her criticisms would probably fall on deaf ears, and even prepared herself for a counterattack from the entrenched system's loyalists. But she felt a responsibility to state her views. With her baby tucked in bed, Margaret stayed up several nights working on her letter. She wanted to be candid but not offensive; she wanted to engage in collective self-criticism, not denigrate the efforts of her colleagues. Having finished, she asked Charles to read the letter and suggest changes in tone and wording. Finally, she delivered it to the committee chairman, tense with anxiety and excitement:

> *Dear Sirs:*
>
> *Certain curricular matters have been of great concern to me during the past several months. These problems have taken shape as I have had the opportunity to work within the system and more important—live among the students. I wish to pass these problems as I see them on to you so that perhaps they may be considered as a part of the larger problem of integration.*
>
> *1. Concerning the crowded schedule and lack of time for creative effort*
>
> *We realize that this is an accelerated program; nevertheless, we certainly defeat our purpose when we rush students from hour to hour of continuous classes with hardly a moment for serious reflection and certainly no time to refer to classical works or current literature. This seems particularly so in the case of the senior students. Their response to the present system is one of disinterest and sometimes outright antagonism.*
>
> *2. Concerning the Presentation of Material*
>
> *The text appears to be holy to the student. His main purpose in life is to read 133 "pages" on a given night with little regard for the material therein. One student even demanded that a given assignment should be found word for word in the table of contents of his text—because "I paid ten dollars for this book." The natural result is a rivalry between student and instructor as to who can outwit whom in the "reading"-"quiz" relationship. All regard for the material being presented seems to have been lost.*
>
> *3. Concerning the "Solid Front"*
>
> *Some of us are very frank in feeling the necessity of presenting a "solid front" to the students. We seem to think that if a student discovers a difference of opinion between two faculty members or be-*

tween instructor and text—that "all is off." The student—if he is wise—either believes that we are dishonest or that we don't recognize that various theories exist. Other students graduate believing that there is only one answer about a stated problem. This latter belief by the way, seems to be characteristic of the results of nursing education. We hope for more from the medical student.

I do not claim to know the answers—but the problems are real ones to me. Concerning the first we might say that some of the students wouldn't use "free" hours properly. We are not, however, setting our standards for the student who might be driven to learn anything. I believe, too, that the student in the clinical years particularly should be given some "free" time—even at the expense of some of our "hours" of classwork.

Concerning the second point, we know that texts are hopelessly inadequate—both in material presented and in their current value. Why then should we point up the importance of any given text and stage a battle royal over its contents?

A quotation: "I'm not trying to learn a subject, I'm trying to outsmart the man." Why not make more use of our own experience in teaching students and of the larger experience of others as set forth in original works and current literature?

We know that many theories exist about almost any phase of medicine. I think we would have better students and better rapport with those students if we shared that secret freely with them.

May I apologize to this Committee for offering my problems and perspectives from so meager an experience.

Very sincerely,
Margaret M. Lawrence

Even as Margaret challenged the Curriculum Committee to consider an educational process that valued inquiry, reflection, and criticism, she knew that Meharry was not alone in sustaining a program that encouraged competition, hierarchies, and antagonism. Had she not been so deeply engaged in trying to master the material and accommodate to the system in her medical student days at Columbia, she certainly would have noticed many of the same stultifying, counterproductive methods. But students trying to negotiate the prescribed requirements don't always allow themselves to notice the contradictions or hypocrisies, so engaged are they in making it through successfully and identifying with their powerful mentors. For Margaret, in her status as a new teacher and outsider from the North, the hypocrisies were visible and troubling. She recognized that the problems were found in most medical schools, but suspected the reason why they might be compounded at Meharry. One of two medical schools for Negroes in the country, it suffered from the assaults of racism, from constant financial fragility, from an inclination toward low self-esteem. This institutional vulnerability seemed to express itself in educational rigidities. In its struggle for credibility and solvency, Meharry became almost a caricature of the worst qualities of most medical schools—more authoritarian, more inflexible, more arbitrary.

For Margaret, who had dreams of integrating research, teaching, and clinical work, who had hopes of creating new institutional forms, who wished to enter into collaborative projects with her colleagues, the institutional rigidities were very discouraging, sometimes eroding to her spirit. She yearned for more open cooperative encounters with other faculty, for more democratic relationships instead of the hierarchies that seemed to reduce productivity and spontaneity. After she had been at Meharry for two years, Margaret wrote another letter, this time to the president, that outlined her feelings of frustration and disappointment:

> ... *At the present time I feel that the restrictions exerted on the individual staff member in the pursuit of his duties are inimical to productive effort. This is true even though the free pursuit of these duties would create no hardship anywhere else in the department. Such restriction was demonstrated in the nursery school projects. Senior students were made unavailable to the project for grossly insufficient and contradictory reasons. There is a lack of cooperative management of the department for the good of all and a lack of freedom of opportunity—also I believe for the good of all. This freedom of opportunity includes freedom to do interesting research in the best manner possible under the current circumstances and equal opportunity to do the more desirable jobs of the department.*
>
> *I would like to see work schedules for the department arrived at cooperatively by its members. . . . We literally carry out instructions which we have little part in devising. . . . The pediatrics department I see as a cooperative venture profiting by whatever each staff member has to offer—guided in a democratic manner by its chairman. I had*

real hopes when I came to Meharry of working under an experienced chief well trained in the modern practice of pediatrics. The patients, students, and staff would gain much in such an environment.

As Margaret recalls the passionate feelings behind these letters, she does not discount the impatience of youth. Neither is she surprised that the letters—so brave in their solo voice and candid language— never received serious response, only begrudging admission that they had been received. The concerns that Margaret expressed in the summer of 1945 remained reverberating themes in her professional life, increasing in amplification as she has gained more experience. At seventy, she still has trouble with unproductive institutional hierarchies. She still chafes at the autocratic pyramids that permit arbitrary decision making and don't encourage the initiative of individuals. She still preaches the "team approach"—cooperative, interdisciplinary, eclectic. She still crosses boundaries that inhibit most of her classically trained colleagues. And she *still* doesn't expect warm response. Now, at seventy and with the genuine respect of her colleagues, she has more freedom to "do her own thing" and carve her niche. But the institutions chug along, remaining relatively unchanged. And Margaret spends less time composing careful letters. She is content to state her position, voice her beliefs, and get to work.

In the same letter, to the president of Meharry, Margaret assured him: "May I state here frankly that I have no departmental administrative ambitions but prefer to be a 'worker.'" Forty years later, she still has no wish to "speak for the institution." "I am a worker," she says with a determination born of an enduring sense of how best to use her strengths. If she can surround herself with a small team of like-minded people who relate to one another in a "democratic manner," and if their work with patients is creative and productive, then she feels satisfied. She may rail quietly to her family and close friends about the institutional constraints, but now she devotes her full energy to the healing of patients, which she sees as inextricably bound to the health and "sentiments" ("meaning mind *and* feeling") of the healers.

In the years since she left Meharry, she has come to understand the peculiar and debilitating pressures that Meharry suffered. She remembers how white professors from Vanderbilt University came across town to teach courses at Meharry for salaries much higher than the black faculty who were working there full-time. They had little commitment to Meharry or their students, and they frequently treated their black colleagues with disrespect, flaunting their higher status and incomes. Their presence made the permanent staff feel diminished and enraged, a silent, seething anger that was never expressed because no one dared offend the white professors who gave the institution legitimacy. With no outlet, the black anger turned back on itself, infecting the life of the community. In retrospect, Margaret can now see the relationship between the invasion of arrogant white professors and the authoritarian manner of her black colleagues toward their students. Feeling the pain of their lowly status in relation to the Vanderbilt professors, the black doctors needed to pass it on to their students. It was very hard for the black staff to break the pattern when, every day, they experienced assaults from the white world.

In 1945, Margaret suggested to the president, "There is need for a better relationship between student and staff on a high level and extending into social life. A definite effort should be made to welcome the student body into the homes and lives of staff families. There would certainly be a more happy, mutual understanding of the problems faced by each group." She may not have fully appreciated the impossibility of what she was asking. "Mutual understanding" is hard to achieve in an environment where the adults are infantilized. As long as the black professors were not permitted to be men, fully empowered in their adulthood, then they could not be expected to encourage their students' manhood.

The denial of their manhood by a racist system may have been one of the reasons why so many of the black professors were preoccupied with "the almighty dollar." Along with the formulas and facts of medical training, the professors seemed to overemphasize the material benefits of being a doctor. One teacher was famous for holding up a hundred-dollar bill in front of his class. "Look at this, gentlemen, this is what you have to look forward to." And several bragged about the numbers of patients they could see in an hour and how much they charged each one. Dollar signs danced in the eyes of the students as they heard such testimony from their professors. Perhaps the rewards of money (and the status it yielded) were a partial consolation for the demeaning environment the black professors had to endure.

Whatever the reasons for these dubious values and the exaggerated materialism, Margaret was horrified by the money waving in classrooms, by the ways students were socialized to believe this was the goal. "I'm going to be a doctor and I'm going to be rich!" Forty years later, Margaret smiles at her horror of the doctors "who were hell-bent on making money" and admits to a softening of her stance. She now sees in her harsh criticism a kind of "puritanical attitude" that was too judgmental. But Margaret still dislikes the money-grubbing parts of medical practice and believes in an ethic of service. She credits her own family legacy for this ethic. "I always had this *missionary attitude* toward the South. Charles and I were going to be missionaries. I probably saw myself as going to Meharry as a missionary, although I wasn't one. I probably saw myself as not being one of those who expected to get wealthy—and I didn't!"

Margaret's criticisms of Meharry were not a reflection of her disinterest or distance from the institution. Quite the opposite. She was vitally interested in the training of black doctors and very much wanted their education to be challenging and productive. She deeply valued Meharry's commitment to community-based, clinical medicine (an orientation not present at the prestigious white medical schools), and she wanted to develop a curriculum that would match those goals. Her frustrations grew out of what she perceived as a dissonance between the professed values of the institution and the educational practices. Perhaps Margaret's criticisms were harsh because she cared too much.

Her keen scrutiny of life at Meharry might also have been related to her token status. As the only woman on the medical faculty, she often felt peripheral to "the action," and this position may have allowed her to take a more critical view. Being the only woman was a new experience for Margaret, who, as far back as she could remember, found pleasure and support in female company. As a young adolescent, new to Harlem, she had reached out to a small group of girls at Wadleigh High who had become "almost like sisters." They offered to Margaret, a recently transplanted, only child, a warm circle of friendship that fueled her independent pursuits. Feelings of alliance with a circle of women were echoed in her medical school experience, where Margaret formed close relationships with most of the other female students. In the vast sea of men at Columbia, the women swam together, buffered against the waves of male presumption and privilege. They provided comfort and solace for one another and supported each other's ambitions. Even during her residency at Harlem Hospital, Margaret had felt a special camaraderie with the few other women physicians. Late at night they would often gather in Margaret's room and talk shop, listen to the radio, knit and sew, and design their futures.

In contrast, Margaret's experience as the only woman physician at Meharry felt lonely. The loneliness was exaggerated by the social practices of middle-class Negro society in Nashville where men and women rarely developed friendships outside marriage. It was considered inappropriate, for example, for Margaret to be close to a male colleague at Meharry. Gestures of friendship would lead to suspicions and embroidered gossip. Margaret still recalls the seething rage of one faculty wife who resented her husband's admiration for the young woman doctor who seemed to combine being a doctor and a mother so gracefully. "He got in a lot of trouble with his wife because he came home saying, 'Dr. Lawrence works everyday doing this marvelous job and she has a baby and doesn't think anything about it!'"

But it was not only the suspicion and wrath of the doctors' wives that kept Margaret distant from her male colleagues. She also felt subtly ostracized within the faculty. She would come up to a group of her colleagues who were enjoying some lively gossip and the conversation would suddenly shift as they noticed her approach. Or she would make an urgent point at a departmental meeting and encounter no signs of response from her colleagues. On the few occasions when her colleagues would forget about her presence, she would feel awkward and out of place as they bantered crudely like athletes in a locker room. In most cases, it seemed wiser and more comfortable for Margaret to keep her distance and not risk the misinterpretations of friendship or expect to feel at home in this male world.

Margaret's feelings of isolation were enhanced as well by the contrast with Charles's work life at Fisk. As a member of a very tightly knit group of researchers at the Race Relations Institute, Charles enjoyed intimacy and camaraderie with his colleagues. The collaborative research, pioneering and exciting, captured the minds and hearts of each participant, weaving work relationships that crossed over easily into friendships. Sometimes Margaret would catch herself feeling envious of these rich contacts. "Charles had good friends over at the Race Relations Institute.... My colleagues were people I didn't feel that close to. Charles had close women friends and men friends, and they adored him and he adored them."

The subtle social exclusion (which Margaret now clearly recognizes as pervasive sexism) affected salary and promotion decisions. After her second year at Meharry, Margaret began to notice troubling inequities. Not only had she been overloaded with responsibilities not required of many of her male colleagues, but her salary did not match those of her peers with similar experience and standing. When she felt satisfied that she had accumulated enough evidence to make a strong case, Margaret wrote to the president describing her institutional responsibilities and her dismay at the inequities she perceived:

June 18, 1945

My work here began July 1, 1943 when I was hired as instructor in pediatrics and public health. My program consisted of a full time faculty schedule in pediatrics, ward and clinic work in pediatrics, and physical examination and immunization of student nurses. During that year I gave routine physical examinations to the children of Grace Eaton Day Home. During this year also Dr. Maddox asked me to make routine weekly examinations on the children of the South Street Community Center nursery school. I have continued this project until the present time.... My contract of July 1, 1944 stated that I was assistant professor of pediatrics....

Seeing the great opportunity for studying growth and development at the nursery school age in the day nurseries, and having a real interest in problems of physical and behavioral development, I decided to use the two nursery schools under my care in such a study.... The Fisk Social Center nursery school was taken on in the same manner. When the program was going on at full tilt we were visiting the South St. Center weekly and the Grace Eaton Day Home and Fisk Nursery every other week. Two senior students scheduled for the pe-

diatric clinic group at Hubbard were taken to these nurseries on each visit. We were a fact finding and reporting group. We saw an amazing lot of medical abnormalities and the nurseries depended on us for the service. This program continues at present with the difference that the senior students component of the examining group has not been available to us; and juniors from the pediatric wards used in their place—though willing—have to be under constant supervision, thus slowing up the work and leaving no time for the research angle. This type of experience is to me plainly an experience for seniors who have mastered the rudiments of examining children and are able to appreciate the usually concealed abnormalities of supposedly healthy children. . . .

This brings me to a few comments on salary and status. Within the past weeks I have been offered a contract for 1945–1946 identical with the one accepted for 1944–45. I have given two years of full time service to the department of pediatrics including very frequent nights and holidays beyond the ordinary working hours. My previous pediatric training consists of six months during a two year hospital service, three months as a New York University fellow working under Dr. Bullowa of Harlem Hospital on whooping cough and pulmonary embolism, and a year of public health training dealing principally with child health. I feel, I hope with some justification, that my past training, my services to the pediatrics department and my ability to give service in the future—if given ample opportunity—entitle me both to an increase in salary and an improvement in rank. I have reached this conclusion not without comparing my qualifications with those of one of my colleagues who is enjoying these advantages. I also consider this discrimination in advancement as adverse criticism of my services here.

. . . I am grateful for the opportunity to state my grievances concerning the conditions of work in our department and the hoped for ideal.

Despite Margaret's heartfelt appeal, the president was unmoved. Her salary for 1945–46 remained $2,700, the same as it had been the previous year, and she was not granted an elevation in rank. By the following year, when she was promoted to associate professor, the disparities were so obvious that the president moved swiftly to repair the impression of discrimination. Her salary was raised to $3,200.

The experience of tokenism was not all bad. Despite her frustration at the discrimination, she enjoyed the high visibility. There was something about being "the only one" that appealed to her. "It was part of my privilege. I didn't suffer for it, and I think I rather liked it." She is reminded of how it sometimes felt in medical school to be the only Negro—both painful and pleasurable. Now, forty years later, she can admit how she relished the limelight, the special glow that often accompanied the uncomfortable exclusion. She wanted the attention and praise—that she now regards as empty and misleading—to assure her of her value and worth. Now she no longer needs that attention and stroking and distrusts it.

Margaret contrasts the empty privileges of tokenism with the genuine pleasure she derived from her identity as a woman. "I liked myself as a woman." This identity was very much related to her enjoyment of motherhood. As she stood up in front of her class, lecturing on pediatrics, she could feel the power of her mother image. However hard the struggle of combining the roles of mother, wife, and doctor, she liked the image of herself as embracing family and work. "I enjoyed the picture of myself as mother." And this side of her was a source of intrigue for the students. Their image of Dr. Lawrence the mother grew right before their eyes as the students watched the steady progression of their teacher's pregnancies. As they learned about the development and diseases of babies in pediatrics, they saw evidence of a real baby's gestation—their professor's very own. Two babies—both girls—were born eighteen months apart while Margaret was teaching at Meharry. Sara Morgan arrived in August 1944 and Paula Jean in January 1946. Margaret laughs at the memory of her students' fascination with the babies' growth and arrival and the exaggerated legend that quickly developed. "There was a story of my saying 'excuse me' during the lecture and simply walking off to have my baby." Although Margaret smiles at the exaggeration, it conveys her students' appreciation of her swift and graceful productivity and her determination to break down the boundaries of work and family. When Margaret left her classes to have her babies, she did not return immediately, but she came back more quickly than most women would have dared. Two weeks after the birth of each daughter, she was back in the classroom lecturing about babies. "The students brought me roses. I remember coming back to lecture after you were born, wearing a nice brown suit and looking very good, weighing about 119 pounds ... I had this image of being the one woman on the faculty but also being wife and mother and carrying it off."

The image of Dr. Lawrence, slim and elegant two weeks after her baby's birth, accepting roses from her grateful students, was not the whole story. The life of Mrs. Lawrence—wife and mother—was complicated and hard. Her serene public image contrasted with her strenuous private life: "Look at Mom, she's laughing!" crowed her three-year-old daughter, so thrilled to see her mother's tired brow and determined mouth ease into a smile.

The family had grown to five, with three children under four years old. Margaret grins mischievously. "It was family planning." And indeed it was. Charles and Margaret had always wanted three children. When they decided to marry and dreamed of the future, their fantasies always included three children. "It seemed like a good balance" is all Margaret can recall as she tries to reconstruct their reasoning. "We knew we didn't just want one. We didn't want a token." Having lived the life of an only child, Margaret wanted to "give my children siblings." She didn't want them to face the loneliness she experienced growing up—the long solitary walks, the endless conversations with herself, the preoccupations with her parents that consumed too much of her young energy. Although she herself had turned loneliness into strength of character, isolation into introspection, she wanted her children to enjoy companions, confidants. She wanted her children to have a childhood. And now that these children are all over forty, Margaret looks back and says, "One thing I'm proudest of is what good *friends* you three are."

Three children seemed the "perfect number" to Margaret and Charles, but their friends and colleagues in Nashville—who watched them appear—thought three was extravagant. In those days "an upper-middle-class Negro family was supposed to have two children." When Margaret was pregnant with Paula, it was not uncommon for some busybody to ask, "How many do you plan to have?", incredulous that this young, ambitious couple would saddle themselves with the extra demands and chaos of more than two children.

In their "family planning," Charles and Margaret not only considered the number of children, but also decided that the children would be close in age. Margaret remembers feeling that if her children were close they would "help to raise one another." With two parents out working in the world, she hoped her children would be good company for one another. A picture flashes in Margaret's mind of a stormy night after the family had moved back north. The snow is falling heavily, and the travel home from work is treacherous. Margaret and Charles arrive home hours late. As the car turns in the driveway, the headlights illuminate three small figures—five, six, and seven years old—huddled on the porch, linking arms, gently rocking to the beat of a song they're singing. Waiting together, scared together, protected by one another.

The rush to have children close together was also related to Charles's anticipated departure. When Charles and Margaret arrived in Nashville with Chuck, they knew Charles might have to leave for CPS Camp any day. "We decided we'd go on and have our second child, because we didn't know how long Charles was going to be away and thought it wouldn't be good for Chuck to be the only child." It somehow seemed better to leave Margaret with two children. A boy baby, all alone with his mother, might be smothered by her feelings of loneliness. Margaret looks back on this concern for *Chuck's* healthy development and exclaims, "There was not very much consideration for what it would be like for me to be raising two children alone! We thought we could do anything. That seemed to be our whole attitude towards the world and towards ourselves."

This expansive attitude was tempered by anxiety, rarely expressed. They moved on with their lives—working, raising babies, digging tenuous roots in the community—against a background of worry. When would Charles have to go off to CPS Camp? Would this be their last week together? Could they do anything to change the minds of government officials? And the news from the bureaucrats kept changing. Just as soon as they would begin to accommodate to one set of plans, a letter would arrive changing Charles's status. Meanwhile, Dr. Johnson and his colleagues kept sending urgent letters to Washington attempting to get Charles reclassified to a status that would allow him to continue his work at Fisk.

At first, Charles had been assigned to a CPS camp in Tennessee. But as soon as the southern officials discovered that Charles Lawrence was a *Negro* conscientious objector—something they had not imagined in their wildest dreams—they refused to accept him. Since he had originally been drafted from New York, great confusion followed; letters and telephone calls raced back and forth between Washington and Nashville, and Charles's case finally arrived on the desk of General Hershey. "Charles became a cause célèbre!" Hershey himself decided that Charles should be sent to a northern camp and assigned him to Big Flats CPS Camp in New York.

Although Hershey's decision was a blow—Margaret had always held out hope that some miracle would save them from Charles's departure—it was also a relief. The constant uncertainty had been very stressful. Now they could make plans. As the departure day approached, the daily rhythms remained unchanged. The busy patterns of their life seemed to provide some comfort. Finally, the day before Charles was supposed to leave for Big Flats, they spent the morning in downtown Nashville buying the supplies he would need for hard, manual camp work. As they collected the heavy workboots, warm workshirts, sturdy khaki pants, Margaret felt her grief rising. They had promised each other that they would never live apart again; and here they were once more facing the separation and the distance between North and South. And this time, she was being left with a child, and soon two children, to care for.

Once she let herself feel the pain, it swept over her. How would she care for her babies? Charles was such a partner, such an enthusiastic and involved father. His absence would leave a gaping hole. Although Margaret had always expected her husband to be a fine father, she hadn't anticipated what energy and commitment he would bring to it. Right from the beginning he took part without inhibition, joyfully. "Charles *wanted* to be the first to bathe Chuck. . . . You hear lots of fathers say that their children have to be walking and talking before they can feel involved. Not Charles. He was immediately *involved* with the babies." Sometimes his enthusiasm made Margaret feel slightly excluded. He'd rush in, gather up the baby in his strong arms, plant kisses all over his face and belly, with loving hugs and exclamations. Margaret, who tended to be quieter and more restrained, would occasionally feel preempted by this joyful, noisy man. She would watch and wait for her turn, experiencing the twin emotions of deep pleasure in Charles's involvement and envy at the exuberance that allowed him the first and biggest hug.

Now she pictured Charles traveling hundreds of miles away to Big Flats, New York. Margaret knew she would miss this big man with big emotions. Having bought the camp supplies in the morning, Charles returned to work in the afternoon, filling the last precious hours with ordinary duties. Margaret went home to face the sadness, to get used to the feel of her house and child without Charles's presence, and to prepare a special bon voyage dinner. The sun went down and she waited for Charles's footsteps at the door, his exuberant homecoming, and Chuck's delight in his father's return. Night fell and she was still waiting. There was no call. The dinner had long since gotten too cold to eat. Chuck had even dozed off to sleep. Margaret waited, alternately worried and angry. Finally, just before midnight, she heard him coming. He opened the door and walked into the room as if nothing was wrong. Not a sign of guilt or remorse on his face.

Margaret tells this story with a dramatic pause. I have heard it many times, and I wait for the incredulous question. "Do you know what he had been doing?" I let her give the unbelievable punch line. "He had been playing volleyball!" There is something about this story—now embroidered into family legend—that still angers and perplexes Margaret. It is a story that *she* would tell and Charles would listen to without expression or explanation. "I was furious!" exclaims Margaret. "I had made a supreme sacrifice. . . . My husband was going off to Big Flats the next morning . . . and there he was playing volleyball!" I follow the script and ask a question I have asked before. "Was this Dad's way of dealing with anxiety?" My mother's reply has always surprised me. "To this day, Charles never told me why."

Early the next morning, Margaret and Charles were sitting in silence at the train station. Margaret could sense Charles' dejection— he hated leaving his family—in the heaviness of his arm as he hugged her. He looked handsome and strong in his traveling clothes, her "big oak tree" leaving. She permitted herself to feel helpless and small, knowing she would not be able to indulge such feelings after he left. Urgent voices suddenly interrupted the silence, echoing through the train station. They were calling for Charles. A couple of his colleagues came running toward them, waving a piece of paper in great excitement. Just a few minutes before, a telegram had arrived at Fisk saying that Charles had been released from his assignment at CPS Camp—his work at Fisk had been reclassified. His college teaching was now judged to be in "the national interest" and would be considered legitimate "alternative duty." The breathless messengers stood there with big smiles frozen on their faces. Margaret and Charles sat in stunned silence, almost not daring to believe this new twist of fate. But the good news was real and final. After the shock, Margaret and Charles recovered quickly and plunged back into their lives, this time without the low-level anxiety they had learned to live with. Now they could settle into the Nashville rhythm, believing that the beat would go on.

By the time their third child was born, the Lawrences were well established in Nashville. While Margaret continued her teaching at Meharry, Fisk tended to be the place where both Lawrences found colleagues and friends. In addition to her teaching and clinic work, Margaret had started a small pediatric practice in their house that grew more quickly than she ever expected. When the children of Fisk faculty got sick, the parents felt very comfortable calling Dr. Lawrence. "People used to call me day and night." The Fisk community began to feel like a large, extended family. Everyone knew "the Lawrences," and many had opinions about this unusual family. "Either we were very much admired or people were very critical, but they were very much *aware* of us. . . ." What amazed people was not merely the fact that Charles and Margaret were both professionals with "real careers" in a community where men tended to be bread-winners and women homemakers. It was also, perhaps primarily, the way Margaret and Charles ran their family life. They were both active and enthusiastic parents and could often be seen together with their flock of children.

The children went everywhere with them—to evening meetings, to concerts, to parties, to church. "We did our work, but when we weren't working, whoever was born went out with us." The five Lawrences appeared at gatherings where people did not generally expect to see, or hear, children. "If you had kids you were supposed to stay home with them." Occasionally, when child-care arrangements would break down and Margaret had duties at the hospital, Charles would take the children to class, get them settled in the back of the room with a few books and toys, and carry on with his lecture with half an eye on his tiny offspring.

Charles and Margaret also drew attention by the unusual way they raised their children. In a community where decorum was of great concern, where correct manners were terribly important, the Lawrence children were raised to be independent and outspoken. In a community where generational lines were clearly drawn between adults and children, the Lawrence youngsters were encouraged to make their way among grown-ups. "As soon as you arrived you came to the table," says Margaret. No matter how chaotic meals became— and they were often wild—the parents valued eating and talking together.

Friends and colleagues often offered unsolicited advice to the young parents. Margaret remembers carrying two-month-old Chuck across the Fisk campus and running into Dr. Johnson. The president gave mother and son a bemused, skeptical look and advised, "Why don't you put some pants on that boy, he's too old to be wearing dresses." The advice often came in this form—half serious, half joking— leaving Margaret to ponder the mixed messages. The wife of a faculty member who lived next-door was "dead serious," however, when she looked at the round, brown infant and snarled, "Don't you think he's too fat for the summertime?"

Sometimes, in this unsolicited advice, Margaret could hear echoes of the church ladies of her childhood in Vicksburg who loved to gossip and pry into the Morgans' business. They, too, were uncomfortable if a child spoke out: "Don't you think Margaret is a little peculiar, Mrs. Morgan?" As Margaret raised her own children, she remembered her mother's response to such officious criticism. In the same way, Margaret quietly defended the honor of her three children by not responding to the intrusive comments of her Nashville neighbors. Never once did she worry that Chuck was "too fat for the summertime," nor did she give the neighbor lady the satisfaction of a response.

From her Vicksburg childhood, Margaret was familiar with the combination of gossip, friendly meddling, and begrudging admiration. But now she and Charles were in this together. Even in the midst of wild baby tantrums or ferocious sibling battles, she could enjoy the fullness and closeness of family life, so different from the strained triangle of her own childhood. The togetherness made Charles's departures especially painful. As part of his work at the Race Relations Institute, Charles often had to travel, to collect data for their study on community organizations in Negro communities, to meet with Negro leadership, and to give speeches to various political, civic, and church groups. These trips usually took him away for three or four weeks at a time, and Margaret would be left to orchestrate the home front.

These weeks, always difficult, sometimes were overwhelming. When she would discover, just before putting dinner on the table, that there was no milk in the refrigerator, she would look at her three hungry children, missing their father, and wonder, "What have we done?" Beyond the daily grind, there were moments of crisis, like the day when Sara toppled off of the high toilet seat, crashed onto the floor, and came up with a bloodied mouth and tooth missing. Paula, a tiny infant, was screaming for attention in the next room. Chuck, having witnessed the calamity and his sister's face bathed in blood, "fell apart." Charles was away in Michigan, and Margaret still shakes her head at the memory of how desperate she felt and how much she missed him.

Margaret and the children received daily letters from Charles, who traveled mostly to the Midwest—Detroit, Ypsilanti, Kalamazoo—with side trips to Richmond, New York, and Washington, D.C. In his letters, Charles reported on his adventures in the field, and spoke of his loneliness for his family and their "bravery" in his absence. Margaret welcomed news of Charles's intellectual and political experiences, for Nashville sometimes felt provincial. She also enjoyed the view of Charles doing the work he loved most—sociological research and fighting for justice:

Ypsilanti
10/17/44

Loveliest of people,
This has been a rather full day. The morning was spent largely in

trying to line up persons for interviews tomorrow. There was also one two hour interview with a personnel manager of one of the large employers of Negroes here in Ypsi. A conference with a union leader led me to a trial being held at the city hall. The proprietors and a waitress in a restaurant were being tried for refusal to serve a Negro. The six man jury—apparently allowed in misdemeanor hearings— looked as if it had been recruited from Hinds and Copiah counties in Mississippi. The defendants were obviously lying with every breath, but they were acquitted. The CIO-UAW was very much interested in the case because they are trying to break down the general pattern of discrimination found in the town. . . .

Ypsilanti
10/18/44

Loveliest of people,

Today has been something of a holiday for me. I worked up until noon and then had lunch (as usual). The whole town seemed to be headed toward Ann Arbor for the Michigan-Purdue football game. Never having seen a big-time match of University mercenaries, I decided to go. The buses headed that way were all full to the brim! Finally some Negroes in a rubbish truck drove alongside and offered me a lift. There was nothing else to do but take it; so I did. I stood on the rear of the truck along with the workmen; and found that I actually enjoyed the invigorating air of a brisk autumn day.

By dent of following the crowd I finally came to the stadium—a huge monument to the high aims of American higher learning, planked down my three bucks and went in. In spite of myself—my critical Thorstein Veblen Theory-of-higher-education-self—I found that I enjoyed the game. Michigan had an 18 year old freshman Negro lad on the first string team, so I lent my very reserved support to them. (He was a very good dependable half-back who made one touchdown and placed the team in scoring position several times.) Michigan which had been rated as the "underdogs" trounced (notice the sports writer terminology) Purdue 40–14. . . .

During the lulls between interviews I am getting a good bit of Myrdal read. It gets better and more challenging as one goes along. Especially interesting is the section in which he stresses the leader-consciousness of Americans and the passivity of the masses that accompanies it. . . .

10/29/44
Ypsilanti

My very Lovely People,

... At this point I am actually further than ever away from a good
notion of how to tackle the situation here. I suspect strongly that it
requires a type of wisdom which I sorely lack. In fact, there are
strong suspicions that not a student of sociology but a miracle man is
needed here....

10/30/44
Ypsilanti

Beautiful People,

After I wrote to you Saturday night, I went over to Carver Center
to a party being given by Negro students here at Normal College.
Somehow it struck me as a very sad affair. Not even at Fisk-our-
Alma-Mater do the women (about 30 of them) seem to have an air
of such utter futility. I sense that the Negroes here are even more set
apart than those of you who were at Cornell; for there is no general
liberal tradition about the campus—there are no radicals with whom
the darker brethren can make common sense. From conversations
with the Negro students I have not yet discovered a faculty member
to whom they can look for genuine understanding....

Kalamazoo
Wednesday morning 11:45

My mighty Lovely People,

We worked so late last night that by the time we finished I was
physically exhausted and mentally unable to function—even up to
my usually poor level. I had worked steadily from 8:00 A.M. until
11:00 P.M. I had to gather a group of people together to compile a
list of names and addresses of Negro families in the community from
which to make assignments to our volunteer interviewers.... At last
night's coaching session, the shortcomings of Chief Long's schedule
became glaringly apparent. There were several persons present who
were trained interviewers, and they began asking very searching questions aimed politely—but pointedly—at the ambiguities in the instrument. You will recall that I talked to you about the defectiveness
of the thing before I left. Without apologizing for the thing, I tried to

help work out ways of handling it that would obviate too much fogginess.

From this point of perspective in the study it looks as if it will be several days after I had planned before I shall be able to get away from here. The entire responsibility of supervising the 56 volunteer interviewers is on my shoulders. In addition, there is the fact that I have been promised to the Detroit FOR [Fellowship of Reconciliation] Conference. Finally, there are a good many data that must be gathered by interviews with industrialists, union people, city officials, and social agencies. . . . It takes constant vigilance and occasional moments of prayer. . . ."

Kalamazoo
Wednesday afternoon 4:45

Loveliest of People,
. . . At odd moments during the last three days I have been writing my manuscript for Friday evening in Detroit. So far I have done nothing about tomorrow's three speeches (a class at Kalamazoo College, 9:00 A.M.; Y's Men's Luncheon, noon; Presbyterian Church Supper, evening). There is also a speech for Sunday evening at the local Congregational Church. Speaking and managing the mechanics of the study just about take up all of the time I have. . . .

Worn out by the long hours, discouraged by the imperfections in the research methods, exhausted by speech making, unsurprised but distressed by the persistence of racism, Charles longed for the support and solace of his family. He also felt some guilt for abandoning Margaret when she needed him most.

10/24/44

. . . I miss you all as much as I knew I would. Sallyboo, I miss your big toothless, burpful smile and your delightful conversations. Chuck, my son, I miss you all the way from a 6:00 A.M. "Daas" to your 9:00 P.M. "night night." As for you, lovely one, I am hopeless in

saying how much I miss you as I am in saying how much I love you. . . .

10/27/44

. . . I especially miss you, Sweetheart, when I go out among other happily married couples; yet I am drawn to them because of the vicarious satisfaction of being with them. To make matters worse, the Haydens have a daughter of two years, and she is quite advanced for her age. Though not nearly as beautiful as our Sally—nor as bright as our Chuck—she is an exceptionally nice child. . . ."

11/10/44

My Beautiful Woman,
* The disappointment which I felt on not finding you at home when I telephoned a few minutes ago was completely mitigated by the knowledge of the fact that you were out re-creating yourself. As Mrs. LaSaine told you, my call was to ascertain that you and the Little Ones were in good health. The fact that you were at a lecture and a reception was all the proof that I needed that everything was ship shape. I missed the ring in your voice, but I'm mighty proud that you could get out—in fact, I'm mighty proud of you (PERIOD). . . .*

9/20/45

. . . Chucky, it is mighty good to know that you are telling everybody about our conversation over the telephone. I shall try to call you up again this weekend; so be ready to talk to me. It's good to know that you are developing so fast, too, Sally. I miss all three and ½ of you more than I can tell you about; but there is great consolation in knowing that you are there and that you are so much help and comfort to one another. . . .

Charles's concern for his family often got expressed in housekeeping directives, usually reminding Margaret to take care of some piece of business that needed doing before his return. These dreary details—that consumed too much of the time Margaret didn't have and that required that she do the things Charles would probably have done if he were home—always caused her fatigue just thinking about them. At the point in each of her husband's letters when he would list the chores, Margaret would groan, a tired note of resignation. So much of family life was full of these routines.

10/24/44

. . . By the way, be sure to follow-through quickly on the inspection of and application for tires. There is no telling when that front right one will blow out; and, at the moment, there is no spare to replace it. . . . I plan to cash at least a forty dollar check either in Ypsi or N.Y. This will mean a replacement of my expense funds and fifteen dollars from our own. I shall let you know the correct amount when I make out the check.

9/20/45

. . . About the car: I'm mighty glad that you got the new battery in and that it is performing satisfactorily. It has been apparent from the beginning that the old battery was not much good. I would suggest that you get a note from Mr. Stone certifying as to the condition of the battery and that it was due to faulty materials or workmanship—there has never been a time when we even allowed the water to run low! If you do not have time to go over and see the Feldman people, write them, enclosing a copy of the note, and tell them that you did not have time to come by and make an adjustment; but that you feel that some adjustment should be made. I think that this should be done soon, lest the time element work too much against us. I feel much better now that I know that you will not be stranded on some side street in East Nashville.

6/46

. . .

1. The check duplication must come from the fact of my new employment status. . . . Please take my check to Mrs. Perry. Should it happen that it is a check due to me, thru some accounting miracle, keep it till I come.

2. Get tires (new synthetic—Don't get Grade III). Sears is perhaps the best place.

3. *I think we should try to give at least five dollars between us to the Community Chest.*
4. *Orndorff's bill sounds right. If you didn't pay today, his address is Highway 81-South, Route 1, Adairville, KY.*
5. *I think the fly wheel ought to be repaired.*

Charles's forays into "the field" made him feel alternately energized and overwhelmed. While they confirmed his commitment to the integration of social science and political action, they also forced him to see all the ways in which he needed further training in order to do justice to the work. He felt particularly inadequate in designing the questionnaires and interviews for his research. Those designed back at the university too often proved fuzzy and naive when they were used in the "real world." Charles struggled to bring greater clarity and sophistication to the research methods but longed for more guidance, direction, and knowledge. Too much of the project's success seemed to hinge on the power of his personality, his intuitive talents of questioning, rather than on systematic principles of inquiry.

The rapid pace of the work was also a problem. Too mired in the details of research, Charles felt that he lost sight of the larger questions. It sometimes felt strange, even irresponsible, to be making big speeches at public meetings—speeches on such broad topics as "The Current Situation in Race Relations," "The State of the Nation," and "One World or None"—when he did not have the time for reflection. But it was not only time that eluded Charles. He was still searching for ways to frame his observations of social reality and articulate his criticisms of current social science, and knew that he had much more to learn.

Returning North

TO MAKE THE WOUNDED WHOLE

O N one of Charles's trips to Ypsilanti, he made special plans to travel over to Ann Arbor, to the University of Michigan, to hear Professor MacIver, one of his advisers and mentors from Columbia, a "towering intellect" whose work spoke directly to his own ideological and intellectual passions. In a letter to Margaret, Charles described the excitement of his reunion with MacIver and the intellectual excitement it stirred in him:

> ... MacIver was speaking to the Michigan State Press Association meeting on "Peace and the Devil." It was a good address the thesis of which is that war-time mentality ill prepares nations to wage peace inasmuch as it requires regarding people of enemy countries as if they were a different order of human being "pulled by different strings." He attacked the Dunbarton Oaks proposal as one which is conceived in this mentality and therefore foredoomed unless it is reconstructed through the power of American public opinion. It was an excellent address.
>
> ... At one point MacIver attacked the timidity of academic men, who although they don't have an election to win, fail to speak out and ask for the very best, hoping at least to get the best possible compromise. It was downright fine to see the manner in which he towered in intellect above the best that the U. of M. has to offer. When the professors left Scotty and I had a session with him on Scotty's thesis proposal. MacIver admonished us both to get through [with writing our theses] with all dispatch. ... It was very good to meet a Great Mind again!!!

In so many ways the meeting with MacIver confirmed Charles's formless worries about his research work. Hearing MacIver's tough criticisms of academic timidity, and marveling at his intellectual range, Charles knew he must return to Columbia University to finish his studies. In addition, MacIver, who recognized their meeting as a critical moment in Charles's career and wanted his graduate student to take full advantage of his potential, urged him on. "Finish with dispatch," he said simply. Charles was ready to hear this advice and decided then and there that he would find a way to return to New York to complete his doctoral work.

At the same time, Margaret was going through private ruminations about her own career. She continued to feel completely engaged by her clinical work with babies and young children but had begun to recognize that much of her time was spent unraveling family stories. More often than not, the parents would arrive with concerns about their baby's physical health, but in trying to uncover the history and causes, the doctor would hear about the family's psychological problems. Margaret noticed the frequency of "family crisis" (and her interest in it) most often in her pediatric work at the child-health stations, where many families arrived at the door in some state of generalized need for help, and where Margaret's supervision of medical students allowed her to see more clearly the diagnostic patterns.

Aware of the emotional as well as physical troubles in her patients and their families, Margaret felt more and more intrigued by tracing their interaction. She also recognized that one reason families expressed their anxieties and struggles to her was her interest in hearing their stories. In her questions and replies, mothers could sense a concern for the "whole child" and felt comfortable revealing the hidden family issues that frequently surround a child's illness. Margaret saw her interests gradually shifting toward the emotional side of health, not necessarily away from pediatrics but toward a medical practice that integrated pediatrics and psychiatry.

When she began to articulate these emerging interests to herself, Margaret could hear the echoes of Benjamin Spock, who gave her "the first firm feelings" of integrating these disciplines. Margaret had watched the attention Spock gave to the complicated stories of family life; she had watched his deft synthesis of the psychological, social, and physical dimensions of each problem, and had been convinced of the power of his eclecticism. She had also heard of Spock's struggles with the medical establishment, which found his integration of disciplines unsettling and forced him to choose one—pediatrics—as his primary professional identity. She had heard of his training in psychoanalysis and admired his search for the roots of emotional health, including his own. She could see that there were costs to these pioneering attempts. Spock faced the skepticism of colleagues threatened by his eclecticism, rejection by pediatricians not convinced that psychoanalysis was a worthy "scientific" endeavor, and the difficult intellectual and clinical problems that inevitably arise in application of new concepts to traditional, reified practice. The costs he faced were probably invisible to those who experienced his generous care, but they were costs, nonetheless, and they no doubt eroded some of his good energies.

As Margaret began to feel the reverberations of Spock's message in her work at the child-health clinics in Nashville, as she moved from appreciating his innovative example to experiencing her own special gifts of integration, the next steps in her career began to take form. Through close observation of the nature of her patients' needs, as well as a recognition of her special talents, she was drawn more and more to child psychiatry.

As we discuss this important shift in her career, Margaret sees that her interest in psychiatry probably had more complex origins. She pauses, then offers a clue: "I wonder now whether part of this interest might have been related to my self-preoccupation." Among her father's many ambitions for Candy Man had been the dream that he might have followed in the Reverend Morgan's footsteps. "If only the boy had lived, he would have become a priest of the church. . . . Certainly, my father from time to time let me know that part of the disadvantage in being a girl was that I couldn't grow up to be a priest." She could, however, do the next best thing: she could become a healer. She could lay on hands like her father did. Psychiatry—with its concern for the emotional well-being of people; with its emphasis on hidden issues, on empathy, and listening; with its great appreciation of history and roots—may have felt closer to the spiritual healing Margaret had witnessed as a child. "In Mississippi of fifty years ago . . . black people turned to religion for comfort in the literal sense of the word; that is, through religion they 'joined' their strength, body, mind, and soul." Perhaps Margaret, in moving toward psychiatry, felt pulled by its "soulfulness," its attention to the depth of being.

Echoes of her mother's sadness could also have contributed to Margaret's interest in psychiatry. Her childhood was dominated by Mary's grief, by images of her mother lying in bed "like she was dead." Her mother's "depression" (no one called it that in Mississippi) terrified and angered the child. The wish to untangle and understand her mixed reactions to Mary's sadness may have contributed to Margaret's developing interest in emotional problems. I also suspect, although this goes unmentioned by Margaret, that Andrew, the schizophrenic uncle who lived out his anguished existence in the Harlem apartment and consumed the love of Mom Margaret, must have played his part. At fourteen, Margaret heard his wild, out-of-control hallucinations and saw the guilt and pain he caused her grandmother. As an adolescent, Margaret was unforgiving. As an adult, psychiatry offered her the possibility of understanding Andrew's hallucinations and of coming to terms with her own embarrassment and fear.

All these family echoes would be enough to explain Margaret's interest in psychiatry. In fact, the choice seemed "overdetermined," as analysts might say. But Margaret continues to refer to "the issue of self-preoccupation" as well. She recalls her adolescent worries that her preoccupations with herself might be "sinful," that her conversations with herself, her private reveries, might be self-indulgent. "I prayed about that and wondered whether I was being selfish." Later, she worried, too, about the pleasure she sometimes got from the high visibility of her tokenism in college and medical school, and her need for the approval and appreciation of others. Psychiatry, perhaps, represented a turning point—an unconscious decision to attend to others, to move beyond her preoccupations with self. It may also have offered Margaret the opportunity to listen to others in a way she had never felt listened to. Her childhood reveries were, after all, in *place of* parents or companions, who were not listening. Her need to "constantly check myself out" may have been related to early mixed messages she had received from her parents, particularly her mother—

messages of respect and admiration but also subtle denigration: "You're absolutely wonderful and we look up to you . . . and on the other hand pick, pick . . . this little thing is wrong."

The mixed messages and lack of a reliable audience in her childhood made Margaret want her own children's experience to be different. She did not want her children to be unclear about their parents' presence and unalterable belief in them. "I joined Charles in this . . . both of us anticipated that all three of you were going to be productive people and you didn't have to do that by yourselves . . . we wanted to be there." A big part of being there was listening. "I was aware of listening to you . . . wanted to know what was going on with you which I don't think my parents knew how to do . . . *I very much got involved*." She speaks with great passion and relief on this point of involvement, as if this is something that marked a major developmental transformation that had implications for her personal and professional life. "Here I was, a person growing up somewhat self-centered, but I got involved along the way with consideration of what somebody else was feeling."

For Margaret, listening to her children required that she treat them individually and be ready to hear the unexpected. "Like the time when Chuck sat down at the little table and suddenly broke into tears. 'I want my Daddy!' Charles was away so much . . . or you, Sara, required special listening because I had never known anyone like you. . . . You were so direct, so outspoken. You *demanded* response. . . . This business of being in a family meant that each child at some time required response from the parent . . . and I learned to pay attention. . . ."

Part of Margaret's pleasure in giving attention to her three children was to give it to each one singly. "I never felt I had to give equal treatment." When she perceived that one of her children needed a time alone with her or did something that required individual celebration, Margaret made a "special, secret plan." Mother and child would drive to town, tour a bookstore, buy a toy, and indulge in a delicious chocolate eclair on the way home. The pastry tasted particularly wonderful because it was secretly consumed, a wonderful silent conspiracy between Margaret and the chosen, deserving offspring. As they arrived home they were careful to remove the last bit of chocolate from around their lips. "Yummy," says Margaret, reliving one of her deepest satisfactions in mothering.

The craft of psychiatric practice seemed very much related to Margaret's motherly talents and gifts. Psychiatry—which requires the building of trust, the development of relationships, perceptive listening, and benign attention—not only allowed Margaret the privilege of making up for what she had not been given in childhood but also allowed her to make connections between her maternal pleasures and her professional identity.

In deciding to head north again, to purse further training, Margaret and Charles came to an important realization. This plan—concocted during their first summer of courtship in Vicksburg, nurtured in order to keep themselves going during times of separation—did not have to be limited to a return to their geographic home. Ever since they had conceived of building the Center for Health and Social Action, they had imagined that their "missionary work" would take place in the Deep South, in Vicksburg, Mississippi. But as they took in the broader social and political scene, they began to see clearly that their mission might be moved to anyplace where there was need for enlightenment and liberation. Harlem was as needy as Vicksburg. New York—with its more subtle forms of racism, with increasingly large numbers of black people migrating from the rural South, with emerging left-wing coalitions fighting for justice and peace—surely offered challenges equal to any that might be found in Mississippi. In Margaret and Charles's minds, then, the plan became less literal and specific. It would take many shapes and forms depending on where vocational opportunity, educational training, and "the Spirit" might take them.

During their years in Nashville, Margaret's father's health had deteriorated badly, to the point where he had to give up the ministry of St. Mary's Church. Reverend Morgan had lost both legs from complications of diabetes, and his wife didn't think she alone could manage his care. At first, the Morgans had urged the Lawrences to come "home" to Vicksburg and live with them in the rectory on North Street. Margaret and Charles resisted. "If we had gone to live in their house, they would have remained the powerful parents. We would have had to live by their values. . . . But if they came to New

York to live in our house, we thought we could live our life our way ... and raise our children in our way." There was never any question of Margaret's responsibility for her parents' care. She was their only child, and she felt both honor and obligation in welcoming them into her household. She also hoped that Mary, who was still healthy and vigorous, who still had a lot of the teacher left in her, might be able to help in child care. But Margaret knew that their already complicated life would be made even harder, and she worried quietly about the generational conflicts that were sure to come up.

In the early summer of 1947, Charles took the train to New York, charged with a long list of tasks including finding a place to live, locating schools and child care for the children, and securing funding for their educational ventures. He had been hired by City College to teach summer school courses, and between classes he pounded the pavement, carrying out his family responsibilities. He wrote his family daily, describing his searches, alternating between optimism about how everything would work out and restrained dread about the doors closed in his face, the high costs, and the tangles of bureaucratic red tape. Despite moments of discouragement, Charles persisted, contacting every person he knew in town and pursuing every option.

June 2, 1947

My Mighty Lovely People,
... There is still no house in sight! But I have been busy at trying to find one. This morning bright and early I was out in Saint Albans following up a lead that Aunt Hazel had had. I walked over to Linden Boulevard and 178 Street and beheld a very lovely, large vacant house—set on a nice lawn. I then beat it back to 167 Street and spoke to the owner, who said it could not be leased. I could, however, buy it—for $18,000.... I then went on to Manhattan, talked to a couple of odd real estate men and ended up at Newton Poyer's office in time to be taken out by him for a very expensive lunch.... Following John Johnson's suggestion, I talked to Mr. Edwards, the real estate operator he mentioned at Christmas. He had nothing; but will give us top preference for the first thing that comes through that we can use.... Walking back to 125 Street I saw the name 'Hawthorne Lee Agency.' I remembered that a person by that name had graduated from Morehouse a year or so before I arrived

*and had remained in Atlanta for a couple of years. When I went in
the office, he was most cordial and helpful, telephoned several of his
friends, and found at least one fellow real estate man who feels less
than hopeless (or more than hopeless, whichever is better) about the
situation. This man, Walter Miller, has a house on Riverside Drive
in which he expects to produce some apartments at least for sub-let-
ting. He also thinks that he might have a first-floor, five-room (three
bedroom) apartment in Brooklyn. (It is being sold, he thinks, to
someone who doesn't want to occupy it; and it is vacant.) Mr. Aus-
tin, another of Rev. Johnson's suggestions was busy; but one of his
lady assistants heard our story and took my name—pleasantly, but
routinely. From the few incidents mentioned, you'd never guess that
the above paragraph covers thirteen hours. . . .*

For most of the month of June, every day was full of "more or
less" hopeless leads. By month's end, Charles wrote a cautiously
optimistic letter, full of details:

*Saturday night, 9:30
28 June, 1947*

Lovely Margaret,
   *I think that I have found a place to live. The catch is that we
shall have to buy it, if we want it. This morning I went out to see
Mr. King—Heubert's father. He has a semi-detached house on 107
Street near Northern Boulevard in Corona (in the borough of
Queens). It sells for 9,750 dollars (he thinks he can get it for
$9,500). It will require $1,500 down and can be carried for a total
of one hundred dollars per month.*

Description

   *It is semi-detached, all-brick. On the main floor there is a five-
room apartment. On the second there is a six-room apartment. The
latter is occupied by tenants who have been in the house for ten years
(Negroes). The owner occupies the lower floor, but will give immediate occupancy on the signing of the deed. The basement is finished
and contains a bathroom and a kitchen. It was formerly a three room
flat; but there was a small fire a few months ago and the firemen
tore the partitions down. On Mr. King's recommendation, the partitions were not replaced. (It had earlier been used as living quarters.)
There are bathrooms on each of the apartment floors. The basement*

seems quite dry and useful—could be converted either into a bed-room or we could use the present kitchen on the main floor—which is reasonably large—into a small bedroom for Chuck and use the basement as a study-playroom-kitchen. It has an automatic oil fur-nace.

Advantages

(1) Mr. King thinks that it will be a most excellent buy, saying that he is quite certain that we could at least get the money back which we have or shall have paid by the end of two years and have virtually two years rent-free. The occupied apartment rents for $45.00 per month and the tenants are willing to go up to fifty. This means that the monthly carrying will be cut down by this amount. (2) We would take over the present mortgage which is being amortized at sixty dollars per month, including taxes, water rent, and insurance. A second mortgage would be executed by the present owner which could be paid off in payments of forty dollars per month, including his interest. (3) The oil burner would mean maximum heating com-fort with minimum effort. (4) The location is convenient to the IND by bus and within easy walking distance of the IRT. (5) Schools are convenient. (6) Charles Frost and Aunts Ninnie and Hazel assure me that the cash payment is extremely low; Mr. King concurs in this judgment. (7) There is every likelihood that it could be disposed of easily; or that we could continue renting it should we wish to move after two or three years. (8) The neighborhood is generally good, with convenient schools and other institutions. (9) There is a small back-yard and an enclosed front porch. (10) It won't need painting or re-decorating this year.

Disadvantages

There are certain shortcomings: (1) Closet space is very small. (2) It means an unexpectedly large initial outlay for us. (3) It isn't a house that we should wish to retain for a long period.

Details

In addition to the $1,500 we should need approximately $150 for various fees. I should think that we might explore the possibilities of securing a loan of five hundred dollars—with the car as surety—from Citizens. You might show Mr. P. the business portions of this letter with that in mind. This would leave us enough of the Inde-pendent Aid getting-started money to move on. I shall telephone you

*on tomorrow evening to get your response to this proposition. If we
agree that it is a good thing—and the more I think of it the more I
think of it—I should like for you to wire me two hundred dollars on
Monday: One hundred with which to bind the deal and one hundred
with which to have the title traced. The owner and I would then fix
a date on which to make a formal contract to buy and a date on
which the deal would be consummated and the house prepared for
occupancy by us. I figure that this can all be done by August 1.*

*Incidentally, the rooms can be so arranged that we can all be
comfortable, I believe. We could use Mother and Dad's refrigerator
and living room suite, our studio couch, gate-leg table, and other odd
effects such as chairs, chests, etc. (stoves come with the house).*

*Think and pray over this today—Sunday—and I shall do likewise.
Considering the difficulty of finding suitable places, this sounds good
to me. Admittedly, it is not an ideal situation. (The tenants upstairs
are two women and one of their sons; and they are said to be very
quiet and well-behaved. There is ample privacy both for them and
us.) The net cost will perhaps be less than renting in Harlem, even if
we should find a place. Moreover, I believe that Mr. King is being
perfectly fair and frank with us. (Frost kept marveling over the small
down-payment).*

The Figures

Cost	*$9,750*
Unpaid balance on first mortgage (to be checked. Will be	*5,700*
* paid at 60 dollars per month)*	
Down payment to owner on his 4,050 equity	*1,500*
Balance to be executed in 2nd mortgage	*2,550*

*I'll call you Sunday evening.
I love you very much.*

Having found the living space, Charles proceeded to fill it with
furniture. First stop: Goodwill.

*My Margaret and our children,
Bright and early this morning—about eight thirty—I was on my
way over to the Harlem store of Goodwill Industries to look for beds
for Sara and Paula. As it happened, I was in luck. We were able to
get a very substantial and large crib for Paula for ten dollars and a
strong youth bed—with a slight defect on one side guard—for
twelve-fifty. Both of these are good substantial pieces of furniture. I*

was tempted to buy a three-quarter bed with an inner spring mattress for $17.50. The bed and mattress were in excellent condition; and there was also in the store a three quarter metal bed-without-ends, also with innerspring mattress for $16.00. I wasn't sure about the propriety of unmatched single beds; but if you think they would do, Margaret, let me know and I'll see if they are still there. Incidentally, the beds on which I placed a total of $12.50 deposit also have comfortable pads on them. (Everything is sterilized before being placed on sale—sterilized under conditions conforming with City Health regulations.)

The search for inexpensive, substantial furniture seemed easy compared with the important and sensitive job of finding a nursery school for their children. At very tender ages—fourteen months for Chuck and sixteen months for Sara and Paula—the children had gone off to the nursery school in Nashville. Henrietta, the director of the Fisk University Nursery School, was the wife of a colleague of Charles and a close neighbor. She watched the way the Lawrences were raising "independent children," disregarded all the minimum age rules, and welcomed each one in turn before their time. "Oh, surely, they'll be fine," she said with certainty. Margaret and Charles grew to love Henrietta, felt comfortable leaving their children in her care, and hated to take them out of this intimate environment. "The whole setting felt welcoming and safe." In looking for a new school in New York, Charles felt uneasy. He missed Margaret's knowing perspective and wanted her there to take some responsibility for the decision:

My Lovely Sweetheart,
I have just returned from a trip to Corona. I went over primarily to talk to Mrs. Crandall, director of the childcare Center at 90th Street and Northern Boulevard. Mrs. Crandall proved to be a very gracious woman. When I stated our case, instead of the usual—and quite justifiable line regarding waiting lists—she began trying to discover when she was likely to have the first openings for our three. They are not taking children now until they are 2½. When I explained that Paula had already had nursery school experience, she thought it could be managed by the time she is two. There will soon be an opening in the three-year-old group. In spite of the waiting list, this will be held for Sara . . . Chuck will get the first opening following this in the four-year-old group; and this should be a matter of

weeks after we arrive, she thinks. Fees are based on a sliding scale according to income. The maximum fee for three children is twenty dollars per week. We shall, of course, be pretty close to the maximum.

The Center appears to have plenty of room for indoor and outdoor activities. I counted five teachers beside (in addition to!) the director. I didn't count the children; but there appeared to be about thirty-five or forty in attendance. Two of the teachers and about a half dozen of the children were Negroes. . . . You can be assured that Dada put on his best "charm," bringing out pictures of the family at the right moment and speaking most casually of things like Babies Hospital and City College! . . .

Weighing on Charles's mind more than anything was the problem of financing their educational endeavors and supporting their family. He spent endless hours trying to figure out where the pieces of income would come from, and a good deal of time conferring with the bureaucrats in charge of fellowships and grants; and he felt at moments that he and Margaret had made the wrong decision leaving the security of their jobs in Nashville for the uncertainty and risks of life in New York.

July 3, 1947

My Lovely Margaret,
I have just returned from Mrs. Furst's office. I arrived at eleven and we conversed until about twelve. . . . I stated the situation just as it is. She assured me that the money was yours to disburse in any way you saw fit toward the preparation for your year of study. She was most gracious about it. BUT, as we talked, it developed that Dr. Davidson of the Infantile Paralysis Fund knows about the grant from IA. This was divulged to him in the course of correspondence re whether or not the NRS fellowship is an individual or institutional grant. Moreover, in one of his letters, he stated that the fifteen hundred would be subtracted from their total grant. He also quoted a total budget figure of around forty-five hundred dollars which you had submitted to them, according to him— or maybe it was nearly forty-eight hundred; and implied that the NRS was planning to award you one-half of this total amount. He also spoke of having met you at Meharry and expressed the opinion that you certainly should be encouraged to continue your study. . . .

If we have to accept an eight or nine hundred dollar fellowship, we can perhaps manage anyway by selling the Packard. In addition, I could try to finish up my work faster in order that I could accept—if offered—a job paying more than 210 dollars per month.

On leaving Mrs. Furst's office, I found that I was sleepy. And I had had plenty of sleep last night and have not felt drowsy since I arrived in NYC, except at bed time!!!! On the other hand, the Lord has been very good to us no matter what. I believe we can manage on whatever we are able to get. Even should we have to go into debt, it will be the usual way of getting advanced training! Perhaps, you will be able to make it clear to NRC people that the fifteen hundred should not affect their grant.

This has not been a joyous letter, I am sorry to say; and I hope that by the time it reaches you, you will have reason to discount any gloom that is contained herein.

One other thing, I don't believe that a viable alternative is that of giving up the house. There really doesn't seem to be anything else in sight or likely to be. It may mean no nursery school for the children; but Mother Mary certainly can handle that situation if she needs to. If worse comes to the foreseeable worst, we are still two of God's luckiest children; and I am certainly the luckiest, the most fortunate, the least deserving of His creatures.

As I remind myself of this, I am much more inclined to try to share in helping think the thing thru than to take a nap.

Kiss our children a special Fourth of July kiss for me.

Charles's summer sojourn in New York was so grindingly serious, so full of adultlike, parental responsibilities, so absent of play, that a trip to Bear Mountain at summer's end felt like a wonderful adventure. After searching for houses, schools, and money, he was thrilled to find peace and beauty, and he took full advantage of the moment.

Atop Bear Mountain
3:45 P.M.

My Lovely Family,
The boat trip up was very pleasant despite the very large crowd and noise. I've never been to Bear Mountain before; and I find it a very lovely place for family outings There are about 20 or so persons who chose to come on the boat ride with the Interracial Fellowship Group. Everyone brought his own lunch. We found three tables fairly

close together and ate together. After lunch, about eight of the "younger" ones of us decided to climb Bear Mountain.

It was a strenuous climb, especially in light of my lack of condition; but it is worth it in terms of coolness and view. One can see for miles up and down the Hudson. Moreover, it is very quiet and peaceful. (At the moment the rest of our party has disappeared and I am apparently alone.)

Being alone—physically alone atop a mountain—reminds me of how seldom one is alone in the sort of urbanized life we live nowadays. (In the middle of the preceding sentence, my ink gave out!) As I sat there, there was a certain peace which I was able to capture for a moment. This physical aloneness is by no means the same as loneliness—not even close kin to it; for I was not alone. In a real sense you were with me— and especially you, Margaret. On occasions when I am able to get to a mountain top, the realization of the nature of the "Mountain-top experience" returns anew. There is a joy in climbing even a little mountain like Bear that comes from having partially "earned" the view. There are many instances of natural beauty which one may gain in autos or trains or planes; but the sweat and hard-breathing and sore muscles testify that the view of a mountain climbed is one whose value is enhanced by its price.

We are back in Manhattan now. Every muscle seems tired; but it has been a good day. In a sense we have been together as you four have looked at the Cumberland and as I have looked upon the Hudson. As I looked down from Bear Mountain, I reminded myself; Chuck and Sally and Paula and Margaret are perhaps standing on Miss Anderson's back porch looking at the Cumberland River and Chuckie is saying, 'Sara, it's magnificent, *isn't it!'*

Her husband, the pathfinder, was magnificent, thought Margaret as she read his words. With most of the major family arrangements settled, she did not feel as anxious about the move as she had anticipated. Even though part of her knew that it was time for them to leave Nashville—they had benefited greatly from the southern experience but had begun to feel the limits of the place—the other part of her wanted to stay in the setting where their life had achieved a kind of balance. They had become valued members of the Fisk community, had made some friends, had managed comfortable childcare arrangements, had settled into reasonable, if precarious, routines. The thought of having to re-create all this again in a much less hospitable place gave Margaret pause.

Margaret also wondered what a return to the passive student role would be like after having grown into the teaching, guiding role at Meharry. And to be training in psychiatry, a discipline that required a psychological return to childhood haunts, might exaggerate feelings of powerlessness and chip away at her adulthood. How would she manage this along with the responsibilities of mothering her three children? What would it feel like to have her parents living with them and be both daughter and mother in the same household?

In the spring of 1947, having applied for a residency at Columbia's Psychiatric Institute, she stayed with Dr. Viola Bernard, "a psychoanalyst with a social conscience" who was eager to attract minorities into the field. No Negroes had ever been accepted into Columbia's psychiatric program, and she was determined to change this situatuion. Dr. Bernard, a strong-willed, forceful woman, had heard about Margaret through acquaintances in "peace work." When Margaret contacted her, she responded generously and vigorously, offering her apartment for a few nights' sleep, contacting her colleagues for interviews, and spending hours talking about psychiatry and psychoanalysis. Viola Bernard argued that if Margaret were truly interested in psychiatry, she should also be trained in psychoanalysis. It was critical, she maintained, that a psychotherapist be self-aware, with a full sense of her own motivations and inhibitions. They had marathon conversations at Vi Bernard's apartment that kept them awake late into the night.

Margaret felt both convinced and resistant. "I was not eager by any means," Margaret recalls. "I had the rest of my psychiatric studies and work. I had three children. How was I going to do all these things?" Her resistance was not only related to her crowded life. She also worried about the intrusive process. "I was not a person to want to put my private life out there." Eventually, she decided to go ahead. "I went reluctantly, with some sense of adventure . . . but a little scared of it, naturally."

In 1948, by the time Margaret began her analysis, she was a fellow in pediatrics at Columbia. Her analytic hours were scheduled in the afternoon, Monday through Friday. All five Lawrences and Reverend Morgan would leave their house in Queens at the crack of dawn with Charles driving the old Packard. Margaret would be dropped off at Babies' Hospital in Morningside Heights; the place that had rejected her as a pediatric intern had welcomed her with open arms eight years later as a fellow. Then Grandfather would be delivered to a rehabilitation center on the West Side where Charles would help him out of the car seat and into his wheelchair, and where Reverend Morgan would practice trying to walk on "wooden limbs." Next stop, a private school in Midtown Manhattan, where the three children had been enrolled on scholarship after spending a year at the Queens nursery school. They would arrive an hour before the opening of school and spend a happy time with the custodian touring the building, making it ready for the school day. Finally, Charles would park the car in front of Margaret's analyst's office way downtown in the West Village. He would then take the subway on to Brooklyn College, where he was teaching sociology. The Packard would be waiting for Margaret after she finished her analytic hour in the late afternoon. "I would get in the car and start the afternoon trek back to Corona." It was a tightly knit schedule that required organization and precision. The grinding, determined pace could not easily be stretched to accommodate mishaps, accidents, illnesses, or bad moods.

Margaret remembers the few times when the clockwork plans were foiled. Once, having taken the subway from Morningside Heights to the Village, with only a couple of minutes to spare before her analytic hour, she stopped in her tracks when she saw the street scene. There was their Packard, sitting all alone in front of her analyst's office, on a clump of pavement. "The whole street was dug up except for the section our car was on, and there was a big ticket on the windshield." On another occasion, when Margaret had been in analysis for about a year, the arrangements for child care were suddenly undone and "there was nothing to do but take you three with me. You were three, four, and five years old." Margaret arrived at the analyst's office with her children, their coloring books and crayons, and the admonition that they must behave themselves quietly in the waiting room. On the couch, Margaret tried to carry on as usual, but her free associations kept wandering back to her children in the next room. "Every once in a while I would say, 'I wonder what they are doing now?'" Her analyst was wondering the same thing and didn't try to hide his distraction and concern. "Finally he said, 'If

you think they are tearing the place up, we might as well stop now.' "
Margaret laughs at the patient and analyst's joint preoccupations and
their relief when they discovered that the children had not torn the
place up, "just rearranged it a bit."

Eugene Milch, Margaret's analyst, was a kind and patient man
whose approach to his work helped ease her trepidations about the
intrusive and revealing process. Trust developed quickly and Margaret felt comfortable with him. "Milch was a good person, easy
going but very much in there.... He was classical in the sense that
you lay on the couch and he said very little. But I was very aware
of his concern. I am like him in the sense that he was always looking
for ego strength in his patients ... not just probing for problems and
difficulties."

Once Margaret had relaxed into the couch and accepted the method,
she discovered her talent for it. She soon got over her reluctance to
reveal herself. "Once I decided to put it out there ... it was right
there," she says with a simplicity which expresses how well she took
to the analytic method. "I would find myself in a state of autohyp-
nosis ... as if I had left the reality of being on the couch...." This
suspended reality felt deeply familiar to Margaret. "Because of being
so much alone as a child and pretty introspective ... this was going
on all the time with me." Her natural inclination to turn inward and
her fascination with dreams and fantasy were the stuff of the analytic
method and served Margaret well.

Unlike her years in medical school and during her pediatric residency, Margaret's training in psychiatry and psychoanalysis could
not be single-minded. She struggled to hold together the pieces of a
very full life and hoped that the daily rhythms would not be destroyed
by some unexpected event in her family life. Her classes at the
Columbia Psychoanalytic Clinic were not memorable. Margaret often
felt tired as she listened to the drone of her teachers and watched
the mostly blank, unmoving faces of her fellow trainees. Classroom
sessions were generally not considered a central or particularly val-
uable piece of the training.

Occasionally a presentation would seem to speak directly to Margaret. She remembers watching Sandor Rado, director of the Psychoanalytic Clinic, work with patients, using what was known as his

"massive dose" direct therapy. On Saturday mornings, Rado ran a case conference for fifteen trainees. Each week one of the trainees was responsible for presenting a patient he (or she) had been working with to the group. The chairs would be arranged in a semicircle, and everyone would be waiting expectantly as Rado would stride in "on the dot of nine o'clock." "He was a most obsessive man." The trainee whose patient was to be seen would offer a summary of the patient's history and review the course of treatment. As Rado listened to the analyst-in-training, he would pace the room, his brow furrowed and his demeanor intense. After the trainee's summary of the case, the patient (who had been carefully prepared for what to expect) would be ushered into the room. Rado would continue to pace as he asked the patient short, penetrating questions. "The presenting doctor was as nervous about this as the patient, probably more so . . . I recall my terror when my turn came." After the relatively brief questioning, Rado would sit down, face the patient, and "lay it all out." He would begin by making a "psychodynamic summary," a synthesis of all he had heard from the doctor and patient, and then talk about "how this had happened and what needed to be done." "He would put it all together, a résumé of the dynamics of the problem, and let the patient see the whole thing."

Rado's performance was extraordinary, sometimes frightening. He moved so boldly, so quickly, drawing out the story, piercing the defenses, uncovering the pain, and spreading it all out—a whole life's picture—before the patient. "Massive dose" therapy, indeed. . . . Margaret marveled at Rado's clinical insights, his keen intelligence, and his speed. Not a moment was wasted. She also understood the risks. "Rado relied a lot on the patient being strong enough to take it . . . being able to withstand the confrontational mode." Echoes of Dr. Rado's Saturday case conferences still reverberate in Margaret's head today, although she generally offers interpretations "more gently" in her work with patients. While aware of the risks, she values the uses of "quick immersion" and clinical courage, especially for those patients who may come seeking help in great pain and "you know you'll never see them again."

More rewarding to Margaret than the classes at the Psychoanalytic Clinic was the supervision of her own psychiatric work with children.

Each week she would meet with David Levy, her supervisor, to review and rework her clinical sessions with patients. He was a quiet listener who knew the precise moment of optimal intervention. Margaret also felt he was a "magnificent teacher" who "made discoveries" along with his trainees. She remembers telling him about her work with a young boy in foster care who had lived through several traumatic dislocations in his short life. The boy, who appeared to be both fragile and resilient, was "making a family play" with Margaret when he began to remember a scene from his infancy, from the time when he was still living at home with his mother. He recalled his mother and her boyfriend fighting loudly, cursing, and wailing and remembered his own screams and cries. When his mother heard the insistent cries of her infant, "the fighting stopped, so she could fetch the baby and feed him." The child's memory of his mother who had cared for him, who stopped her fighting to feed him, was a vital discovery. "The boy knows he has been loved and he can repeat it in later relationships." Levy listened to Margaret's rendition of the family play and was excited by the doctor's discovery of the patient's discovery, and also by what he learned through hearing the narrative. "Levy called himself a child analyst, but he did not believe in putting the couch in the playroom . . . He believed in being an *active* therapist, setting things up and making things happen. He always said, 'Be sure that at least *one* thing happens during the hour.'" Margaret remembers Dr. Levy's supervision with affection and admiration, acknowledging his continuing influence on her work.

At the center of her memories of the Psychoanalytic Clinic was, of course, her own training analysis with Eugene Milch. The analysis—although often difficult and painful—felt productive. Margaret's relationship to Milch was certainly the most trusting and open she had with any of her mentors during training. She felt his loyalty and his affection even as they were going through the most difficult stages of her analysis. For these reasons Margaret had turned to Milch when, at the end of her training, Dr. Rado had delivered his unbelievable ultimatum. But even with Milch, her trusted analyst, Margaret sometimes caught herself feeling suspicious. "Once, riding on a crowded bus at the end of a day, I hung uncomfortably on a strap. Suddenly heat suffused my body. It was anger. Had my analyst accepted me because of his curiosity about a Negro woman?"

These momentary worries about intent and motivation (even in reference to her trusted analyst) were the jagged expression of an anxiety that always rested uncomfortably below the surface. Even when Margaret says to me resignedly, "The years passed by and I felt very comfortable at the clinic," her voice seems to express a guardedness that was always present—"comfortable" but not fully free of suspicion. She knew better than to let down all of her defenses.

In her initial interview at the Columbia Psychiatric Institute, before she had been accepted as a student, Margaret went to see the director, Dr. Nolan Lewis, for an interview. As she entered the office, she started to raise her arm to shake hands with the man. He did not shake her hand; instead he motioned with his head for her to have a seat and walked immediately over to the window, which he opened wide. "That was a funny, funny experience," says Margaret without the trace of a smile. "I had a notion that this man might have a problem with my being black." Whether Dr. Nolan was offended by the presence of the Negro woman in his office, or whether he just needed some fresh air, remains a mystery. As an opening gesture, however, it prefigured Margaret's double-edged experience in the psychiatric program, an experience that forced her constantly to de-code the mixed messages, search out the underlying meanings—and never know whether she was interpreting them correctly. This was particularly ironic in an environment where people professed to take the unconscious seriously, where awareness of ambivalence, inhibitions, slips of the tongue, was supposedly the stuff of the trade. In this world, the ground felt even less secure than usual, certainly more shifting and treacherous than the clear-cut prejudices of the southern society in which Margaret had grown up.

While watching for unexpected minefields, Margaret also saw the competition among her peers and consciously decided not to partic-ipate. "There was the story of my 'brother in analysis' [also in analysis with Dr. Milch], who was more competitive with me than I was with him. Apparently on the couch he said to Eugene Milch, 'Did you know that Margaret Lawrence is religious?' He hoped that if he revealed Margaret's "dependent attachment" to religion to their analyst that he would be seen as the "good child," the more mature and productive analysand. Milch's response must have annoyed and perplexed him: "Oh, did you think I wasn't?" responded the analyst casually.

Margaret also watched the jockeying for position among her teachers, who were pioneering a relatively new field and who occasionally expressed their insecurities in competition among themselves. They even sometimes revealed these tense relationships to their students. One senior analyst described to Margaret another of his colleagues, with whom he had violent disagreements, as "that short Jew." Margaret was amazed and amused by the outburst (from one who himself was "a short Jew"). "Somehow he didn't like him!"

Margaret successfully negotiated this treacherous ground. She took what was worthwhile—the analysis, the supervision, the craft, the occasional productive insight—and left the rest behind—the mostly male competitiveness, the murky, mixed messages. She expressed part of herself there—developing the language of psychoanalytic expression—and kept part of herself hidden from view—her spirituality, her religious fervor. She accepted some of the theory—the power of the unconscious, of childhood trauma and recognized how useful and creative free association could be. But she rejected the overemphasis on the verbal articulation of emotion, the exclusive focus on white, middle-class populations, the opaque jargon that often seemed to mask the interesting, divergent realities of people's lives.

And when Margaret grew weary of separating out what she would take and what she would leave behind, or when she felt burdened by the reverence and deadly seriousness of it all, the comic aspect of it all came to her rescue. On December 15, 1949, at midnight, about a year and a half after the beginning of her training, Margaret sat down to write a letter:

> Dear Dr. Rado:
> This comes from one of your appreciative and very questioning students. It is in lieu of an interview that I fear I may never have. It is in envy of your right to stay abed on Saturday morning the while

your young seek to fathom the sloughs thru which the psychoanalytic movement struggled and never quite extracted itself. . . .

Margaret's words trailed off. She never finished the letter, although she recalls the constant urge to "speak my piece." "I was always wanting to question Rado's assertions, although I rarely said anything. I don't even know if he knew who I was. *No one* questioned him out loud."

New Beginnings

M_Y mother and I are sitting in my father's study. It is seventeen days after his death. We had made this date to work on the book before he died. In fact, the last time I heard his voice—spirited and hopeful—was when I had called to check our calendars. As always, he anticipated the visit with enormous pleasure: "Can't wait to see you, girl!" This time, as we settled on a mutually convenient day, his voice rang with a special enthusiasm. "You know, we always enjoy these sessions," he said, and judging from his typical style of understatement I knew that he had been captured by the journey we were on. The chance to talk about his life as well as my mother's, to return to old haunts, rehearse old legends, and reclaim his youth, had meant a lot to him. I hung up the phone still feeling his excitement and my own deep satisfaction at the joy he expressed.

I can see him, weak and thin from his illness but clear-headed, his gaze strong as ever. He leans forward at his desk, eager to hear my questions, test his memory, and tell his story. The magenta azalea planted in a small pottery bowl on his unusually tidy desk seems to symbolize the promise of life. His study, newly cleaned and organized, has an orderly look that his busy life never allowed and that his temperament never had the patience for. Margaret's touch is now evident in this room—family photographs carefully arranged, an Indian rug draped over the chair, pictures and diplomas hung at satisfying intervals, and flowers. And Charles, in his gratitude for all of his wife's labors and in his wish to respect the promise of a more peaceful and elegant life ahead, has worked to keep the place un-cluttered.

Until now we have always met for our talks in Mom's office, filled with all her memories. But today we find ourselves here. We have wandered the house looking for a place to settle, like aimless creatures trying to find a sunny refuge. First we go to our usual spot, but the air seems cold. Then we try the living room, then the dining room, looking for the appropriate conditions for work—a table on which I can spread out my notes, a nearby plug for the tape recorder, and a central spot for the microphone. Eventually we both feel drawn to Dad's study. "Is it too cold in here?" Mom asks. "No, it feels fine to me," I reply but the room actually feels a bit eerie and uninhabited. And yet as we take our seats, we both feel some protective warmth enveloping us. I sit in the chair with the Indian rug draped over it, and Mom sits in Dad's chair behind the desk. The azalea is still flourishing.

On this early spring day, Margaret is learning how to embrace the solitude and inhabit the spaces she and my father shared for almost fifty years. "I find myself visiting each room, trying to *occupy* the house . . . I often tell my patients that when they have dreams about houses they are likely to be referring to their selves . . . the house representing the person. . . . So I guess, as I move through this house trying to occupy it, that I'm really trying to reoccupy myself. . . ." Today we push this new frontier into Dad's old territory, his study. Here is our chance, our great opportunity, to reclaim our lives in his absence. As we return to our search in this new setting, we feel both brave and terrified.

I ask Margaret the question that we had chosen to discuss the last time we met, a topic she herself had initiated. But today the question seems blunt and insensitive. How can I ask her about "trauma as a theme in her personal and professional life," so soon after the most devastating loss she will ever face? I offer her a way out. "Do you really feel like talking about this today, Mom?" She looks out the window at the daffodils she planted, at the woods beyond, which are just about to burst with new leaves. The woodpile at the edge of the lawn reminds us both of Dad. He enjoyed splitting logs for the fire, and we can see him out there, axe swung high in his muscular arms.

He would split the wood with one stroke and throw it on the wheel-barrow.

Margaret must see these images as she hears my question float by her. Her eyes are glazed with tears as she begins slowly. "We are sitting in the study of Charles Radford Lawrence the Second. Following a day during which we went out to a festive lunch at a lovely restaurant, spent two hours over our meal talking about a report from the Episcopal Peace Fellowship, had a light supper of tuna sandwiches made by Charles and served by me, looked at the Bill Cosby show, and laughed and laughed . . . Charles Lawrence died." This is an abbreviated version of their last day together—a story Margaret has told her three grown children in full and vivid detail, but which must be rehearsed in order for us to begin. Tears roll gently down Mom's face and my tears join hers. "I think I have to say that," says Margaret as a way of explaining the nearly ritualized story of their last day together. Then she straightens up, wipes away the tears, and surveys Dad's study. "This is a great room and I will use it. It will be my computer room . . . I'll do my writing here."

Despite her grief, Margaret picks up the thread of our last conversation and returns to it now without prompting. Trauma is indeed a major link between her experience growing up and the work she has chosen. Now, in her seventy-third year, the traumas of her youth know no time, although they have left deep imprints. Margaret will always see her mother "lying in bed like dead," hear the words of the dean of the medical school assuring her that she has been an inspired and capable student but that they will not be able to admit her because, twenty-five years before, they had enrolled a Negro man and "it didn't work out . . . he died of tuberculosis." She will always picture the train that carried her and her mother north, from Vicksburg to New York, and the raging white man who threatened "to kick it in the head" if she didn't move out of her seat.

In her work with children, Margaret the psychiatrist and psychoanalyst uses these deeply painful experiences to help her understand the process of healing. In order to survive the "noxia," "the severe physical or emotional injury," she explains, the child (or the adult) must confront the deep wound, experience the knifelike pain, move through the zombielike period of "depersonalization," speak about the event, act it out, cry over it, stomp on it, and finally emerge from it—usually with a scar.

Although Margaret's own experience has been one of transcendence, she knows of enduring scars, and also of the lives, such as her Uncle Andrew's, in which pain is the victor. Cases in which therapy was ill-timed or insufficient continue to haunt her:

> ...the father who came home stoned one night and picked his eighteen-month-old boy out of his crib, cradled him in his arms, walked out on the fire escape, and started to jump; that boy never developed speech.... We lost contact with that little boy when he was three, then found him again when he was eight. He was psychotic and had to be hospitalized.

Many of her stories are of victory over trauma—the slow, difficult recovery that can occur when children are given the opportunity for catharsis, followed by support and reinforcement. In one story, the recovery seemed to echo back through generations:

> Susan, four years old, was left chiefly in the care of her grandmother. She had no father. Her mother was a fearful, dependent person who functioned best when she was working, and therefore not threatened by the need to care for her child, although her four-year-old was no more than normally dependent. I visited the grandmother's neat home and was graciously served tea. When I asked the grandmother where she grew up, she responded, "In a little Georgia town. I always say that my mother gave me away to my grandmother. My mother raised my child, though."
>
> Susan had come to our attention in a day-care center. Her anger, self-destructive fantasies, and demands to be fed brought her into therapy at our Developmental Psychiatry Clinic, but only after a year's delay due to scheduling problems. In therapy she dictated this poem, which speaks of the absent "ego ideal"—the mother—and the disappearance of the child's own ego:

> *They were walking along*
> *They had no mother*
> *They got so tiny, that*
> *Children couldn't see them.*
> *They got so tiny*

that they disappeared.
They were never
back again.

During therapy with black and white co-therapists, Susan's cries and rage found acceptance. In a second verse of her poem, to which she gave the title "Susan and Bobby," her "twin" ideals grew tall:

> *They cried and cried*
> *And cried*
> *They cried so loud*
> *that they grew*
> *Real Big*
> *They grew so tall*
> *That they bumped their heads*
> *Up on the sky.*

Three months after her first poem, Susan dictated:

> *Linda*
> *A little girl*
> *She was walking*
> *Along*
> *She had lots*
> *of sisters*
> *And she had*
> *A thousand*
> *Mothers.*
> *She had*
> *Two Aunts*
> *And*
> *She was cute*
> *And*
> *She was happy*
> *And they all*
> *Lived together*
> *In a little*
> *Yellow house.*

Three generations of loss haunted this family. But as Margaret helped Susan battle the family legacy, she searched for the potential strength. Trauma and strength are always twin forces in Margaret's attempts to reconstruct and rechannel young lives. She finds these interlocking themes particularly important in Harlem, where too many professionals assume the trauma but neglect the strength.

> Strength abounds in Harlem. Three hundred years of oppression and it survives. This is the task in Harlem, to see strength where it exists, to expect it to be there, right there, next to, and a part of nature, nurture, and noxia. Even anger may show strength. It can sustain a child and protect him until he is helped to find more suitable vehicles for his ability to love and to act.

Until she retired from Harlem Hospital in the year of her seventieth birthday, Margaret Lawrence had spent much of her working life in the community where she had come from Mississippi to live with her grandmother and aunts as a young adolescent, and where she had returned as a pediatric resident and again to direct the developmental psychiatry clinic. Her journey kept looping back around to Harlem, forming a circle of images and memories, a history that seemed to pull the "missionary doctor" home.

After finishing her psychiatric and psychoanalytic training, Margaret had divided her work life between the city and a small country town that years later grew into a metropolitan suburb. In Manhattan she organized consultation units, to neighborhood day-care centers for poor and minority families, at the Northside Child Development Center, a pioneering institution started by Drs. Mamie and Kenneth Clark. In Rockland County, thirty miles northwest of the city, where her young family had moved in 1951 to be a part of a newly settled cooperative community, Margaret helped to organize the Community Mental Health Center. She became the director of its School Mental Health Unit, which evaluated public school classes for the retarded and "helped schools to integrate the formerly hidden children in educational settings where their gifts could more easily flower." In each of these settings, she created therapeutic teams—psychiatrists, neuropsychologists, social workers, nurses, and teachers—that worked together, and gained strength through the collaboration.

In addition to her work within institutional settings, Margaret started a part-time private practice in Rockland County that soon flourished as word spread about the new doctor's skill and commitment to her patients. She was the first child psychiatrist to practice in Rockland County and worked hard to dispel stereotypic myths about psychiatry and to introduce people to the nonmysterious, nonmagical dimensions of her work.

Even after building her dream office, which allowed her to separate her practice from family life, Margaret knew that she would never limit her work to these surroundings. She was enlivened by the range of institutional settings in which she worked and by the varieties of families she saw in them. In moving from her roomy suburban office with its view of the woods to a cramped kitchen in a city day-care center, there were no shifts of tone or expectation. Although the equipment and surroundings in her office offered greater comfort and more choices, Margaret felt perfectly happy working in a bare room, reaching into her large African bag for the "essentials"—little people, both brown and white, a few sticks of doll furniture, crayons and paper, balloons, and something to eat, apples, raisins, and cookies. The African bag—full of goodies—has become part of our family lore, a symbol of the legacy of one generation to another.

My sister, Paula, Margaret's third-born—always thought of as the mirror image of our mother—has captured the meaning of our mother's overflowing bag in a recently published essay. Paula speaks of her own carpet bag as a kind of autobiography:

> I was taking a crowded train home from school at rush hour, carrying my carpet bag of stuff.... An elderly black gentleman got up from his precious seat and tipped his hat in a gesture that offered his seat to me. As I was about to refuse, he said, 'You must be a teacher.' I looked down at myself, sort of expecting to see peanut butter smeared all over me. Or I thought maybe my carpet bag had given me away.
>
> I said to him, 'How did you know that?' And he said, 'It's the way you carry yourself'....
>
> There is a living room full of instruments in my carpet bag, and nights full of music.
>
> There is a family table groaning with food, lively with conversation, the stage for famous imitations of our teachers.
>
> In my carpet bag I carry the warmth of my father's fires that are the center of my childhood home and the spirituals he fell asleep

singing to his wakeful children as he held all of us at once in his big chair.

I carry that tattered bag on hikes with my husband and children—into deserts, and canyons whose colors are heightened by the unexpected rain; and the laughter that split the cool, crisp air above the river as we rafted the cascades.

I've got Bach preludes in there, Ray Charles and Stevie Wonder, and thanks to my children who insist that I listen to what they hear, Phil Collins, Philip Bailey, Sting, and Huey Lewis, too.

And everywhere I have worked I have carted with me a sepia-toned, old photograph of my mother at age twenty-eight with her Harlem Hospital resident's coat on, leaning over a healthy, little sweetheart of a girl. Mom's healing hands are barely touching her. Though the uproar of the pediatric ward of that uptown New York hospital must have surrounded them, there is tenderness and warmth and quiet in that healing moment. That is in my carpet bag.

Chuck, Margaret's firstborn, has always carried a dual legacy. It is not hard to see the influence of both my father and my mother on Chuck's career as a law professor, which combines scholarship and social activism. He is skeptical of legal doctrine that claims to be fair but expresses profound historical inequalities; his teaching is an eclectic blend of history, anthropology, law, even psychoanalytic theory. The title of his recent monograph in the *Stanford Law Review,* "The Id, the Ego, and Equal Protection: Reckoning with Unconscious Racism," reflects this rich mix.

As I think of my sister and brother, I realize that my attempt to record my mother's story, also a blend of disciplines—sociology, biography, and a "second analysis"—is an extension of this same legacy. I, too, carry the African bag, now a metaphor in our family for struggle and resilience, courage and safety. Our inheritance of teaching and healing survives another generation.

So it is not just dolls and crayons that travel in Margaret's large woven bag and can be transported to the most barren of settings; it is her special approach to healing, her particular values, experience, and craft, come with her. Whether in her private office or in the clinic, Margaret uses the same approach. She assumes that all of her patients—black or white, poor, wealthy, or middle-class—are capable of expression, reflection, and introspection. She assumes that within all families the doctor can search for, uncover, and reinforce strength. She takes the traumas of childhood very seriously and has enormous respect for the child's vulnerability, pain, and anger. At the same time, she believes that children are extraordinarily resilient. She remembers Benjamin Spock's lesson about the feeding of babies, and sees it as a metaphor for the broader challenges of parenting. "He assured mothers that their children would not starve ... that they did not have to push food on their children ... the cure is to help the mother relax and the child will be all right." Helping families involves supporting the ordinary insights of parents and urging them to believe in their own power. This faith permeates Margaret's practice, whatever the setting.

The tiniest object in Margaret's dream office is a delicately detailed porcelain doll—a black baby dressed in a white lace baptismal gown. For Margaret the doll symbolizes the deep religious roots of her healing practice. In 1963, after twenty-one years of being away, Margaret returned to Harlem Hospital to head the Developmental Psychiatry Service. As we look at the doll, she describes her decision to circle back to Harlem: "I had a dream. I was walking along happily cuddling a brown baby in my arms. I looked down. To my horror I had dropped her." Margaret did not resist the message of her dream. As a child, she had learned to have a healthy respect for "the Word," however mysteriously it was transmitted. When her father listened carefully to "the Spirit," he saved more souls. Reverend Morgan counted on the Spirit to guide and direct him in his ministry. Listening to dreams and listening to the Spirit are harmonious endeavors for Margaret. She has incorporated the Spirit and the unconscious as guiding forces in her life and work.

Margaret's mother, Mary, clung to the traditional belief that a child born with a caul would lead a life "in touch with the spirits." When Margaret as a nine-year-old child claimed to have seen the reflected image of a dead woman, her parents were not surprised. Although Margaret smiles at the story, she does not dismiss the illusion entirely.

The black southern tradition of "spirits," the deep belief in "God the Spirit," the endless parade of funerals, bodies laid out in open coffins, echoes of Reverend Morgan's big bass voice "bellowing the hymns," along with the choir, followed Margaret to New York. Her faith endured even the inhospitable environment of the Psychoanalytic Clinic. Throughout her analytic training, she simply kept her contrary theology quiet, continued to go to church every Sunday at St. Martin's in Harlem, continued to "be in touch with the Spirit," and continued to rehearse the words of her father's favorite psalm, "The Lord is my light and salvation."

Margaret's cultural and religious roots actually became even more important during her analytic training. She never questioned the validity of the psychological drama, nor the need to find ways of expressing the complex of feelings in a patient's life. But she did sometimes find the analytic process empty of soul. "Soul was a matter of being," whereas the purely verbal articulation of feelings often seemed superficial to Margaret. For her, analytic training was not a matter of disposing of old beliefs and neatly replacing them with the new. It was a more complex task of incorporating two theologies, living with both, and choosing carefully when and where to express them.

As Margaret's clinical experience deepened, as her demanding personal life mellowed, Margaret found these apparently contrary and distinct beliefs in her life blending. As she found her own way, she rid herself of the constraints and inhibitions of former authorities. One day not long ago, Margaret stood onstage at Columbia University School of Medicine, before an audience of young, eager, black and brown faces. She was preparing to speak to hundreds of minority college students interested in applying to medical school, and they were waiting to hear from this "ancient pioneer." On that day, the "missionary doctor" could feel the threads of her life coming together; she could feel "the expression of soul" as she began her speech to these premedical students in a most unorthodox fashion. She sang a black gospel hymn.

> *Plenty good room*
> *Plenty good room*
> *Plenty good room*
> *In my Father's kingdom*
> *Plenty good room*
> *Plenty good room*
> *Just take your place*
> *And sit down.*

The journey had come full circle as Margaret clapped her hands, swayed gently to the rhythmic, soulful beat, and let the music—the black church music—speak the message.

Margaret held onto religion, clung to it for solace and comfort, particularly when her education seemed to be leading her away from the soulful center. She quietly, but stubbornly, continued "to believe" and expected that her travels would return her to her roots in ritual, music, mystery, and ministry. But journeys do not always return full circle. Some of Margaret's travels required deliberate departure from well-worn paths. In some ways, she worked to undo her Mississippi roots. The most vivid departure was her marriage. Margaret wanted to live a life very different from her parents' and wanted her children not to suffer the conflict she had experienced in the Morgan family.

When Margaret "spaced out" on her wedding day, her anxiety was justified. She dreaded repeating the Morgan family drama. She also had to blot out her aunts' dim view of men, their image of marriage as certain doom. This was especially difficult since she admired these women—admired their strength, their grace, and their stamina against odds. All of the important women in her life had an imposing strength. Mom Margaret, the most powerful—large, demanding, sometimes mean—had held her family together despite a reckless, philandering husband. She had raised beautiful, educated, dignified daughters and given her heart to her wounded son. Even in the worst times, she had managed to put food on the table, dress her children well, and insist upon decency and manners. Her daughters, each one, carried on her strength in more muted forms, even as they lived under her dominance.

Mary Elizabeth was strong in her teaching, uncompromising in her insistence that all of her students learn. At three, Mary taught Margaret to read, and for the first time the daughter could feel her mother's special power and the rewards that come from knowing you have fully satisfied your parent. As a dutiful, precocious student, Margaret had the love and undivided attention of teacher Mary.

Aunt Ninnie was strong in her devotion to her mother, a blind devotion that would not let her give her love to anyone else until she was sixty-three and her mother was dead. And Aunt Hazel was strong in her glamorous dignity. With long, bright-red hair, swept up in exotic styles, she was a sight to behold. She, too, loved her mother fiercely and loved her husband for the generous space he gave her to be herself. Margaret admired the power and drive of these women but grew to understand that theirs was a brittle strength, derived partly from its distance from and distrust of men. She wanted a strength for herself that did not rule out intimacy and a good marriage.

Right from the beginning, Charles had seemed like a man with whom such a dream would be possible. Even though their courtship was intense, even though they both knew by the end of the summer's romance that they wanted "to be together always," Margaret never felt a sense of claustrophobia. For the first time, Margaret experienced trust and reciprocity. For the first time, she did not worry that a man would block or denigrate her path. "He immediately *joined* my dream," said Margaret. Through her love for Charles—with its twists and turns over nearly half a century—Margaret discovered that men and women can express their autonomy and achievement precisely because of the power of their relationship. Intimacy and trust were not the enemies of strength and independence, as the Smith ladies had taught her. It was the opposite: out of a deepening love relationship came the courage to pursue independent endeavors.

Early on, before most men dared to make such protestations, Charles took pride in calling himself a feminist. As a young boy in rural Mississippi, when Charles delivered his prize-winning orations, he remembers referring to the need for "women to gain equal status and opportunity." Later on, when he was on speaking tours for the Race Relations Institute at Fisk, he often joined the issues of race and sex discrimination and railed against both kinds of oppression. And at home—a much more rare achievement for his time—Charles lived by his professed values. He participated in raising his children, in bathing, diapering, reading stories, and bedtime rituals. He shared equally in household chores. More important, he encouraged his wife's ambitions and achievements ("I have exhibited the *Times* clipping until it is worn and frayed") and felt strongly identified with Margaret's success.

But even with a dedicated feminist for a husband, equality sometimes felt elusive to Margaret. For more years than she likes to admit, she felt inhibited by her perception of the quality of Charles's mind and by the way he used it. But slowly, with struggle and determination (Margaret's struggle, for Charles always regarded her as "brilliant"), she gained respect for her own mind and began to see the contrasts with Charles as enlivening and enriching to their union. She began to recognize the value of her intuitive, relational intelligence, her metaphorical insights, her ability to search out the connections between intellect and emotion. With this hard-won confidence, Margaret finally grasped the equality that had always existed within her marriage.

In trying to forge her new path, Margaret was determined that her children would not be hurt by old stereotypes. First of all, she did not want her daughters to find pleasure or strength in the ridicule of men. Because this meant so much to Margaret—she could still hear the taunting voice of Mom Margaret as she strutted around imitating her father Reverend Morgan—she was sometimes heavy-handed in her insistence that it be different for her children. If she ever caught us belittling a man—particularly a black man—she would speak sharply, with an intensity that baffled us: "I do not want to hear that!" I remember riding through Harlem one afternoon when I was twelve or thirteen years old. Paula and I were in the back seat taking in the scene, and Mom was driving. We had spent most of our growing-up years in the country, in a predominantly white community, and so Harlem was not home for us in the same way it was for our mother. This was a strange world—ominous, noisy, exciting, seductive. Our curiosity and fears made us feel guilty. And perhaps Mom felt guilty at having created a life for her children that prevented them from feeling at home in Harlem. All these raw feelings were just below the surface as we drove through the hot city streets on our way to visit some favorite relatives.

Paula and I had spotted some men drinking and carousing on the corner, a scene we had passed several times already, taking the action in quietly, our faces impassive, our minds racing. But as we peered out at this particular group of boisterous drinkers, one of them caught us staring and made an outrageous gesture toward us. Was it dirty? we wondered. This caught us both off guard and released all our inhibitions. We began to laugh uncontrollably. We could not have stopped ourselves for anything. Then we followed our howls with cynical comments about the drunken men. Mom, who had been silently negotiating the crowded city streets, peered back through the rearview mirror, whipped her head around in an angry stare and abruptly pulled the car over to the curb. Now she had turned all the way around facing us, her face creased with rage. "I never, never want to hear that again." She launched into a passionate sermon about not denigrating "Negro men," and waited for our response. We assured her we understood; we would not do it again. But we were perplexed—not by our mother's correcting us for poking fun at the men ("compassion for those less fortunate" was one of the cardinal values of our family), but at the intensity of her anger. Even at the time I recall feeling that her response was exaggerated, way out of proportion to our giddy transgressions. Now I understand some of her fury.

There were other ways in which Margaret was determined that her children's experiences would not parallel hers, in which she made a conscious decision not to listen to the lessons of her youth. Both she and Charles, for example, wanted all of their children to feel supported and unconditionally loved. "Both of us anticipated that all three of you were going to be productive people, and you didn't have to do that by yourselves . . . we wanted to be there." Margaret had never felt that kind of clear, unequivocal support from her parents. Even her father—whose love and respect for her "were assumed" even if they were not freely expressed—sent out mixed and troubling messages. However good Margaret tried to be, she could not undo her father's disappointment at Candy Man's death; she could never fulfill his dream of a son who would become "a priest of the church." Margaret was determined that her children would not have to earn their parents' love. She wanted her daughters never to experience the preference for sons, never strive for parental love that depended on achievement.

More invidious was love tied to lightness of skin. Beautiful Candy Man, white-skinned and golden-haired, was adored without measure. Could Mary, also fair-skinned, ever love her brown-skinned daughter as much? This, of course, was not merely a family issue. Skin color was a potent force in Vicksburg and Harlem when Margaret was growing up. It was better to be lighter and long-haired, better to be more like white folks. There was status in fair skin, and the Smith ladies had traded on the dignity that came with their lightness. And they had all married men whose darkness was a source of both attraction and repulsion. While Mary never said anything about her daughter's color, Margaret could hear how she felt in the way she insisted, for example, that Margaret wear dark colors—blues, browns, and dark greens—so that her "brown skin wouldn't stand out so much."

Margaret promised herself that her daughters would wear colors— bold, intense colors, colors that would show off their beautiful brown skin. She was determined that her daughters would "know that they were beautiful." She knew, of course, that the whole world might not value our beauty, that as Negro girls we would suffer society's preoccupation with white skin, blond hair, and blue eyes. But she wanted us to be assured of our beauty within the family. She and Charles would let us know how lovely we were—clearly, continuously, authentically—so that even with the contrary messages from the wider world, we would believe in our beauty.

Again, Paula and I felt our mother's heightened sensitivity on this matter. On Halloween—the day of the year when children relish the chance to be outlandish, weird, scary—our mother would insist that we dress up in costumes that were beautiful. She did not even want us to pretend to be ugly. Not even for an evening did she want us to enjoy the pleasure of acting out a denigrating caricature. On what we came to call the "Halloween situation" my mother was insistent and unyielding. Since our experience was so different from hers, we resisted mightily. Why couldn't we be drunken hoboes or fiery dragons or slimy snakes or scary monsters for one lousy, pretend evening a year?

Now I understand. My mother was struggling with old, genera- tional demons—real ones, not those that appear in costume once a year. Now, on Halloween, when my mother calls and inquires pleas- antly, "What are the children going to dress up as this year?", I feel relief when I can report, "Martin is going to be a fireman and Tolani will be the Good Witch Glenda from the *Wiz*." I am glad both have chosen proud, strong figures. But I also know that if they chose to be the slimiest, scariest, ugliest creatures in the world, I would give them my permission and blessing. My generation may be somewhat less haunted by the pejorative, historical symbols. We may be ready to act ugly and crude once a year.

It is the spring of 1987 and Margaret is preparing a paper to present at the annual meeting of the American Academy of Psychoanalysis in Chicago. The title of the conference is "Psychoanalysis: An Extended Vision," a theme Margaret interprets as an opportunity "to take some risks," to do something offbeat. We spend hours playing with possible angles and perspectives. Our conversations return again and again to our work on the book, to the intriguing experience of "a second analysis," to the mother-daughter dialogue that has taken us in unexpected directions. This chance to sit and talk face-to-face, with a common goal, has been a rich and rare experience for both of us.

I look into my mother's eyes and see my own reflections—not mirror images but refracted, varied. I feel the stubborn lineage that has survived generations—passed down from Mom Margaret, Mary Elizabeth, Mama Lettie—but I also sense the ways in which our temperaments, our family dramas, our choices, and the historical timing have made us different from one another. "I had never known anyone like you," recalls Margaret about how my demands and outspokenness sometimes baffled her when I was a young child and adolescent. Now we have grown toward one another. There are fewer surprises and deeper understandings. Mother and daughter have both changed. At seventy-two, Margaret laughs more, weeps more—tears of joy, anger, and sadness—demands more from life, plays more, and speaks out more than she did when she was a mother of young children. "I no longer have to be careful," she says with exuberance. At forty-two, I continue to be the kind of person who speaks out in ways my mother "had never known" but feel the strain of putting together all the pieces, or of energy wrapped up in single-minded concentration. My mother looks into my eyes and sees her own reflections.

Margaret labors over the speech, working on the computer in Dad's study, which has now been transformed into her writing room. She calls the speech "The Integration of Psychoanalysis in One Life Story" and looks forward, with excitement and anxiety, to delivering it to her colleagues. When the day comes, she stands before them in a Guatemalan dress that I have given her. The magenta tones around her face make her glow, and the silver ornaments on the soft yoke of the dress sparkle when light hits them. Her paper traces the connections among her life story, which she sketches briefly, her perspective on early developmental patterns in children, and the centrality of the mother-infant bond. Bravely, she tells her own story— not case materials from patients in her care—as a way of examining the themes of trauma, survival, and ego strength. Margaret retells the dream that we have explored many times during our book interviews. She tells it simply, without embellishment:

I was nine years old when I had the dream. It took place in and around the rectory where my mother, my father, and I lived. . . . The year was 1923 . . . I was laid out in the middle of the living room as was the custom of the time when a family member died. On the wall of the living room facing the casket was a life-sized picture of my brother. The picture was in its usual place.

Then I was walking along the fence that bordered my front yard. I seemed to be an early adolescent. I opened the gate, walked up the steps to the porch, walked to the front door which opened into the living room, and rang the bell. My mother opened the door promptly. I could see the casket and the picture. I felt no sadness but heightened expectancy. "Mrs. Morgan," I said compassionately, "I heard that Margaret died. I'm sorry." Intently I searched my mother's face. The dream ended. . . .

. . . Even the newborn sees her image reflected by the mirror of the mother's, father's, or caregiver's face. On the other side of the mirror, the nonreflecting, see-through side, lie generations of related images with a long history, representing the cultures of which they are a part, and their traditions. These images carry their religious traditions and their mother tongues as well. They find their end point in the mother's own image. The infant fastens her attention on the mother's face, absorbing the image which becomes her own. There is mutual engagement of the two images, mother's and daughter's. There is vitality that flows between the two images and the inner lives they represent. It is through this flow that the value of each is confirmed. . . .

Having spoken "the Word," Margaret Cornelia Morgan Lawrence pauses, takes a deep breath, and looks out at her audience. This time, the faces of her colleagues—the gray-haired, bearded, pipe-smoking ones and the new, earnest, eager ones—are responsive. "There wasn't a dry eye in the house!" she reports to me later. We look at one another, and smile—a promising conclusion to our day's work. As we get ready to leave my mother's office, our eyes land on a picture of my children that sits on her desk. Their beaming faces take us backwards into the future.

Index

Luddington, Miss (teacher), 127–128
Luke, Jean, 155, 199
Lyle, Kitty, 163

M

McAdney, Pleasant, 130–131, 138
McCarthy, Mr. (chauffeur), 50, 51
McClarren, Mrs. (dressmaker), 67
McIntosh, Rustin, 185
MacIver, Professor, 274–275
MacVay, Anna Pearl, 85–86, 92
Magnolia High School, 18, 83–84, 85, 87, 100, 105
Marshall, Thurgood, 145
Maryville College, 121, 122
Mattis, Eunice, 76–77, 90, 102
Mayo, Baby Lee, 78
Mayo, Erma, 77–78
Mayo, Grannison, 78
Meharry Medical College, Margaret's teaching position at, 242–246, 249–260, 265, 288
Merrick, Sadie, 62–63, 105–106
Merton, Robert, 232, 233–234
Michigan, University of, 274
Middleton, Clarence, 61–62
Milch, Eugene, 180, 181, 182, 183, 290, 293–294
  Margaret's analysis with, 290, 292–293
Milch, Mildred, 180, 182
Montgomery, Isaiah T., 44
Morehouse College, 104, 108, 110, 205
  Charles Lawrence's attendance at, 141–142, 144–151
Morgan, Hattie (aunt), 31, 32
Morgan, Leah (aunt), 32, 41

Morgan, Mary Elizabeth Smith (mother), 21–22, 23, 25, 28, 306
  birth of children of, 34, 35
  depressions suffered by, 37–39, 45, 46, 277
  her devotion to teaching, 39–40
  dramatic readings of, 113
  her friendships with women, 62–64
  her imprint on Margaret, 111, 236–237
  later life of, 279–280
  and Margaret's pregnancy, 237–238
  and Margaret's wedding, 160
  marriage of, 20–21, 34, 66
  in Mound Bayou, Mississippi, 44, 45
  New York trips of, 66–70
  racism experienced by, 165, 166
  her suspicions of husband's wandering affections, 42–44, 156
  in Vicksburg, Mississippi, 45–54
  in Widewater, Virginia, 36–44, 45
Morgan, Sandy Alonzo (father), 28–30, 206–207
  birth of children of, 34, 35
  his career in ministry, 31–34
  deterioration of health of, 279, 288–289
  marriage of, 20, 34, 66
  in Mound Bayou, Mississippi, 44
  in Vicksburg, Mississippi, 45–53
  in Widewater, Virginia, 36–44
Morgan, Sandy Alonzo, Jr. (Candy Man, brother), 54–55, 66, 110, 114–115, 276
  congenital illness of, 34, 185
  death of, 34–35, 70, 72, 309
Morgan, Sarah (grandmother), 30–31, 41
Morgan, William (grandfather), 30
Mosely, Mrs., 45

FOR THE BEST IN PAPERBACKS, LOOK FOR THE

In every corner of the world, on every subject under the sun, Penguin represents quality and variety—the very best in publishing today.

For complete information about books available from Penguin—including Puffins, Penguin Classics, and Arkana—and how to order them, write to us at the appropriate address below. Please note that for copyright reasons the selection of books varies from country to country.

In the United Kingdom: Please write to *Dept. JC, Penguin Books Ltd, FREEPOST, West Drayton, Middlesex UB7 0BR.*

If you have any difficulty in obtaining a title, please send your order with the correct money, plus ten percent for postage and packaging, to *P.O. Box No. 11, West Drayton, Middlesex UB7 0BR*

In the United States: Please write to *Consumer Sales, Penguin USA, P.O. Box 999, Dept. 17109, Bergenfield, New Jersey 07621-0120.* VISA and MasterCard holders call 1-800-253-6476 to order all Penguin titles

In Canada: Please write to *Penguin Books Canada Ltd, 10 Alcorn Avenue, Suite 300, Toronto, Ontario M4V 3B2*

In Australia: Please write to *Penguin Books Australia Ltd, P.O. Box 257, Ringwood, Victoria 3134*

In New Zealand: Please write to *Penguin Books (NZ) Ltd, Private Bag 102902, North Shore Mail Centre, Auckland 10*

In India: Please write to *Penguin Books India Pvt Ltd, 706 Eros Apartments, 56 Nehru Place, New Delhi 110 019*

In the Netherlands: Please write to *Penguin Books Netherlands bv, Postbus 3507, NL-1001 AH Amsterdam*

In Germany: Please write to *Penguin Books Deutschland GmbH, Metzlerstrasse 26, 60594 Frankfurt am Main*

In Spain: Please write to *Penguin Books S. A., Bravo Murillo 19, 1° B, 28015 Madrid*

In Italy: Please write to *Penguin Italia s.r.l., Via Felice Casati 20, I-20124 Milano*

In France: Please write to *Penguin France S. A., 17 rue Lejeune, F–31000 Toulouse*

In Japan: Please write to *Penguin Books Japan, Ishikiribashi Building, 2–5–4, Suido, Bunkyo-ku, Tokyo 112*

In Greece: Please write to *Penguin Hellas Ltd, Dimocritou 3, GR–106 71 Athens*

In South Africa: Please write to *Longman Penguin Southern Africa (Pty) Ltd, Private Bag X08, Bertsham 2013*